In the NEWS

In the NEWS

*American Journalists
View Their Craft*

Jerry W. Knudson

A Scholarly Resources Inc. Imprint
Wilmington, Delaware

Scholarly Resources Inc.
104 Greenhill Avenue
Wilmington, DE 19805-1897
www.scholarly.com

Library of Congress Cataloging-in-Publication Data

Knudson, Jerry W.
  In the news : American journalists view their craft /
Jerry W. Knudson.
       p.   cm.
  Includes bibliographical references and index.
  ISBN 0-8420-2760-2 (alk. paper). — ISBN 0-8420-2761-0
(pbk. : alk. paper)
  1. Journalism. 2. Journalism—United States—History.
3. Journalists—United States. I. Title.
PN4775.K54   2000
071'.3—dc21   99-36464
                                                        CIP

∞ The paper used in this publication meets the minimum
requirements of the American National Standard for perma-
nence of paper for printed library materials, Z39.48, 1984.

For

Calder M. Pickett

teacher, colleague, friend

Contents

————<◆>————

Preface

————⟨◆⟩————

H. L. Mencken once observed, "The only opinion that counts is that of the fellow at the other end of the workbench." In other words, one must labor in the vineyard to know if the wine will be good. That concept is the premise of this book—how do journalists of any given historical period view their own work, or that of others? There is continuity to be found here, as well as relationships not previously explored. Thus, this collection of readings atttempts to offer professional insights for the student of the history of American journalism.

The idea for this volume came about quite accidentally. While pursuing another research topic, I came across an interview with William Randolph Hearst by Lincoln Steffens in *The American Magazine* of November 1906. Here were two giants of American journalism—the powerful newspaper publisher and the powerful muckraker—exchanging their views on journalism. These were not people simply writing about journalism, but the candid insights of those who had experienced the reality of meeting deadlines, dealing with space limitations, and searching for information.

Preparing this volume has been a long haul. Journalists are notoriously reticent to talk about their own work or to criticize that of others. In a few cases I have had to settle for brief samples of their work to illustrate a point. And I regret that there is not room to pay greater attention to magazines and the electronic media. As for the latter, although they permeate our lives today they have not yet had an impact comparable to that of 250 years of print—which of course has had much smaller audiences but perhaps greater impact: Even when printing first appeared in England in the sixteenth century, it was regarded as a "social engine" that could undermine authority.

This work has truly been a group effort, stemming partly from the efforts over the years of graduate students in my seminar "Literature of Journalism" at Temple University and graduate and undergraduate students in my courses on the history of journalism. The introductions to the selections that follow rely on the work of many scholars, some of whom are given credit in the text, the others being mentioned in the notes at the end of each chapter. To avoid clutter, only direct quotations are supplied with endnotes. The press does not function in a vacuum, and these introductions are meant to provide the historical framework.

The question arises—why study the history of journalism? George Santayana, poet and philosopher, said it best: "Those who do not know the past are doomed to repeat it." There are blemishes in press history and the mass media today that cannot be ignored, but perhaps acknowledging them will prevent their reoccurrence. Journalists themselves, contrary to popular belief, are the most loving critics of their craft— and that characteristic is the reason for this book. Scholars are still debating whether the press tends to shape society or simply to reflect it. In my view, history is concerned—or should be concerned—not only with what actually happened at any given time or place but also with what people thought was happening—as revealed to them by the means of mass communication that may have conditioned their subsequent actions. Thus, the perception of events "filtered" through the press may have changed historical outcomes. Accordingly, it matters a great deal whether the news was false or distorted, if readers believed it and acted on their belief. Whether the bearer of good or bad tidings, newspapers and the later electronic media have largely determined where we are today. And the messenger should not be ignored.

There are many persons and institutions to thank for their help with this work. I am especially grateful to Susan G. Williamson, librarian at the Annenberg School for Communication at the University of Pennsylvania, and the late Bob Roberts, who was librarian at the School of Communications and Theater, Temple University. David Dillard of Paley Library at Temple University has done several fruitful computer searches for me, and the staff at Van Pelt Library at the University of Pennsylvania has also been helpful. In addition, one must mention the Free Library and the Library Company, both of Philadelphia. For access to their collections, I am also greatly indebted to the Library of Congress; Rutgers, the State University of New Jersey; the State Historical Society of Wisconsin; the Kansas State Historical Society; and the Illinois State Historical Library.

For particular help on the African-American press, my thanks go to Christopher C. De Santis of the University of Kansas; for the Colonial period, David Copeland of Emory and Henry College; for columnists, Sam Riley of Virginia Tech; and for the frontier press, Ruth Laird, professor emerita of South Dakota State University, and Wallace Clayton, editor of the *Tombstone Epitaph*. Henry Walton did yeoman service in word-processing part of the manuscript and in untangling my computer errors.

Then, there is that group of persons—former colleagues and students—who have sustained me through the years. I cannot thank them individually, but they know who they are. Some may find this collection too critical of the press; others, too lenient—but the journalists themselves will have the last word.

Philadelphia   *Jerry W. Knudson*

1

Colonies and Revolution

Prelude to Press Freedom

———⟨◆⟩———

While Jamestown, Virginia, that brave outpost of empire and the first English settlement in North America, was struggling to survive after its founding in 1607, thirty young men were competing for a poetry prize at the Royal and Pontifical University of New Spain in Mexico City. We tend to measure time to suit our own limited worldview, but long before the English arrived, the Spanish had established the widest empire in human history, reaching from California and Florida to Tierra del Fuego at the tip of South America, and from the Caribbean to the Philippines. Yet many Americans are not aware of their rich Hispanic heritage, even though demographers say that Latinos will be our most numerous racial minority by the year 2010. In fact, the first printing press was introduced into Mexico in 1535, to print ecclesiastical and literary works; Harvard College, on the other hand, was not established until 1636—a century later—and acquired the first printing press in the British colonies in 1638. Its function, too, was to produce religious texts needed in schools and seminaries.

In both Spanish and British North America, however, the press was closely regulated, from Henry VIII on, because of its potential as a "social engine" to undermine the government or create domestic turmoil. The first formal restrictions on the British colonial press were imposed in 1662 in the Massachusetts Bay Colony. A quarter of a century later, printer Benjamin Harris brought forth the first American newspaper, on September 25, 1690; *Publick Occurrences, Both Forreign and Domestick*. It was immediately suppressed because of "reflections of a very high nature" against the French royal court and

Britain's Indian allies. The size of a page of typing paper, *Publick Occurrences* was printed on only three sides (the paper being folded) so the reader could use the blank fourth page to add his own news before passing it on. Harris planned to publish his paper monthly, "or if any Glut of Occurrences happen, oftener." All copies of this newspaper were destroyed except the one sent—according to law—to the British Records Office. In 1990 the British lent it to the Library of Congress for its exhibit on three hundred years of American journalism.

However, it is important to realize the time lag in communications in the seventeenth century. The first English newspaper, the *Oxford Gazette*, was founded in 1665, a full quarter of a century before Benjamin Harris's little venture on this side of the Atlantic. It is also essential to remember that these were Englishmen imitating English forms in a "new England." For almost two centuries they copied British polemics such as the "Cato Letters" (1720–1723), which heralded representative democracy and freedom of the press, before developing a political vocabulary of their own.

In retrospect, the press can be characterized as having passed through three major stages of development—the commercial or mercantile, the political, and the mass-information press. The Colonial press fell largely in the first category, until the stirrings of independence, when many newspapers carried the word "Advertiser" in their mastheads. These papers were expensive but could be consulted at the local coffeehouse or tavern, mainly by the business class. Despite widespread illiteracy, circulation of the news by word of mouth was considerable. Advertisements were usually carried in a separate column at the back of the paper, such as this item in the *Virginia Gazette* of September 10, 1736:

> We are inform'd, from several Parts of the Country, that there will be a great scarcity of Cider, this Year, the Apple-Orchards having generally fail'd: So that 'tis believ'd it will bear a good Price to those who will bring it from other Parts to sell.

It was fourteen years after Benjamin Harris before the first continuously published American newspaper appeared, John Campbell's *Boston News-Letter*, in 1704. It was by all accounts quite dull, endeavoring not to offend anyone. After 1692, when the first official postal service was established, many printers were also postmasters, and they did not hesitate to bar their competitors from the mails. It must be borne in mind that at this time there was no conception of "editor" or "journalist." Printing was a business, and printers borrowed copiously from newspapers exchanged with other printers in the days before copyright laws. For the Colonial entrepreneur, printing was usually simply another adjunct to his shop, an activity he included along with job orders, bookselling, and the distribution of various foods and medicinal remedies.

John Campbell cleared all his copy with the royal governor, or with his secretary, and it made for a tedious and lifeless newspaper. For fifteen years Campbell's journal was the only one in the Colonies. Yet his circulation rarely exceeded three hundred, and twice a government subsidy rescued him from bankruptcy. Why such a lackluster beginning for American journalism? One must consider that newspapers were both a relatively new form and also subject to the chilling effects of colonialism. Yet, despite the short life span of most colonial newspapers, the *Boston News-Letter* managed to survive for seventy-two years, the first fifteen as something of a public enterprise.

Much would change, however, with the advent of the *New England Courant* in 1721, published by James Franklin, older brother of Ben. Although his newspaper, sprightly and loaded with entertaining tidbits as well as serials of British literary works, lasted for only five years, it established for all time the entertainment function of a newspaper. Moreover, James Franklin, later briefly imprisoned, boasted that he published not by authority but in spite of it. (Although licensing or governmental permission to print had lapsed in England in 1695, it persisted in the Colonies until 1730.)

In the theocracy of Massachusetts, James Franklin picked a fight with the spiritual overlords of the colony, Increase and Cotton Mather, coming down on the wrong side of a serious social issue—inoculation against smallpox. The clergymen were in favor of inoculation, but since they represented the aristocratic party, James Franklin opposed it, thereby numbering the days of his otherwise distinguished newspaper.

As resentment against British trade restrictions mounted, the Colonial press entered the political phase with gusto. As press historians William David Sloan and Julie Hedgepeth Williams have pointed out: "Of special importance were political situations—ones that either provided a supportive climate or were so controversial as to provoke publishers into action. Furthermore, the role of the individual publisher should not be overlooked. The recent emphasis among journalism historians on environmental factors has diminished the importance attached to individuals."[1]

Benjamin Harris Plants a Seed

News values—what are regarded as newsworthy items—have changed little from the time when news ballads were sung in medieval English country fairs and markets, later printed as broadsides. They recounted murders and hangings and other aberrations of human behavior, along with natural catastrophes—what Max Lerner has called "the daily disaster diet." People have always responded with interest to news about the downfall of prominent persons, about conflict, confrontation, action, and violence (all the ingredients of today's local television news, in which fires and crime are the mainstays, perhaps because it is easier to cover them than to dig into complex social, political, and economic problems).

In the late seventeenth century, timeliness in newspapers was not important. After the four-to-six-week Atlantic crossing, the news was stale when it reached America, and people had limited resources for acting upon what they read. Newspapers were regarded as chronicles of events, as weekly encyclopedias—much as the *New York Times* still regards itself as a "newspaper of record." One Colonial printer got six months behind in presenting the "news" but kept plugging away from where he had left off rather than presenting the "freshest" news first. Benjamin Harris's prospectus (opening statement) for *Publick Occurrences, Both Forreign and Domestick* of September 25, 1690, however, reveals a remarkably modern attitude regarding the news.

It is designed, that the Countrey shall be furnished once a moneth (or if any Glut of Occurrences happen, oftener,) with an Account of such considerable things as have arrived unto our Notice.

In order hereunto, the Publisher will take what pains he can to obtain a Faithful Relation of all such things; and will particularly make himself beholden to such Persons in Boston whom he knows to have been for their own use the diligent Observers of such matters.

That which is herein proposed, is, First, That Memorable Occurrents of Divine Providence may not be neglected or forgotten, as they too often are. Secondly, That people every where may better understand the Circumstances of Publique Affairs both abroad and at home; which may not only direct their Thoughts at all times, but at some times also to assist their Businesses and Negotiations.

Thirdly, That some thing may be done towards the Curing, or at least the Charming of that Spirit of Lying, which prevails amongst us, wherefore nothing shall be entered, but what we have reason to believe is true, repairing to the best fountains for our Information. And when there appears any material mistake in any thing that is collected, it shall be corrected in the next.

Moreover, the Publisher of these Occurrences is willing to engage, that whereas, there are many False Reports, maliciously made, and spread among us, if any well-minded person will be at the pains to trace any such false Report so far as to find out and Convict the First Raiser of it, he will in this Paper (unless just Advice be given to the contrary) expose the Name of such person, as A malicious Raiser of a false Report. It is suppos'd that none will dislike this Proposal, but such as intend to be guilty of so villanous a Crime.[2]

The Broader Colonial Scene

Journalism history can best be demarcated by landmark technological developments. Colonial printers worked with essentially the same type of manually operated flatbed presses used by Johannes Gutenberg two-and-one-half centuries earlier. At first, the presses themselves and the type, along with paper and ink, had to come from England. Made mostly of wood, these presses had a manually operated lever that brought the platen down to the form on the bed of the press. A boy smeared the type with a stick tipped with a ball of ink-soaked wool, and a strong man could make two hundred impressions, or "pulls," an hour on wet sheets of paper, which were then hung up to dry. As the Revolution approached and imported newsprint became ever scarcer, printers resorted to rag-content paper—a boon to future historians. Rag paper resisted the years, whereas wood-pulp paper—for example, from the time of the Spanish-American war—is now yellowed and falls apart in one's hands.

Nevertheless, the American press was becoming an institution. Printers—still not editors—copied shamelessly from each other, a scissors-and-paste operation. Why did they go into the printing business? Was it to save society from itself? Thomas Fleet, printer of the *Boston Evening-Post*, answered the question in his edition of March 27, 1741: "I had a prospect of getting a Penny by it." Others inflated their calling with such hyperbole as that of William Parks, printer of the *Virginia Gazette*, who said on August 10, 1739, that his paper was filled with "inexhaustable Treasures, out of which may be extracted everything that is necessary for the Suport of Virtue, the Suppression of Vice, the Promotion of Learning, Wit, Ingenuity, &c."

Doggerel poetry appeared quite often, and the following, which appeared in many Colonial newspapers, illustrates better than anything how printers viewed their trade in 1770, on the eve of the American Revolution:

> News'papers are the spring of knowledge,
> The gen'ral source throughout the nation,
> Of ev'ry modern conversation.
> What would this mighty people do,
> If there, alas! were nothing new?
> A News-paper is like a feast,
> Some dish there is for ev'ry guest;
> Some large, some small, some strong, some tender,
> For ev'ry stomach, stout or slender;
> Those who roast beef and ale delight in,
> Are pleas'd with trumpets, drums and fighting;
> For those who are more puny made,
> Are arts and sciences, and trade;
> For fanciful and am'rous blood,
> We have a soft poetic food;
> For witty and satyric folks,
> High-season'd, acid *Bitter Jokes*;
> And when we strive to please the mob,
> A jest, a quarrel, or a job.

If any gentleman wants a wife,
(A partner, as 'tis term'd for life)
An advertisement does the thing,
And quickly brings the pretty thing.
If you want health, consult our pages,
You shall be well, and live for ages. . . .
Our services you can't express,
The good we do you hardly guess;
There's not a want of human kind,
But we a remedy can find.[3]

Benjamin Franklin: The Press Gains Respectability

What can be said of Ben Franklin that has not already been said? We all know the story of his early efforts to make a name for himself with the anonymous series of Silence Dogood papers (the writings of a fictitious scullery maid), slipped under the door of his brother James's *New England Courant*, which became the talk of Boston. Later Ben skipped out on his apprenticeship while James was in jail, arriving in Philadelphia almost penniless. In 1729, after some maneuvering, the twenty-four-year-old Ben became publisher of the *Pennsylvania Gazette*, deemed the best newspaper in the Colonies. Contemporary accounts of life in Philadelphia in the early eighteenth century depict the young Franklin trundling newsprint in a wheelbarrow from the docks to his print shop.

Despite Ben's scientific achievements and inventions and his diplomatic successes—first as agent of Colonial Pennsylvania in England and later as the ambassador to France—he made his living, and his fortune, exclusively by journalism until the age of forty-two. Actors or troubadors were regarded at that time as being lowest on the social scale, and before Franklin itinerant printers were not regarded much more highly. He not only established the first embryonic "chain" of newspapers, setting up young men as printers, but also the first foreign-language journal, in Germantown. Franklin outstripped his seven almanac competitors in Philadelphia with *Poor Richard's Almanack* and tried but failed to launch the first American magazine, a luxury the colonists could ill afford. Patron of learning and the arts—and father of the University of Pennsylvania—Ben Franklin, despite all his accomplishments, wanted to be remembered in his epitaph primarily as a printer.

In the following selection on the Colonial press, written toward the close of his life, Franklin was ambivalent. On the one hand, he first extolled the "watchdog" concept of newspapers, the "Court of the Press," echoing the European idea of newspapers as the Fourth Estate (the other three being the church, the nobility, and the commons), whose job it was to keep excessive government in check. But, on the other hand, Franklin abhorred, although with tongue in cheek as to the remedy proposed below, the rough-and-tumble personal journalism of his day, which was to become even more vitriolic after Ben's death at eighty-four. When William Cobbett, for example, the leading Anglophile printer, attacked Franklin's grandson, Benjamin Franklin Bache ("Lightning Rod Junior"), editor of the *Aurora*, he vented his spleen on Bache's "crafty and lecherous old hypocrite of a grandfather, whose very statue seems to gloat on the wenches as they walk the State House yard."[4]

AN ACCOUNT OF THE HIGHEST COURT OF JUDICATURE IN PENNSYLVANIA. THE COURT OF THE PRESS.

POWER OF THIS COURT

It may receive and promulgate accusations of all kinds, against all persons and characters among the citizens of the state, and against all inferior courts; and may judge, sentence and condemn to infamy, not only private individuals, but public bodies, &c. With or without inquiry or hearing, at the court's discretion.

WHOSE FAVOR OR FOR WHOSE EMOLUMENT THIS COURT IS ESTABLISHED.

In favor of about one citizen in five hundred, who, by education, or practice in scribbling, has acquired a tolerable style as to grammar and construction, so as to bear printing; or who is possessed of a press and a few types. The five hundredth part of the citizens have the liberty of accusing and abusing the other four hundred and ninety-nine parts at their pleasure; or they may hire out their pens and press to others, for that purpose.

PRACTICE OF THIS COURT.

It is not governed by any of the rules of the common courts of law. The accused is allowed no grand jury to judge of the truth of the accusation before it is publicly made; nor is the name of the accuser made known to him, nor has he an opportunity of confronting the witnesses against him, for they are kept in the dark, as in the Spanish court of inquisition. Nor is there any petty jury of his peers sworn to try the truth of the charges. The proceedings are also sometimes so rapid, that an honest good citizen may find himself suddenly and unexpectedly accused, and in the same moment judged and condemned, and a sentence pronounced against him that he is a rogue and a villain. Yet if an officer of this court receives the slightest check for misconduct in this his office, he claims immediately the rights of a free citizen by the constitution, and demands to know his accuser, to confront the witnesses, and have a fair trial by the jury of his peers.

THE FOUNDATION OF ITS AUTHORITY.

It is said to be founded on an article in the state constitution, which establishes the liberty of the press—a liberty which every Pennsylvanian would fight and die for, though few of us, I believe, have distinct ideas of its nature and extent. It seems, indeed, somewhat like the liberty of the press, that felons have, by the common law of England, before conviction; that is, to be either pressed to death or hanged. If by the liberty of the press, we understood merely the liberty of discussing the propriety of public measures and political opinions, let us have as much of it as you please; but if it means the liberty of affronting, calumniating, and defaming one another, I, for my part, own myself willing to part with my share of it, whenever our legislators shall please to alter the law; and cheerfully consent to exchange my liberty of abusing others, for the privilege of not being abused myself.

BY WHOM THIS COURT IS COMMISSIONED OR CONSTITUTED.

It is not by any commission from the supreme executive council, who might previously judge of the abilities, integrity, knowledge, &c. of the persons to be appointed to this great trust, of deciding upon the characters and good fame of the citizens: for this court is above that council, and may accuse, judge, and condemn it at pleasure. Nor is it hereditary, as is the court of dernier resort in the peerage of England. But any man who can procure pen, ink, and paper, with a press, a few types, and a huge pair of blacking balls, may commissionate himself, and his court is immediately established in the plenary possession and exercise of its rights; for if you make the least complaint of the judge's conduct, he daubs his blacking balls in your face wherever he meets you: and besides tearing your private character to splinters, marks you out for the odium of the public, as an enemy to the liberty of the press.

OF THE NATURAL SUPPORT OF THIS COURT.

Its support is founded in the depravity of such minds as have not been mended by religion, nor improved by good education.

> *There is a lust in man no charm can tame,*
> *Of loudly publishing his neighbor's shame.*

Hence

> *On eagle's wings immortal scandals fly,*
> *While virtuous actions are but born and die. —Dryden.*

Whoever feels pain in hearing a good character of his neighbor, will feel a pleasure in the reverse. And of those who, despairing to rise in distinction by their virtues, are happy if others can be depressed to a level with themselves, there are a sufficient number in every great town to maintain one of these courts by subscription. A shrewd observer once said, that in walking the streets of a slippery morning, one might see where the good-natured people lived, by the ashes thrown on the ice before the doors: probably he would have formed a different conjecture of the temper of those whom he might find engaged in such subscriptions.

OF THE CHECKS PROPER TO BE ESTABLISHED AGAINST
THE ABUSES OF POWER IN THOSE COURTS.

Hitherto there are none. But since so much has been writen and published on the federal constitution; and the necessity of checks in all parts of good government, has been so clearly and learnedly explained, I feel myself so far enlightened as to suspect some check may be proper in this part also; but I have been at a loss to imagine any that may not be construed an infringement of the sacred liberty of the press. At length, however, I think I have found one, that instead of diminishing general liberty, shall augment it; which is, by restoring to the people a species of liberty, of which they have been deprived by our laws—I mean the liberty of the cudgel! In the rude state of society prior to the existence of laws, if one man gave another ill language, the affronted person might return it by a box on the ear; and, if repeated, by a good drubbing; and this without offending against any law; but now the right of making such returns is denied, and they are punished as breaches of the peace, while the right of abusing seems to remain in full force; the laws made against it being rendered ineffectual by the liberty of the press.

My proposal then is, to leave the liberty of the press untouched, to be exercised in its full extent, force, and vigor, but to permit the liberty of the cudgel to go with it, *pari passu*. Thus, my fellow-citizens, if an impudent writer attacks your reputation—dearer perhaps to you than your life, and puts his name to the charge, you may go to him as openly, and break his head. If he conceals himself behind the printer, and you can nevertheless discover who he is, you may, in like manner, way-lay him in the night, attack him from behind, and give him a good drubbing. If your adversary hires better writers than himself to abuse you more effectually, you may hire as many porters, stronger than yourself, to assist you in giving him a more effectual drubbing. Thus far goes my project as to *private* resentment and retribution. But if the public should ever happen to be affronted, as it ought to be, with the conduct of such writers, I would not advise proceeding immediately to these extremities, but that we should in moderation content ourselves with tarring and feathering, and tossing in a blanket.

If, however, it should be thought that this proposal of mine may disturb the public peace, I would then humbly recommend to our legislators to take up the consideration of both liberties, that of the press, and that of the cudgel; and by an explicit law mark their extent and limits: and at the same time that they secure the person of a citizen from assaults, they would likewise provide for the security of his reputation.[5]

The Press and the American Revolution

Bruce Catton, the distinguished historian, once wrote that for many Americans, the events leading up to independence were like a marble frieze with heroes marching inexorably toward a foregone conclusion. It was not that way at all. Benjamin Franklin, for instance, was seventy years old when he signed the Declaration of Independence, along with others risking everything, "our lives, our fortunes and our sacred honor," in the revolutionary cause. These men did not know at that time how things would turn out. Fueled by Colonial newspapers, they took an extreme position that might have caused them to be hanged on the gallows if England had won the conflict.

In the escalating estrangement between mother country and colonies, a decisive turning point came with the Stamp Act of 1765, which (although England had had such a tax since 1712) alienated the two most influential groups in the

Colonies—the printers and the lawyers—both of whom were required to purchase specially stamped paper for their transactions. Colonial printers were up in arms. Not a single newspaper was printed over the hated stamp, using various subterfuges to avoid it. To these printers the measure was the worst symbol of British oppression, and opposition became a form of civil disobedience. From that point on, events moved rapidly, leading to the litany of patriotic acts that to the English were sheer brigandage. Shots rang out at Lexington and Concord on April 19, 1775, but the colonists still did not declare their separation from England. The shooting war had been going on for more than a year when Thomas Paine urged the Second Continental Congress to sever ties with Britain in his famous "Common Sense," published both as a pamphlet and serially in newspapers up and down the seacoast. Appearing early in January 1776, Paine's work sold more than 120,000 copies within three months, unprecedented in the limited marketplace for printed matter in Colonial America.

The Declaration of Independence soon followed, drafted mainly by Thomas Jefferson. It frankly stated in its opening sentence that "a decent respect to the opinions of mankind requires that they [the rebels] should declare the causes which impel them to the separation." Encapsulating the American dream, Jefferson borrowed from John Locke's phrase defending the Glorious Revolution of 1688: from revolt being justified when rulers imperiled "the life, liberty and property" of their subjects, Jefferson instead insisted upon "life, liberty and the pursuit of happiness." The Declaration of Independence was not always revered, at the time or later. In the subsequent Federalist period, for example, Joseph Dennie of the *Philadelphia Port Folio* lashed out at it as "that false, and flatulent, and foolish paper." It did accomplish its mission of soliciting international support, however, a bid consummated when France entered the conflict on the side of the patriots in 1778. For the first time, the rebelling colonists had obtained recognition as a belligerent power, and not merely as a group of international outlaws. It was a decisive turning point in the war.

Philip Freneau Takes Aim at "Turncoat" Hugh Gaine

Public opinion in pre-Revolutionary America was generally split three ways—the patriots, or radicals, on the left, desiring a forthright break from England, and at the other end of the political spectrum the Tories, or royalists, who sought to hold the empire together. The middle ground was composed of the Whigs, or moderates, and it was that sector the other two sought to win over by propaganda. As it turned out, patriot newspapers and pamphlets proved the more effective, because it is always easier to oppose one's enemies than to defend one's friends. Jefferson and his colleagues realized this while drafting and adopting the Declaration of Independence, wherein the attack was focused on the person of George III as well as his policies.

This drama was enacted in miniature in the feud between Philip Freneau, known as "the poet of the American Revolution," who survived a stint aboard a British prison ship, and Hugh Gaine, the royalist printer who seemed only to follow the dollar and whose print shop bore the Bible and Crown on its signboard. After independence, Freneau was on the payroll as a French translator for only $250 a year in the State Department while Jefferson headed that office, but in actuality he had been hired to found and edit the Jeffersonian *National Gazette*. Washington called him "that rascal Freneau" for his attacks on the Federalists, but Freneau had earlier sharpened his pen on printers such as Gaine, who had opposed the Stamp Act but took his *New-York Mercury* over to the royalists when the British occupied New York. After the war, Freneau wrote a long satirical poem pretending to be Gaine petitioning the New York legislature for permission to remain in the state. Actually, according to Paul Leicester Ford, editor of Hugh Gaine's journals, there never was such a petition, although it keeps popping up in textbooks. Freneau apparently used the fictitious petition as a peg upon which to hang his lengthy fifteen-page poetic attack on Gaine, which included the following lines:

> As matters have gone, it was plainly a blunder,
> But then I expected the Whigs must knock under,

> And I always adhere to the sword that is longest,
> And stick to the party that's like to be strongest.

The confusion seems to have arisen from the title of the poem, "Hugh Gaine's Petition to the New York Assembly by Philip Freneau." The following lines further illustrate the tenor of journalistic banter during this period:

> *So said, and so acted—I [Gaine] put up a press,*
> *And printed away with amazing success;*
> *Neglected my person and, looked like a fright,*
> *Was bothered all day, and was busy all night,*
> *Saw money come in, as the papers went out,*
> *While Parker and Weyman were driving about,*
> *And cursing, and swearing, and chewing their cuds,*
> *And wishing Hugh Gaine and his press in the suds:*
> *Ned Weyman was printer, you know, to the king,*
> *And thought he had got all the world in a string,*
> *(Though riches not always attend on a throne)*
> *So he swore I had found the philosopher's stone,*
> *And called me a rogue and a son of a bitch,*
> *Because I knew better than him to get rich. . . .*

> *My press, that has call'd you (as tyranny drove her)*
> *Rogues, rebels, and rascals, a thousand times over.*
> *Shall be at your service by day and by night,*
> *To publish whate'er you think proper to write;*
> *Those types which have rais'd George the Third to a level*
> *With angels—shall prove him as black as the devil,*
> *To HIM that contriv'd him, a shame and disgrace,*
> *Nor blest with one virtue to honour his grace!*

> *Who knows but in time, I may rise to be great,*
> *And have the good fortune to manage a STATE?*
> *Great noise among people great changes denotes,*
> *And I shall have money to purchase their votes—*
> *The time is approaching, I'll venture to say,*
> *When folks worse than me will come into play,*
> *When your double-fac'd people shall give themselves airs*
> *And AIM to take hold of the helm of affairs,*
> *While the honest, bold SOLDIER, that sought your renown,*
> *Like a dog in the dirt, shall be crush'd and held down.*[6]

The First Strike for Press Freedom

The name of John Peter Zenger rings through the corridors of American journalism history like a bell, but perhaps its resonance has been overstated. Zenger was a German immigrant printer who became embroiled in factional New York politics when the popular party persuaded him to start the *New York Weekly Journal* to oppose the autocratic royal Governor William Cosby. Zenger himself was not a writer of note, but the contributions of his political friends kept the governor in a rage. Specifically, their articles asserted that the property and liberties of the people of New York were endangered by the royal government, and that Governor Cosby had encroached upon the rights of trial by jury and free and honest voting. Two grand juries failed to indict Zenger for criminal or seditious libel, whereupon the governor's council itself issued an information, or warrant, for his arrest. Zenger spent nine months in prison awaiting trial in 1734–35 while his wife, Anna, continued editing the paper, missing only one issue and receiving instructions from her husband "thro' the Hole of the Door of the Prison."[7]

When the case came to trial, Zenger faced seemingly insurmountable obstacles. At that time the jury, which could be expected to be on Zenger's side, was allowed to decide only the fact of whether or not he had indeed published the material in question. The judge would decide whether it was libelous; moreover, truth was no defense. Indeed, the rule was, the greater the truth, the greater the libel. The renowned Philadelphia lawyer Andrew Hamilton (no relation to Alexander Hamilton) made the arduous journey from Philadelphia to New York at the age of eighty to defend Zenger. At the most dramatic moment of the trial, Hamilton turned abruptly from the judge, who had already admonished him twice, and appealed directly to the jury to decide the law and to urge that truth be deemed an absolute defense. In Hamilton's stirring summation, the conclusion of which is reproduced here, Zenger was acquitted amidst great popular rejoicing, but the jury's decision did not become precedent. Not until 1790 did Pennsylvania become the first state to include in its constitution the principles of truth as a defense and the right of the jury to decide both the law and the fact, followed by New York in 1805.

At the time, however, the Zenger case did create great popular awareness of the importance of freedom of the press. The trial also had a chilling effect on arbitrary governmental actions, according to journalism historian Frank Luther Mott, for no other Colonial court trial of a printer for seditious libel after 1735 has been discovered. Some printers were found to be in contempt by their own Colonial legislatures or governor's council, but none were tried by the Crown. Hamilton proclaimed:

Power may justly be compar'd to a great River, while kept within it's due Bounds, is both Beautiful and Useful; but when it overflows, it's Banks, it is then too impetuous to be stemm'd, it bears down all before it, and brings Destruction and Desolation wherever it comes. If then this is the Nature of Power, let us at least do our Duty, and like wise Men (who value Freedom) use our utmost Care to support Liberty, the only Bulwark against lawless Power, which in all Ages has sacrificed to it's wild Lust and boundless Ambition, the Blood of the best Men that ever liv'd.

I hope to be pardon'd Sir for my Zeal upon this Occasion; it is an old and wise Caution. *That when our Neighbours House is on Fire, we ought to take Care of our own.* For tho' Blessed be God, I live in a Government where Liberty is well understood, and freely enjoy'd: yet Experience has shewn us all (I'm sure it has to me) that a bad Precedent in one Government, is soon set up for an Authority in another; and therefore I cannot but think it mine, and every honest Man's Duty, that (while we pay all due Obedience to Men in Authority) we ought at the same Time to be upon our Guard against Power, wherever we apprehend that it may affect ourselves or our Fellow-Subjects.

I am truly very unequal to such an Undertaking on many Accounts. And you see I labour under the Weight of many Years, and am born down with great Infirmities of Body; yet Old and Weak as I am, I should think it my Duty if required, to go to the utmost Part of the Land, where my Service cou'd be of any Use in Assisting to quench the Flame of Prosecutions upon Informations, set on Foot by the Government, to deprive a people of the Right of Remonstrating, (and complaining too) of the arbitrary Attempts of Men in Power. Men who injure and oppress the People under their Administration provoke them to cry out and complain; and then make that very Complaint the Foundation for new Oppressions and Prosecutions. I wish I could say there were no Instances of this Kind. But to conclude; the Question before the Court and you Gentleman of the Jury, is not of small nor private Concern, it is not the cause of the poor Printer, nor of *New-York* alone, which you are now trying: No! It may in it's Consequence, affect every Freeman that Lives under a British Government on the main of *America*. It is the best Cause. It is the Cause of Liberty; and I make no Doubt but your upright Conduct, this Day, will not only entitle you to the Love and Esteem of your Fellow-Citizens; but every Man who prefers Freedom to a Life of slavery will bless and honour You, as Men who have baffled the Attempt of Tyranny; and by an impartial and uncorrupt Verdict, have laid a noble Foundation for securing to ourselves, our Posterity, and our Neighbours, That, to which Nature and the Laws of our Country have given us a right—the Liberty—both of exposing and opposing arbitrary Power (in these Parts of the World, at least) by speaking and writing Truth.[8]

William Cobbett: "Peter Porcupine" Bristles

Newspapers of this period both gave rise to political parties—such as the Whigs and Tories, earlier in England—and nurtured their growth. Indeed, Colonial newspapers thrived on controversy, doubling in number from twenty-one in 1763 to forty-two by 1775. After the Revolution and the failure of the Articles of Confederation, journals hammered out the issues involved in the adoption of the Constitution in 1789. For better or worse, this began the split of political parties into Federalists and Jeffersonian Republicans. The foremost luminary among the former was William Cobbett, whose vitriolic pen won him the sobriquet "Peter Porcupine" by his opponents for the stinging darts or quills reserved for his enemies, a designation he proudly adopted as the name of his newspaper, *Porcupine's Gazette*, launched in 1797 in Philadelphia.

Cobbett was a prolific and gifted writer, who wrote both in the United States and later in England. Mott calls him one of the half-dozen best satirists in the English language, and there are more than three hundred entries under his name in the Library of Congress. Before fleeing this country Peter Porcupine was involved in two high-profile libel suits. One, resulting in a fine of five thousand dollars, was brought by Dr. Benjamin Rush, Philadelphia's most celebrated physician, who had advocated bleeding and mercurial purges to stem a yellow fever epidemic; the other arose for his allegedly libeling the king of Spain and the Spanish ambassador to the United States in 1798. Cobbett's reply in the latter case was a spirited defense of freedom of expression—even though coming from an arch-conservative and monarchist. It was published as a pamphlet, *The Democratic Judge: Or the Equal Liberty of the Press*, an excerpt of which follows.

The press has been, and still is, restrained in this country. 1st, by the notion, which has been, for evident motives, inculcated by artful men, that no *private character* ought to be publickly censured. 2nd, by the very dangerous privilege, which *foreign agents* possess, in having *a choice of governments*, under which to bring their prosecutions. And, 3rd, by the terror, necessarily excited in every printer, by the *disgraceful and cruel punishment*, to which he is liable.

As to the first of these restraints, nothing can give us a better idea of the extent to which it is carried, than the bold assertions contained in the Chief Judge's [Thomas McKean's] Charge. He tells us that though a publication may not reflect any moral turpitude on the party, it may yet be libellous, if it *thwarts the said party's desire to appearing agreeable in life.* This is a very comfortable doctrine to every *scoundrel*, and particularly to every *whore*, for you will not find one of either description, who does not desire *to appear agreeble in life*. The reasonableness of this doctrine his Honour supports by telling us, that if any man does wrong, recourse may be had to the courts of justice, and that there can be no necessity, *nor reason*, for appeals to the people in *news-papers* or *pamphlets*.

Thus, you see, if his Honour shuts up the press, he has the goodness to open his court to us. But, if I were to see one officer of government go staggering drunk through the street, on his return from a civic festival; or another from the same cause, reeling into his seat, must I hold my tongue, or go to law with them? If a swindler, a man of the basest character, the most treacherous and corrupt of mortals, were to propose himself as a candidate for a seat in the Legislature, must I say nothing about him; must I not throw out even a hint to the people to warn them of their danger? If a Judge, or any other awful character, were to be detected in shop-lifting, or in the commision of any such base and infamous crime; or if a lady were to choose, now and then to relieve her husband by retiring a few months to the arms of a friend, must I sew up my lips, and must my press be as tame and contented as the cuckold himself?

Such may, indeed, be the practice of the American press; but is it that of the press of Great Britain. Only compare one of the London papers with an American paper, and you will soon see which comes from the free-est press. Is there a crime, is there a fault or a folly, which the editors and print-sellers in London do not lash? They dive into every assembly and every house; they spare characters neither public nor private; neither the people, the gentry, the clergy, the nobility nor the royal family itself is sheltered from their ridicule or their censure.[9]

Crucible of Liberty: The Alien and Sedition Acts

In the early national period a backlash to the assertiveness of the late Colonial period was embodied in the Alien and Sedition Acts (1798–1801), passed by a Federalist congress fearful of becoming involved in the Napoleonic wars at a time when the new nation was young and weak. At the time there were 25,000 aliens in the United States, but the measure seemed aimed mainly at the opposition Jeffersonian Republican newspaper editors, who were the only ones prosecuted. The Sedition Act called for imprisonment of not more than two years and fines of not more than two thousand dollars for anyone writing, printing, or making any "false, scandalous, and malicious" statement "against the Government of the United States, or either house of the Congress of the United States, with intent to defame . . . or to bring them . . . into contempt or disrepute." There were some twenty-five arrests under the Sedition Act, fifteen indictments, and eleven trials, resulting in ten convictions, eight of them involving newspapers.

At the same time, the act did admit truth as a defense and provided that the jury was empowered to determine both the law and the fact—principles first advanced in the Zenger case—and it did not provide for prior censorship. Patently unconstitutional, the Alien and Sedition Acts were enacted before the Supreme Court arrogated to itself the right of judicial review first enunciated by the Court in Marbury vs. Madison in 1803. The acts were the most serious threat to freedom of the press in the United States until the Pentagon Papers case of 1971, in which the federal government did try to impose prior restraint.

At the time of the Alien and Sedition Acts, the Jeffersonian Republicans reacted swiftly, James Madison writing the Virginia resolutions and Thomas Jefferson the Kentucky resolutions, both of which asserted the right of the states to nullify oppressive federal laws. The Kentucky document virtually became Jefferson's platform in the election of 1800, which he narrowly won after thirty-five ballots in Congress, marking the first transfer of political power in the young nation after twelve years of uninterrupted Federalist rule. In office, Jefferson pardoned all those who had been convicted under the Alien and Sedition Acts, which expired on March 3, 1801, and authorized that their fines be repaid to them.

Harry Croswell and the Sting of the "Wasp"

Jefferson, vilified more than perhaps any other president except Lincoln, countenanced a few "salutary" prosecutions in the states under the common law of seditious libel for attacks against his administration. In 1804, Harry Croswell, editor of the satirical newspaper the *Wasp* of Hudson, New York, was indicted for printing that "Jefferson had paid [James Thomson] Callender for calling Washington a traitor, a robber, a perjurer." (Actually, Jefferson had befriended Callender and advanced him small sums of money for humanitarian as well as partisan purposes before he defected to the Federalists, but not specifically to blacken Washington's character.) Croswell lost the trial case but on appeal had a champion in Alexander Hamilton, the brilliant secretary of the treasury under Washington and leader of the Federalist Party. Hamilton himself had founded the *New York Evening Post* in 1801, among other newspapers.

Croswell lost his appeal as well, but in the course of the proceedings Hamilton delivered one of the most eloquent defenses of press freedom in American history, upholding truth as a defense if published "from good motives and for justifiable ends." That sentiment was written into statute by the legislatures of New York and other states and influences libel law to this day. For practical results, the Croswell case was thus more significant than the Zenger trial. Following is an excerpt from Hamilton's plea.

The Liberty of the Press consists, in my idea, in publishing the truth, from good motives and for justifiable ends, though it reflect on government, on magistrates, or individuals. If it be not allowed, it excludes the priviledge of canvassing men, and our rulers. It is in vain to say, you may canvass measures. This is impossible without the right of looking to men. To say that measures can be discussed, and that there shall be no bearing on those, who are the authors of those measures, cannot be done. The very end and reason of discussion would be destroyed. Of what consequence to shew its object? why is it to be thus demonstrated, if not to show too, who is the author? It is essential to say, not only that the measure is bad and deleterious, but to hold up to the people who is the author, that, in this our free and elective government, he may be removed from the seat of power. If this be not to be done, then in vain will the voice of the people be raised against the inroads of tyranny. For, let a party but get into power, they may go on from step to step, and, in *spite* of canvassing their measures, fix themselves firmly in their seats, especially as they are never to be reproached for what they have done. This abstract mode, in practice can never be carried into effect. But, if under the qualifications I have mentioned, the power be allowed, the liberty for which I contend will operate as a salutary check. In speaking thus for the Freedom of the Press, I do not say there ought to be an unbridled licence; or that the characters of men who are good, will naturally tend eternally to support themselves. I do not stand here to say that no shackles are to be laid on this licence.

I consider this spirit of abuse and calumny as the pest of society. I know the best of men are not exempt from the attacks of slander. Though it pleased God to bless us with the first of characters [George Washington], and though it has pleased God to take him from us, and this band of calumniators, I say, that falsehood eternally repeated would have effected even his name. Drops of water in long and continued succession will wear out adamant. This therefore cannot be endured. It would be to put the best and the worst on the same level.

I contend for the liberty of publishing truth, with good motives and for justifiable ends, even though it reflect on government, magistrates, or private persons. I contend for it under the restraint of our tribunals.—When this is exceeded, let them interpose and punish. From this will follow none of those consequences so ably depicted. When, however, we do look at consequences, let me ask whether it is right that a permanent body of men, appointed by the executive, and, in some degree, always connected with it, should exclusively have the power of deciding on what shall constitute a libel on our rulers, or that they shall share it, united with a changeable body of men, chosen by the people. Let our Juries still be selected, as they now are, by lot. But it cannot be denied, that every permanent body of men is, more or less, liable to be influenced by the spirit of the existing administration: that such a body may be liable to corruption, and that they may be inclined to lean over towards party modes. No man can think more highly of our judges, and I may say personally so, of those who now preside, than myself; but I must forget what human nature is, and what her history has taught us, that permanent bodies may be so corrupted, before I can venture to assert that it cannot be. As then it may be, I do not think it safe thus to compromit our independence. For though, as individuals, they may be interested in the general welfare, yet, if once they enter into the views of government, their power may be converted into the engine of oppression. It is in vain to say that allowing them this exclusive right to declare the law, on what the Jury has found, can work no ill; for, by this privilege they can assume and modify the fact, so as to make the most innocent publication libellous. It is therefore not a security to say, that this exclusive power will but follow the law. It must be with the Jury to decide on the intent, they must in certain cases be permitted to judge of the law, and pronounce on the combined matter of law and of fact.[10]

Notes

1. William David Sloan and Julie Hedgepeth Williams, *The Early American Press, 1690-1783* (Westport, CT: Greenwood Press, 1994), 13.

2. Benjamin Harris, *Publick Occurrences Both Forreign and Domestick*, in Willard Grosvenor Bleyer, *The History of American Journalism* (New York: Houghton Mifflin Company, 1927), 46.

3. David A. Copeland, *Colonial American Newspapers: Character and Content* (Wilmington: University of Delaware Press, 1997), 231–32.

4. *Porcupine's Gazette*, July 31, 1797.

5. *The Life and Essays of Dr. Benjamin Franklin* (Philadelphia: J. and J. L. Gihon, 1852), 145–48.

6. Paul Leicester Ford, ed., *The Journals of Hugh Gaine, Printer*, vol. 1, *Biography and Bibliography* (New York: Dodd, Mead and Company, 1902), 74, 83.

7. Frank Luther Mott, *American Journalism: A History of Newspapers in the United States through 260 Years: 1690 to 1950* (New York: Macmillan Company, 1950), 34.

8. Livingston Rutherford, *John Peter Zenger, His Press, His Trial and a Bibliography of Zenger Imprints, also a Reprint of the First Edition of the Trial* (Gloucester, MA: Peter Smith Publisher, 1963), 238–40.

9. William Cobbett, *The Democratic Judge: Or the Equal Liberty of the Press* (Philadelphia: Peter Porcupine, March 1798), 89–90.

10. *The Speeches at Full Length . . . of General Hamilton, In the Great Cause of the People, against Harry Croswell, on an Indictment for a Libel on Thomas Jefferson, President of the United States* (New York: G. and R. Waite, 1804), 63–64.

2

Partisan Press to Penny Press

———<◆>———

The partisan press—newspapers founded or subsidized to further the political fortunes of individuals or parties—was forged during the Colonial and Revolutionary era, shaped with the debate over the adoption of the Constitution, and sharpened by the Federalist-Republican rivalry during the early national period. Primarily propaganda organs with "news" and comment mixed indiscriminantly in their columns, partisan newspapers reached a peak under Andrew Jackson's presidency (1829-1837). Presidents then had their own newspaper spokesmen—official, semiofficial, or unofficial. Thomas Jefferson (1801-1809) had the sedate *National Intelligencer*, edited by Samuel Harrison Smith, as his official organ after the capital moved from Philadelphia to Washington, DC, in 1800, and the unofficial robust party scrapper *Aurora*, edited by William Duane in Philadelphia, the most effective source of Jefferson's newspaper support. The practice of using presidential spokesmen declined with the years: Abraham Lincoln had no official newspaper but relied instead on his contacts within the New York Associated Press, and Andrew Johnson was the last president to have a shadow of an official newspaper.

The Center for the Study of Democratic Institutions recently recommended revival of a governmental newspaper, arguing that it might be more direct and honest than the manipulation of the commercial press by government officials, and one would at least know whose views were being presented. Max Lerner has pointed out in *America as a Civilization* that the European press is explicitly political—there are eleven daily newspapers in Copenhagen, for example, each representing a different political party—while the press in the United States is implicitly political, claiming independence but sometimes harboring hidden agendas.

The decline of the partisan press can be attributed to several factors—the rise of the penny press after 1833, technological developments that made an early mass press possible, discovery of the common people as an audience during the Jacksonian period, and the establishment of the Government Printing Office in 1860. Previously, federal departments and agencies had handed out their own printing contracts as political plums.

By far the most important of these developments, however, was the rise of the penny press. After Benjamin H. Day launched his *New York Sun*, the first successful penny paper, on September 3, 1833, American journalism was never again the same. The *Sun*'s motto was "It Shines for All." Previously, mercantile newspapers had been more or less for the elite, still containing mainly commercial and foreign news. Newspapers were sold only by subscription—and they cost eight to ten dollars a year—whereas the prevailing wage for workers was only eight dollars a week. No one could afford a week's salary to subscribe to a newspaper, the contents of which were of little interest to most people, anyway. Single copies, when they could be obtained, cost six cents. Day followed earlier attempts to establish a penny press by lowering the price for the first time and having newsboys hawk the papers on the street. This strategy, coupled with an emphasis on human interest and sensationalism, made the paper a phenomenal success. Circulation grew by leaps and bounds, and as newspapers attracted more advertising they became less reliant on political sponsorship and subsidies.

This dawning of a mass press could not have been possible, however, without technological improvements in printing. The first newspaper in the United States to install a steam-driven cylinder press was the *New York Daily Advertiser*, which in 1825 acquired a Napier press capable of printing two thousand papers an hour. In 1832, Richard Hoe, a New York manufacturer, perfected a double-cylinder press capable of running off four thousand newspapers an hour. The early Industrial

Revolution also brought about much-needed improvements in paper, ink, and typecasting.

The Crucible of Jefferson and the Press

To understand clearly what partisan newspapers were like before the advent of the penny press, three illustrations from Thomas Jefferson's presidency will be considered—his election in 1801, newspaper reaction to the return of Tom Paine from France in 1802, and allegations that Jefferson had fathered five children by his slave Sally Hemings. Jefferson, one of the most vilified of presidents, was not the last to be the object of personal abuse, nor has gossip been unusual in American journalism. The opposition Whigs charged that Jackson had lived in adultery with his wife, Rachel, before she received a divorce from her first husband (the charge apparently resulting from a legal misunderstanding), and the Democrats countered that John Quincy Adams (1825–1829) had had premarital sexual relations with his wife. Late in the twentieth century, "keyhole journalism" destroyed the presidential candidacy of Senator Gary Hart of Colorado and has blemished the image for many Americans of President William Jefferson Clinton.

Jefferson was narrowly elected president in 1801 despite the Federalists, who controlled four-fifths of the 235 newspapers in the young country, many of which regarded him as a dangerous radical. The *New-England Palladium*, for example, proclaimed in "news" columns: "Should the Infidel Jefferson be elected to the Presidency, the *seal of death* is that moment set on our holy religion, our churches will be prostrated, and some infamous prostitute, under the title of the Goddess of Reason, will preside in the Sanctuaries now devoted to the Most High."[1]

Vicious partisan attacks continued while Jefferson was in office, notably the assault on Tom Paine when that old revolutionary returned to the United States in 1802. Opposition to Paine was based not so much on his participation in the French Revolution, his having been elected to the French Convention and later imprisoned, nor for his defense of that upheaval in *The Rights of Man*, but rather for what was regarded as a deistic assault on organized religion, *The Age of Reason*. In the Federalist prints, the man who had done so much to obtain independence for all Americans was denounced as irreligious, depraved, unworthy to associate with the president of the United States, the assassin of Washington's character, and a journalistic hack who peddled his wares to the highest bidder.[2] Tom's fondness for brandy also came under attack in the *Gazette of the United States & Daily Advertiser* (July 22, 1801): "It is probable enough that the obscene old sinner [Thomas Paine] will be brought over to America once more, if his carcase is not too far gone to bear transportation." Paine was even denied the right to vote at his residence in New Rochelle, New York (the town granted him posthumous citizenship 139 years later, in 1948), and he lived in ignominy until his death in 1809. Denied burial in Quaker consecrated ground, Tom Paine was interred in the corner of a windswept field on the farm given him earlier for his Revolutionary services. Of the handful of persons present, only Mme. Nicolas de Bonneville, a French refugee whom Paine had befriended, had the good sense to say, "Oh, Mr. Paine, my son stands here as testimony of the gratitude of America, and I for France!"

The character of Tom Paine had been singled out for demolition by a partisan press in order to attack Jefferson. The defense of Paine in the Jeffersonian Republican journals was not nearly as effective, however, and next it was open season on the character of the president himself. In 1802, James Thomson Callender, a printer whom Jefferson had earlier befriended, turned against his former benefactor and started printing stories in his *Richmond Recorder* alleging that the president had fathered five children by his slave Sally Hemings at Monticello. This controversy continues today, fueled by a recent DNA study that seems to bear out Jefferson's paternity of one or more of Sally Heming's children. At the very least, Callender exploited the issue, embittered because of a delay in repaying his fine under the Alien and Sedition Acts, Jefferson's refusal to give him money for a new press, and denial to him of the postmastership at Richmond. In his newspaper, Callender openly stated time and again that he was bent on vengeance.

Jefferson himself, who never answered these newspaper attacks, in later life became at least temporarily disillusioned with the excesses of the openly partisan press, even though the Virginia Dynasty held power for almost a quarter of a century (from 1801 to 1825), with two terms each for Jefferson, James Madison, and James Monroe. The Jeffersonian Republicans finally balanced the number of their newspapers against those of the Federalists in 1812, and that party fielded its last presidential candidate in 1816.

Jackson and His Corps of Newspapers

It is no coincidence that the penny press was born and flourished during the presidency of Andrew Jackson (1829–1837), a frontiersman from Tennessee and hero of the victory over the British at the battle of New Orleans in 1812. Major interpretations of Jacksonian democracy, such as Arthur Schlesinger, Jr.'s *Age of Jackson* and Alice Felt Tyler's *Freedom's Ferment*, stress the emergence of the common people into the political arena. The air was vibrant with change, and that was reflected in the excitement of new expectations, which the penny press helped to satisfy. Earlier views of Jackson were quite different. The Whigs, who under the leadership of Henry Clay and Daniel Webster opposed the Democrats under Jackson after 1824, depicted him as an uncouth, despotic King Andrew who did little more than initiate the spoils system. With the blessing of Horace Greeley of the *New York Tribune*, our first national newspaper, the Whig Party was a formidable opponent, electing four presidents in the first half of the nineteenth century.

Later, the Progressive historians of the agrarian democratic school considered Jackson a second Jefferson, whereas others such as Schlesinger noted the incipient labor movement of this period and maintained that it was not a problem of sections but of classes. Certainly the first labor publication, the *Journeyman Mechanic's Advocate*, came out briefly in Philadelphia in 1827, and the first successful labor newspaper was the ably edited *Mechanic's Free Press*, launched by the Mechanic's Union of Trade Associations in 1828, the year of Jackson's election. It lasted until the Panic of 1837.

Although still small by modern standards, the circulation of newspapers in the United States during this period and the number of those newspapers were both the highest in the world. After Henry Clay threw his support to John Quincy Adams in the three-way election of 1824 that was decided by the House of Representatives, the defeated Andrew Jackson realized the necessity of a strong press to back his bid for 1828. Indeed, it was fitting that it was in the *Argus of Western America* of Frankfort, Kentucky, that the frontier hero had first outlined his views on government as early as 1825. Its editor, Amos Kendall, and his successor, Francis Preston Blair, became the key cogs in Jackson's political machine, ushering in an era that has not been surpassed for its close links between government and the press.

Recognizing the need for a national newspaper located at the capital, Jackson and his friends induced Duff Green (called by his opponents "Rough Green"), a St. Louis lawyer, journalist, and promoter, to launch the *United States Telegraph* in 1826. The move was astute, because in the election of 1828, according to Claude Bowers, Jackson was opposed by two-thirds of the newspapers, four-fifths of the ministers, virtually all of the manufacturers, and seven-eighths of the banking capital. Yet with the *Telegraph* and its satellites giving voice to the common people and their concerns, Jackson was elected.

One good thing to be said for the partisan press was that it focused attention on national politics rather than the court intrigues of Europe. Congress, for example, had not always been open to reporters. The House of Representatives opened its doors to the public in 1779, two days after the first session, but Philip Freneau of the *National Gazette* had to fight for two years to open up the Senate—a feat he accomplished in 1794. The highly capable shorthand reporters Joseph Gales, Jr., and William W. Seaton, successors for forty-eight years to Samuel Harrison Smith as editors of the *National Intelligencer*, began the *Register of Debates* in 1824, which in 1873 became the official *Congressional Record*. The former was a valuable source of information for newspapers in the hinterlands, and by about 1825 the first newspaper correspondents from elsewhere in the country appeared on the scene in Washington.

It was the Jackson administration newspaper, however, that was the oracle of public opinion to which loyal Democratic editors everywhere turned. When Duff Green and the *United States Telegraph* went over to the John C. Calhoun faction at the beginning of the sectional struggle, Jackson founded the *Washington Globe* in 1830, which became much more powerful. Francis P. Blair, who had succeeded Amos Kendall as editor of the *Argus of Western America*, was called to edit this new publication, and together with Jackson the two men dominated Washington and national politics. When the *Globe* was established, for example, federal officeholders earning one thousand dollars or more a year were expected to subscribe to and promote the interests of the newspaper. It was Blair who originated the technique of planting items in rural Democratic newspapers and then reprinting them in the *Globe* as evidence of a groundswell of public opinion. Jackson also controlled the press by shunting critics into government appointments or similarly rewarding the party faithful. The *National Intelligencer* in 1832 printed a list of fifty-seven journalists who had been given federal appointments by Jackson.

Third of the triumvirate who marched and countermarched Democratic editors through their paces at both state and national levels in the columns of the *Globe* was John C. Rives, who rounded out the "Kitchen Cabinet." The *Globe* later became the spokesman for Martin Van Buren, who succeeded Jackson, but as no other newspaper before or since, the *Globe* served as disciplinarian for a major political party.

Meanwhile, the opposition was not sitting on its hands. In the celebrated show of strength between Jackson and Nicholas Biddle over rechartering the Bank of the United States, the banker in the early 1830s spent $29,600 of public money to defend the institution by bribing newspaper editors for favorable publicity. Jackson wanted to decentralize the money system through state banks for debtor relief, among other reasons, and Amos Kendall drafted the message of July 10, 1832, vetoing the bill to recharter the Bank of the United

States. In his autobiography, from which the following selection is taken, we have firsthand insights into the political and press infighting of the day.

Even before the organization of General Jackson's administration, General Duff Green, the editor of the "United States Telegraph," had lost, if ever he enjoyed, the confidence of many of the General's supporters. A majority of them in the Senate, at the session of 1828–29, were supposed to be averse to electing him their printer. Mr. Amos Kendall, being then in Washington, was informed by Major Eaton that he could have the printing of that body if he would consent to take it. He replied that he would consent only on condition that General Green should be consulted, and should give his assent; but he declined to consult Green himself, and requested that what had passed as far as he was concerned should not be communicated to that gentleman.

On a subsequent occasion, Major Eaton reported that Green had been consulted, and refused his assent; but it was proposed to elect Mr. Kendall notwithstanding, when the latter peremptorily refused to let his name be used. This refusal arose, not from any repugnance to the appointment in itself, but from an indisposition to interfere in any way with Green's expectations, however extravagant; for it could not be denied that he had established himself at Washington, risking everything in a doubtful contest, and there would be a seeming unfairness in depriving him of the anticipated reward of his labors, though his views might be grasping and unreasonable. Such an act, it seemed to Mr. Kendall, would sow the seeds of discord at the very outset of General Jackson's administration, to which he did not then doubt General Green's fidelity. . . .

As to Mr. Kendall himself, Green remarked that if rejected by the Senate for the Fourth Auditorship of the Treasury, to which he had been appointed, he might return to Kentucky and resume his editorial profession. When told that Mr. Kendall did not intend in that event to return to Kentucky, a new idea seemed to strike him, and it was singular that, when the vote was taken on his nomination, the Senate was equally divided, and he was confirmed by the casting vote of Mr. Calhoun, then Vice-President.

These incidents, and more of like tendency, created an impression among the friends of General Jackson that General Green was more the friend of Mr. Calhoun than of the President, and was already embarrassing the administration by intrigues looking toward the succession. It was their desire that General Jackson should be elected for another term, that he might establish the policy in relation to the Bank of the United States, and other subjects which he had initiated, and they apprehended that in this important measure they would not have the support of the "United States Telegraph." It seemed to them important, therefore, that another paper should be established at Washington, devoted exclusively to the support of the administration and its leading measures, without regard to the succession. It was not their object or desire to supersede the "Telegraph" as an official paper, or to deprive General Green of the printing of Congress, should he remain faithful, but to furnish an auxiliary paper, published semi-weekly, and sustained by its subscriptions, advertising, and job work.

When the project was broached to General Jackson, he entirely disapproved of it. He still had faith in the fidelity of the "Telegraph," and he feared collision between the papers should another be established. It was not long, however, before he began to realize the necessity of such a paper as was proposed, and finally gave the project his tacit approval.

The several public offices were visited for the purpose of ascertaining whether they would give such a paper a portion of their printing. The responses were generally favorable; but Mr. Van Buren, then Secretary of State, replied that he not only would not promise, but would not give the paper a dollar's worth of printing should it be established. The reason he gave was, that were such a paper established its origin would be attributed to him and he was resolved to be able to say truly that he had nothing to do with it.

In a consultation on the subject, Major W.T. Barry, then Postmaster-General, named Francis P. Blair, who was then writing for Mr. Kendall's paper in Frankfort, Kentucky, as a suitable person for editor, and Mr. Kendall undertook to correspond with him on the subject. Mr. Blair hesitated, and was induced to accede only by Mr. Kendall's assurance that he would bear an equal share in the responsibilities, upon the condition that he should at any time have the privilege of resigning the office he then held and becoming an equal partner in the new establishment.

This assurance was given, not because Mr. Kendall had any inclination to avail himself of the privilege, but only to overcome the hesitation of Mr. Blair, who thereupon determined to assume the position, writing Mr. Kendall that he should hold him responsible for the result.

Neither Mr. Blair nor Mr. Kendall had any capital to invest in such an undertaking. One condition insisted upon by Mr. Blair was that no publicity should be given to the project until he could have an opportunity to compound with his creditors, and particularly the Bank of the United States, to which he was heavily indebted. Under these circumstances, it was essential to make the new paper self-sustaining from the start. Its terms of subscription required payment in advance, and a printer was hired to print it. All the arrangements were made by Mr. Kendall before Mr. Blair's arrival, and he had only to ratify and execute what had already been planned. Only the name of the paper and its motto remained to be fixed upon. Mr. Kendall and Mr. Blair concurred in the name and in the sentiment embraced in the motto, "The world is governed too much"; but the phrase in which it is so briefly expressed was the work of Mr. Kendall.

Mr. Blair communicated frankly to General Green the objects of his location at Washington, so far as they had reference to the public printing and the official position of the "Telegraph," and he was advised studiously to avoid any expression to which General Green could justly take exception. But the latter evidently had no faith in Mr. Blair's professions, and looked upon the new paper as intended to supersede his establishment and promote the elevation of Mr. Van Buren to the Presidency in opposition to his own favorite, Mr. Calhoun.

The first number of the "Globe" appeared on the 7th of December, 1830. Little notice was taken of it by the "Telegraph" until February, 1831, when General Green was elected printer to both Houses of Congress. Upon that event the "Globe" congratulated the friends of the administration on the disappointment of its enemies, who had anticipated divisions from the establishment of a new Jackson press at Washington. But the prospect of harmony, if there really was one, was of short duration. No sooner had the printing of Congress been secured, than the "Telegraph" began to throw out innuendos against the "Globe," of which the latter, however, took no notice. In a few days after the election of printer, Mr. Calhoun committed the fatal error of bringing before the public, both in pamphlet and through the "Telegraph," his correspondence with General Jackson touching the events of the Seminole war. On the 19th of February, 1831, the "Globe" came out with an article exposing Mr. Calhoun and vindicating the President. The "Telegraph" had already ranged itself on Mr. Calhoun's side. A sharp controversy ensued, which in a short time led to the repudiation of the "Telegraph," and the adoption of the "Globe" as the organ of the administration.

The "Globe" was still a semi-weekly paper, printed by contract. The position to which it had now attained required that it should be placed on an independent footing and published daily; but Mr. Blair had not the means to purchase the necessary materials. To raise the funds, he called on the friends of the President in Washington and elsewhere, who subscribed and paid in advance for six hundred copies of the "Daily Globe," at ten dollars per annum, and by this aid the "Globe" was made a daily paper. Thus, first and last, the "Globe" was established without a dollar of capital furnished by its proprietor, and, as Mr. Blair used to say, like the great globe we inhabit, was created out of nothing.

Mr. Benton is entirely mistaken in attributing the origin of the "Globe" to General Jackson. General Green is equally in error in attributing it to Mr. Van Buren or his friends. It originated with those friends of General Jackson who regarded measures more than men, and desired his re-election for another four years, not so much for his own sake as to effect reforms in the government which no other man was capable of bringing about; chief of these was its severance from the banking power organized and exercised under the charter of the Bank of the United States. The "Globe's" subsequent support of Mr. Van Buren was occasioned by later events, which seemed to indicate that his administration would, so far as measures were concerned, be in effect a continuation of that of General Jackson.[3]

The *New York Sun* and Its Successors

There were ten newspapers in New York City when Benjamin H. Day launched the *New York Sun* on September 3, 1833, the first successful penny newspaper, which stated as its object "to lay before the public, at a price within the means of everyone, all the news of the day." This idea did not originate with Day, however. The formula had been tried by the *Cent* in Philadelphia, the *Bostonian* in Boston, and the *Morning Post* in New York City—all of which failed, perhaps because they emphasized more the low cost than the content of their papers. Day had served as an apprentice on the *Springfield* (Massachusetts) *Republican*, founded by Samuel Bowles in 1824; under Bowles and his descendants the *Republican* was a training ground for many top journalists of the period.

As the penny press evolved in New York, it succeeded because it conveyed news, however roughly, rather than views, with an emphasis on what would interest the average person in the street: local or hometown news, crime and sex, and what later would be called "human-interest" stories. George W. Wisner, a young veteran Bow Street police station reporter in London, joined the *Sun* staff when the newspaper was less than a week old. The following is an example of one item from his column simply headed "Police Office" from the issue of July 4, 1834: "William Luvoy got drunk because yesterday was so devilish warm. Drank 9 glasses of brandy and water and said he would be cursed if he wouldn't drink 9 more as quick as he could raise the money to buy it with. He would like to know what right the magistrate had to interfere with his private affairs. Fined $2—forgot his pocketbook, and was sent over to Bridewell." Such items were amusing for working people who had few other sources of entertainment. For his efforts, Wisner received four dollars a week and a share of the profits. Within a year he was co-owner of the newspaper. With this concept of the news, one essentially still with us today, circulation of the *Sun* skyrocketed. Within four months it had reached five thousand whereas those of the earlier partisan newspapers, William Coleman's *New York Evening Post* and William Duane's *Aurora* in Philadelphia, did not exceed fifteen hundred.

When Richard Adams Locke wrote his famous hoax for the *Sun* that life had been sighted on the moon, circulation for that issue (August 28, 1835) zoomed to 19,360, allowing Day to boast that his newspaper had the highest circulation in the world, surpassing the 17,000 of the *London Times*. Edgar Allan Poe later wrote, "From the epoch of the hoax, 'The Sun' shone with unmitigated splendor. The start thus given the paper insured it a triumph. . . . Its success firmly established 'the penny system' throughout the country."[4] By 1837, at the end of Jackson's second term, the *Sun* issued 30,000 copies a day, more than all New York dailies combined when it had first come out. Such success spawned imitators. In 1833 there had been about 1,200 newspapers publishing in the United States. Despite a high mortality rate, twenty years later— thanks to the impact of the penny press—there were 2,500 newspapers, 250 of them dailies, publishing a million copies a day.

Others fell by the wayside because marketing alone—one-third of the *Sun* was filled with advertising—could not save a newspaper if it lacked the editorial genius of a James Gordon Bennett or Horace Greeley, children of the penny-press era who became two of the most powerful journalists of the nineteenth century. Bennett appeared on the scene first, having come from Scotland at the age of twenty-four and becoming first associate editor and then Washington correspondent for the *New York Enquirer*, whose merger with the *Morning Courier* he engineered in 1829. The combined newspaper became a staunch Jackson supporter and the leading newspaper in the East, but Bennett wanted to strike out on his own. Denied a position in the Jackson administration and an association with Day on the *Sun*, Bennett launched the *New York Herald* in 1835. Never known for his modesty, the ambitious Scotsman proclaimed in the issue of October 29, 1836, "I am building up a newspaper establishment that will take the lead of all others that ever appeared in the world in virtue, in morals, in science, in knowledge, in industry, in taste, in power, in influence." He nevertheless surpassed the sensationalism of the *Sun* with even more blatant exploitation of crime and sex news. These excesses led to the boycott of the *Herald* by civic and religious groups in the "Moral War" of 1840, which cost Bennett one-third of his subscribers.

On the other hand, Bennett did much to shape the modern newspaper. Timeliness of news continued to gain in importance, and after the first steamship crossed the Atlantic in 1838, Bennett established correspondents in Europe and in leading American cities, including a bureau in Washington. He even used a small fleet of boats to meet incoming ships from abroad to rush the news to the presses before the vessels entered New York harbor. Later, he fielded sixty-three war correspondents to cover all major theaters of the Civil War.

James Gordon Bennett believed that journalism in general, and that he in particular, had a mission: to revitalize and reform American society. He once had argued before the U.S. attorney general the right of the press to report on a famous murder trial of the day without permission of the court by advancing the argument that newspapers are "the living jury of the nation," a concept that some future historian might apply to television in the O. J. Simpson murder trial and other notorious legal battles of the 1990s. Bennett also introduced in the *Herald* the first financial section, letters to the editor, theater reviews, society news, and sports news. By 1860 the *Herald* had outstripped the *Sun* in circulation, but this explosion of public opinion and entrepreneurial zeal rested upon penny-press techniques. As Allan Nevins phrased it, "With all his errors, he [Bennett] had been perhaps the chief figure in a great and democratic revolution in journalism, a natural and beneficial concomitant of the rise of Jacksonian democracy."[5] In the following selection, taken from his *Memoirs*, Bennett describes the birth of modern journalism, the penny press.

Mr. Day's usual business becoming less and less profitable, he determined to issue the *Sun*. He knew that much labor and the strictest economy would be requisite to make it successful. He engaged a stranger, Mr. Benton, as a paragraphist, but he was not equal to the task, though stimulated by a conditional arrangement. Mr. Day, alone, then edited the paper. See him now placing the foundation of the most gigantic institution known to civilization—one that has swayed the people of the New World, and which eventually will move the chief nations of Europe. He commences his work at daylight—takes his news from the large morning papers, and has it ready for his apprentices. At nine o'clock the forms of type are on the press, at which each person in the office, in his turn, works. The circulation in a few days, increases. A thousand copies are wanted! . . .

Newsboys are unknown in 1833. At the steamboats, the newspaper carriers are finding that they can sell a few copies, at six cents each—probably to hungry politicians, who are hurrying away to Albany or to Washington; or, perhaps, to merchants who wish to see the ship news, or the prices current—and the publishers will print, for the carriers, only a few extra copies. It is quite uncertain if the papers can be sold, even if they contain libels on the President, or his family, or on a score of politicians. A first rate murder, well described, may make the sale of a hundred copies quite possible! These carriers will not touch the *Sun*. What! at a cent? It is too small a business.

Men live in this world to learn; and often find that oaks spring from acorns. Mr. Day will demonstrate this. He advertises for boys to work by the week. He has six or eight of them engaged, at two dollars a week, to distribute the *Sun* of September the third. Each one goes out to sell one hundred and twenty-five copies, in a designated district, which is not to be deserted during the day, unless the papers are all sold. There are several active boys in the squad. They have been gone two or three hours, and have not a paper on hand. Mr. Day compliments these with more copies, at nine cents a dozen. Two or three of the boys now earn five dollars in a week. . . .

It is to Mr. Day's persistent course that society is to attribute the consequences now seen in the successful establishment of numerous daily newspapers, at low prices, in the large cities of the United States. He it was that began to prepare the public for a profitable and civilizing habit of reading, which has now become fixed and universal. Even slander was slow in sale at sixpence!

Mr. Day purchased Mr. Wisner's share of the *Sun* in July, 1835, for fifty-three hundred dollars, and subsequently, in 1838, sold the whole establishment to Moses Y. Beach, for thirty-eight thousand dollars—eight thousand dollars for the materials, and the remainder for the right and good will. The paper had a circulation, then, of thirty-four thousand copies! Such was the result of a visionary scheme.[6]

The Penny Press Reaches Maturity

As Bennett was building up the reputation of the *Herald*, another newcomer entered the arena of New York City journalism—Horace Greeley, who failed at his first venture to put a penny paper on the streets because of a snowstorm, but who later started the famous *New York Tribune* as a penny paper in 1841, the only Whig newspaper in New York at that time. Greeley and Bennett dominated American journalism until late in the nineteenth century when Pulitzer and Hearst magnified many of the trends of the original penny press in their so-called New Journalism. An echo of Bennett and Greeley exists today in the merged *International Herald-Tribune*, published in Paris.

The *Tribune* trailed both the *Sun* and *Herald* in daily circulation, but its national influence rested on the weekly edition with its astonishing circulation for that period of 200,000. It was read primarily in the rural Midwest, being receptive to Greeley's plans for social betterment that Easterners dismissed as "crackpot" or "scatter-brained" (it should be noted that later the Populist and Progressive movements also found strongholds in the Midwest). By 1854 the *Tribune* employed fourteen local reporters, twenty American correspondents, and eighteen foreign correspondents, including Karl Marx of London, who wrote almost five hundred columns on European politics. In addition to the news, the *Tribune* also published lectures, serialized novels, excerpts from books, poems, and book reviews.

The penny press strategy—lower cost, greater circulation—was applied to the weekly edition as well. For two dollars a year (or one dollar when clubs of twenty members subscribed), loyal heartland readers looked to Greeley for political guidance and advice on other matters. More than anyone else up to his time, he made the function of the editor personal by signing his editorials, traveling widely, and making many speeches. With his unpretentious clothes, chin whiskers, steel-rimmed glasses, and cherubic face, Greeley was a figure whom everyone recognized. He was also the best writer since William Cobbett, in the judgment of E. L. Godkin, editor of both the *Nation* and the *New York Evening Post*. Farmers and others declared that they could not do without their Bible, their Shakespeare, and "Uncle Horace's" *Tribune.*

Some critics denounced his "beneficent capitalism" as socialism, but Greeley is more accurately described as a pragmatic humanitarian. In 1850, for example, he became the first president of the New York Printers' Union, and when he led the movement to free Jefferson Davis from prison after the Civil War, the *Tribune* lost more than half its circulation. He ran on the Liberal Republican presidential ticket in 1872 and lost amid such mud-slinging that he later expressed uncertainty whether he had been running for president or the state penitentiary. He died a few weeks after the election.

One of Greeley's legacies was his training of a young reporter, Henry J. Raymond, who with George Jones in 1851 was to found the *New York Times*, which tended to counter the excesses of the other penny papers and to specialize in foreign news. Raymond demanded fair, careful, and accurate reporting by his staff, which the *New York Times* today continues to insist upon, although the present *Times* did not begin to take shape until Adolph S. Ochs bought it in 1896. An assessment of Raymond's abilities is included in the following account by Greeley of the founding of the *New York Tribune*. It is taken from his autobiography, *Recollections of a Busy Life.*

On the tenth day of April, 1841—a day of most unseasonable chill and sleet and snow, our city held her great funeral parade and pageant in honor of our lost President [William Henry Harrison] who had died six days before. General Robert Bogardus, the venerable Grand Marshal of the parade, died not long afterward of exposure to its inclemencies. On that leaden, funereal morning, the most inhospitable of the year, I issued the first number of The

New York Tribune. It was a small sheet, for it was to be retailed for a cent, and not much of a newspaper could be afforded for that price, even in those specie-paying times. I had been incited to this enterprise by several Whig friends, who deemed a cheap daily, addressed more especially to the laboring class, eminently needed in our city, where the only two cheap journals then and still existing—*The Sun* and *The Herald*—were in decided, though unavowed, and therefore more effective, sympathy and affiliation with the Democratic party. . . .

My leading idea was the establishment of a journal removed alike from servile partisanship on the one hand and from gagged, mincing neutrality on the other. Party spirit is so fierce and intolerant in this country that the editor of a non-partisan sheet is restrained from saying what he thinks and feels on the most vital, imminent topics; while, on the other hand, a Democratic, Whig, or Republican journal is generally expected to praise or blame, like or dislike, eulogize or condemn, in precise accordance with the views and interest of its party. I believed there was a happy medium between these extremes, a position from which a journalist might openly and heartily advocate the principles and commend the measures of that party to which his convictions allied him, yet frankly dissent from its course on a particular question, and even denounce its candidates if they were shown to be deficient in capacity or (far worse) in integrity. I felt that a journal thus loyal to its guiding convictions, yet ready to expose and condemn unworthy conduct or incidental error on the part of men attached to its party, must be far more effective, even party-wise, than though it might always be counted on to applaud or reprobate, bless or curse, as the party's prejudices or immediate interest might seem to prescribe. . . .

I had been ten years in New York, was thirty years old, in full health and vigor, and worth, I presume, about two thousand dollars, half of it in printing materials. . . .

On the intellectual side, my venture was not so rash as it seemed. My own fifteen years' devotion to newspaper-making, in all its phases, was worth far more than will be generally supposed; and I had already secured a first assistant in Mr. Henry J. Raymond, who—having for two years, while in college at Burlington, Vt., been a valued contributor to the literary side of *The New-Yorker*—had hied to the city directly upon graduating, late in 1840, and gladly accepted my offer to hire him at eight dollars per week until he could do better. I had not much for him to do till *The Tribune* was started: then I had enough: and I never found another person, barely of age and just from his studies, who evinced so signal and such versatile ability in journalism as he did. Abler and stronger men I may have met; a cleverer, readier, more generally efficient journalist, I never saw. He remained with me nearly eight years, if my memory serves, and is the only assistant with whom I ever felt required to remonstrate for doing more work than any human brain and frame could be expected long to endure. His salary was of course gradually increased from time to time; but his services were more valuable in proportion to their cost than those of any one else who ever aided me on *The Tribune*. . . .

About five hundred names of subscribers had already been obtained for *The Tribune*—mainly by my warm personal and political friends, Noah Cook and James Coggeshall—before its first issue, where I printed five thousand, and nearly succeeded in giving away all of them that would not sell. I had type, but no presses; and so had to hire my press-work done by the "token"; my folding and mailing must have staggered me but for the circumstance that I had few papers to mail, and not very many to fold. The lack of the present machinery of railroads and expresses was a grave obstacle to the circulation of my paper outside of the city's suburbs; but I think its paid-for issues were two thousand at the close of the first week, and that they thenceforth increased pretty steadily, at the rate of five hundred per week, till they reached ten thousand. . . .

The idea is rather to embody in a single sheet the information daily required by all those who aim to keep "posted" on every important occurrence; so that the lawyer, the merchant, the banker, the forwarder, the economist, the author, the politician, etc., may find here whatever he needs to see, and be spared the trouble of looking elsewhere. A copy of a great morning journal now contains more matter than an average twelvemo volume, and its production costs far more, while it is sold for a fortieth or fiftieth part of the volume's price. There is no other miracle of cheapness which at all approaches it. The Electric Telegraph has precluded the multiplication of journals in the great cities, by enormously increasing the cost of publishing each of them. *The Tribune*, for example, now [1868] pays more than one hundred thousand dollars per annum for intellectual labor (reporting included) in and about its office, and one hundred thousand dollars more for correspondence and telegraphing,—in other words, for collecting and transmitting news. And, while its income has been largely increased from year to year, its expenses have inevitably been swelled even more rapidly; so that, at the close of 1866, in which its receipts had been over nine hundred thousand dollars, its expenses had been very nearly equal in amount, leaving no profit beyond a fair rent for the premises it owned and occupied. And yet its stockholders were satisfied that they had done a good business,—that the increase in the patronage and value of the establishment amounted to a fair interest on their investment, and might well be accepted in lieu of a dividend. In the good time coming, with cheaper paper and less exorbitant charges for "cable despatches" from the Old World, they will doubtless reap where they have now faithfully sown. Yet they realize and accept the fact, that a journal radically hostile to the gainful arts whereby the cunning and powerful few live sumptuously without useful labor, and often amass wealth, by pandering to lawless sensuality and popular vice, can never hope to enrich its publishers so rapidly nor so vastly as though it had a soft side for the Liquor Traffic, and for all kindred allurements to carnal appetite and sensual indulgence.

Fame is a vapor; popularity an accident; riches take wings; the only earthly certainty is oblivion; no man can foresee what a day may bring forth; while those who cheer to-day will often curse to-morrow: and yet I cherish the hope that the journal I projected and established will live and flourish long after I shall have mouldered into forgotten dust, being guided by a larger wisdom, a more unerring sagacity to discern the right, though not by a more unfaltering readiness to embrace and defend it at whatever personal cost; and that the stone which covers my ashes may bear to future eyes the still intelligible inscription, "Founder of *The New York Tribune*."[7]

Jane Grey Swisshelm and Women's Rights

Before the advent of the penny press, numerous specialized newspapers dotted the landscape of American journalism, such as religious and agricultural publications, and the success of the leading penny papers encouraged the creation of many more. As sectional conflict propelled the country closer to civil war, antislavery became a leading issue. Women such as editor Jane Grey Swisshelm entered the abolitionist struggle with force and vigor. As Ida M. Tarbell (see Chapter 6) later wrote in her series on "The American Woman" for *American Magazine*, "The first decided jar the American woman gave her country was when she showed her determination to work in [any way] she chose for the correction of any evil which stirred her soul. The specific wrong on which she first fixed her attention was slavery."[8]

Swisshelm became active in the antislavery cause at the age of fourteen and a year later taught and managed the only school in Wilkinsburg, Pennsylvania. Later she also took up the causes of the rights of married women and property rights of all women. After establishing the *Pittsburgh Satur-day Visiter* (*sic*) in 1847 with a legacy from her mother, she advocated woman's suffrage as well as championing the antislavery and temperance causes. Moving to Minnesota in 1858, she started the *St. Cloud Visiter*, closed by a libel suit in several months and replaced by the *St. Cloud Democrat*, which she edited until 1863. Like editors before and after her, she used her newspapers at times in personal quarrels, as with the mayor of St. Cloud or in attacks on Daniel Webster's private life. During the Civil War she did clerical work in Washington, DC, and as a volunteer in a war hospital there. In 1866 she attacked President Andrew Johnson with such vehemence in her *Reconstructionist* that he dismissed her from government service.

In the selection that follows, taken from her autobiographical *Half a Century* (1880), Jane Grey Swisshelm gives her opinion on "Bloomers and Woman's Rights Conventions." She urges women to focus on the issues rather than on superficial matters such as dress. When a national convention promoted the cause of women's bloomers (modified trousers), Swisshelm warned, "It will open a door through which fools and fanatics will pour in, and make the cause ridiculous." She also advised wise use of the many new journalistic voices made possible in the era of the penny press.

The appearance of *The Visiter* was the signal for an outbreak, for which I was wholly unprepared, and one which proved the existence of an eating cancer of discontent in the body politic. Under the smooth surface of society lay a mass of moral disease, which suddenly broke out into an eruption of complaints, from those who felt themselves oppressed by the old Saxon and ecclesiastical laws under which one-half the people of the republic still lived.

In the laws governing the interests peculiar to men, and those affecting their interests in common with women, great advance had been made during the past six centuries, but those regarding the exclusive interests of women, had remained in *statu quo*, since King Alfred the Great and the knights of his Round Table fell asleep. The anti-negro-slavery object of my paper seemed to be lost sight of, both by friends and foes of human progress, in the surprise at the innovation of a woman entering the political arena, to argue publicly on great questions of national policy, and while men were defending their pantaloons, they created and spread the idea, that masculine supremacy lay in the form of their garments, and that a woman dressed like a man would be as potent as he.

Strange as it may now seem, they succeeded in giving such efficacy to the idea, that no less a person than Mrs. Elizabeth Cady Stanton was led astray by it, so that she set her cool, wise head to work and invented a costume, which she believed would emancipate woman from thraldom. Her invitation was adopted by her friend Mrs. Bloomer, editor and proprietor of the *Lily*, a small paper then in infancy in Syracuse, N.Y., and from her, the dress took its name—"the bloomer." Both women believed in their dress, and staunchly advocated it as the sovereignest remedy for all the ills that a woman's flesh is heir to.

I made a suit and wore it at home parts of two days, long enough to feel assured that it must be a failure; and so opposed it earnestly, but nothing I could say or do could make it apparent that pantaloons were not the real objective point, at which all discontented women aimed. I had once been tried on a charge of purloining pantaloons, and been acquitted for lack of evidence; but now, here was the proof! The women themselves, leaders of the malcontents, promulgated and pressed their claim to bifurcated garments, and the whole tide of popular discussion was turned into that ridiculous channel.

The Visiter had a large list of subscribers in Salem, Ohio, and in the summer of '49 a letter from a lady came to me saying, that the *Visiter* had stirred up so much interest in women's rights that a meeting had been held and a committee appointed to get up a woman's rights convention, and she, as chairman of that committee, invited me to preside. I felt on reading this as if I had had a douche bath; then, as a lawyer might have felt who had carried a case for a corporation through the lower court, and when expecting it up before the supreme bench, had learned that all his clients were coming to address the court on the merits of the case.

By the pecks of letters I had been receiving, I had learned that there were thousands of women with grievances, and no power to state them or to discriminate between those which could be reached by law and those purely personal; and that the love of privacy with which the whole sex was accredited was a mistake, since most of my correspondents literally agonized to get before the public. Publicity! publicity! was the persistent demand. To meet the demand, small papers, owned and edited by women, sprang up all over the land, and like Jonah's gourd, perished in a night. Ruskin says to be noble is to be known, and at that period there was a great demand on the part of women for their full allowance of nobility; but not one in a hundred thought of merit as a means of reaching it. No use waiting to learn to put two consecutive sentences together in any connected form, or for an idea or the power of expressing it. One woman was printing her productions, and why should not all the rest do likewise? They had so long followed some leader like a flock of sheep, that now they would rush through the first gap into newspaperdom.[9]

Notes

1. Quoted in the Hudson *Bee*, September 7, 1802.

2. Jerry W. Knudson, "The Rage around Tom Paine, Newspaper Reaction to His Homecoming in 1802," *New-York Historical Society Quarterly* 53, no. 1 (January 1969): 34–63.

3. William Stickney, ed., *Autobiography of Amos Kendall* (Gloucester, MA: Peter Smith Publisher, 1949), 370–74.

4. Quoted in Frank M. O'Brien, "Benjamin Henry Day," *Dictionary of American Biography*, 20 vols. (New York: Charles Scribner's Sons, 1931), 3:155.

5. Allan Nevins, "James Gordon Bennett," *Dictionary of American Biography* (New York: Charles Scribner's Sons, 1928), 1:199.

6. James Gordon Bennett, *Memoirs of James Gordon Bennett and His Times* (New York: Stringer and Townsend, 1855), 180–81, 184.

7. Horace Greeley, *Recollections of a Busy Life* . . . (New York: J. B. Ford and Company, 1868), 136–40, 142–43.

8. Ida M. Tarbell, "The American Woman," *American Magazine* 69, no. 3 (January 1910): 363.

9. Jane Grey Swisshelm, *Half a Century* (Chicago: Jansen, McClurg and Company, 1880), 139–42.

3

The Civil War

———————⟨◆⟩———————

When the English novelist D. H. Lawrence visited the United States in 1922 he thought this country could become a great civilization, but first it had to undergo "a vast death happening." In other words, the people had to suffer as in Europe before they would lose their innocence and mature. Had he never heard of the Civil War? On September 17, 1862, at the battle of Antietam alone, the bloodiest encounter of a long and bloody war, 12,410 Union and 13,724 Confederate soldiers perished.

An event of such cataclysmic proportions as the Civil War elicited various historical interpretations as the years passed. At first, through the 1890s, the American attitude toward the Civil War and events leading up to it was that the conflict was a "moral crusade" between the virtuous, antislavery North and the evil, slave-holding South. On the other hand, Southern defenders such as Jefferson Davis and Alexander Stephens blamed the war on a "conspiracy" of wicked Northern politicians.

The first crop of young Northerners who returned from Germany with Ph.D.s refuted these amateur propagandists on both sides and declared that secession had to have been stopped because sovereignty had been regarded as indivisible by the Founding Fathers. The second generation of trained historians concentrated on economic motives. This interpretation emphasized the sectional struggle: The South joined with the West to dominate the North in national politics until the election of Lincoln in 1860, when the West defected to the North.

Wounds were gradually healing. The third generation of historians, both North and South, decided that the Civil War could only be understood as caused by a "blundering

generation," in the words of James G. Randall, the culmination of long and sustained propaganda both by the abolitionists and those who defended "the peculiar institution" of
slavery. But the fourth generation, after World War II, again
regarded the Civil War as a "good fight." Arthur Schlesinger,
Jr., has called the Civil War "a necessary war, a war between
morality and evil." Thus, we have come full circle back to the
issue of slavery as the primary cause of the conflict. Certainly
it is a thread running through all the other explanations,
whether secession (to protect the slave system), sectional
(should Western territories enter the Union as free or slave
states?), or propaganda (focusing on the slavery issue). But if
we accept the "blundering generation" school of thought, the
press of the North and the South must partly shoulder the
blame for tearing a nation asunder. Politically partisan journalism had not run its course despite the growing reliance of
the penny press on advertising, and the creation of the Government Printing Office, in 1860, which took politics out of
official printing contracts.

The appearance of embryonic editorials in the first decade
of the nineteenth century—separating comment from news—
took some, but by no means all, of the heated rhetoric out of
the news columns. After Abraham Lincoln was elected, belli-
cose feelings in the Southern and border states ran white hot.
Consider, for example, these excerpts from the *Richmond Examiner*, printed only days after South Carolina forces fired
on Fort Sumter in Charleston harbor:

> From the mountain-tops and valleys to the shores of the sea,
> there is one wild shout of fierce resolve to capture Washing-
> ton City, at all and every human hazard. That filthy cage of
> unclean birds must and will assuredly be purified by fire.
> . . . It is not to be endured that this flight of abolition harpies
> shall come down from the black North for their roosts in the
> heart of the South, to defile and brutalize the land. . . . Our
> people can take it [Washington, DC],—they *will* take it,— and
> [General Winfield] Scott the arch-traitor, and Lincoln the
> beast, combined, cannot prevent it. The just indignation of
> an outraged and deeply injured people will teach the Illinois
> ape to repeat his race and retrace his journey across the

borders of the free negro States still more rapidly than he came. . . .

Great cleansing and purification are needed and will be given to that festering sink of iniquity,—that wallow of Lincoln and Scott,—the desecrated city of Washington; and many indeed will be the carcasses of dogs and caitiffs that will blacken the air upon the gallows before the work is accomplished. So let it be.[1]

Northern writers could be just as emotional, as was the case with Horace Greeley's celebrated editorial "Prayer of Twenty Millions" in the *New-York Tribune* of August 20, 1862, which (like Tom Paine's *Common Sense* of the Revolutionary era in regard to independence) argued that the Civil War had been under way for more than a year and that the time had come to free the slaves in the territories held by the Union. It was once thought that Greeley's editorial spurred Lincoln to issue the Emancipation Proclamation of September 22, 1862, for all slaves in rebelling states, an edict described by Dumas Malone as "a dramatic gesture and a declaration of intention." It appears, however, that Lincoln had made up his mind before the editorial appeared. Greeley had founded the *Tribune* as a penny paper in 1842, and it became our first national newspaper. Its circulation was strongest in the crucial West but minuscule in the South, and with abolitionist literature barred there, that region was isolated from other viewpoints.

It was not among the newspapers, however, that the lines were drawn. That distinction belongs to Harriet Beecher Stowe's novel *Uncle Tom's Cabin, or Life among the Lowly*, which was first published as a serial in the antislavery paper *National Era* of Washington, DC, in 1851–52 and then as a book in the latter year. No one expected a big splash, but within a week 10,000 copies were sold, and 300,000 in the first year—an unprecedented press run for that period. Some million and one-half pirated copies were sold in England, and the novel, which appealed to the romantic sentiment of the day, was translated into a score of languages. Mrs. Stowe based her book on *American Slavery as It Is*, by the more moderate abolitionist Theodore Dwight Weld, and a brief visit to a Kentucky plantation. In it she produced a morality play that captured the imaginations of millions, both with her novel and as one of the most popular plays ever produced on the American stage. She tried to be fair—some Southerners come off quite warmly and, after all, the evil slave-master Simon Legree was a transplanted Northerner. Nevertheless, readers and playgoers remembered most the desperate flight across the ice-strewn Ohio River to freedom by the slave Eliza and her child. When Mrs. Stowe finally met Lincoln, the president said, perhaps being gallant, "So you're the little woman who wrote the book that made this great war."[2]

The Civil War and what led up to it was fraught with images—from Little Eva and Uncle Tom to word portraits of John Brown, who was hanged for leading an abortive slave uprising at Harper's Ferry, Virginia, on October 16–18, 1859. Henry David Thoreau in his last protest excoriated the "slave power" for executing Brown, and thereafter Union troops chanted, "John Brown's body lies a-mouldering in the grave, His soul is marching on. . . ." Julia Ward Howe, who with her husband edited an antislavery newspaper, *The Commonwealth*, heard soldiers singing this marching song at night while visiting a Union camp near Washington, DC. Inspired, in the darkness of her tent, by the powerful cadence of the old folk tune, she scribbled down new words for it, "The Battle Hymn of the Republic," which still stirs emotions among many Americans today.

The war also inspired the creation of powerful visual images. Mathew Brady and his assistants captured on wet-plate emulsions some thirty-five hundred Civil War scenes. The process was slow—coating a pane of glass with a light-sensitive silver-iodide solution immediately before a rather lengthy exposure—so Brady was unable to photograph action scenes. His photos were limited to portraits, camp life, and the aftermath of battles with corpse-strewn landscapes. And his work was available only to those who visited his small gallery in New York, where the curious might see, for example, a photograph of a basket of amputated arms and legs at the foot of a field operating table. It was not until 1878 that Frederic Eugene Ives invented the halftone, so that photographs could be reproduced in newspapers. At the time of the Civil War, Northern readers could see pictures of the conflict only through zinc etchings—sometimes unrealistically heroic—that were published in *Harper's Weekly* and *Frank Leslie's Illustrated Newspaper*, based on sketches by field artists.

Still, the Civil War was an epic in its own time. It was a holy crusade for the North to preserve the Union and free the slaves, and the defense of their homeland and way of life for the South. Above all, it was a conflict of words and images that escalated into a point of no return. One unknown soldier poet, for example, eased his soul by writing these words:

> Slaves rise up men; the olive waves,
> With roots deep set in battle graves.[3]

A Black Journalist Meets John Brown

The hanging of John Brown by the state of Virginia in 1859 after his ill-conceived and unsuccessful raid on Harper's Ferry, which he had hoped would ignite a slave uprising throughout the South, crystallized the abolitionist sentiment that had been brewing for decades. Ralph Waldo Emerson described him as "a pure idealist of artless goodness" whose execution "made the gallows glorious like the cross," while to others he was a fanatic if not outright insane. The latter does not seem likely from the interview with John Brown by the well-known black editor Frederick Douglass in Springfield, Massachusetts, before Harper's Ferry, or from the charismatic Brown's forays into "bleeding Kansas" where a foretaste of the coming national drama was being played out by guerrilla warfare over the issue of whether Kansas should enter the Union as a free or slave state. After proslavery forces from Missouri sacked Lawrence, Kansas, in May 1856, Brown's sons under the leadership of their father in retaliation killed five proslavery settlers on the Osawatomie River in the same area, making "Old Osawatomie Brown" a national figure, the scourge of God bent on eradicating slavery at any cost.

Frederick Douglass found quite a different figure in Springfield, as the following selection indicates. The interview with John Brown by the distinguished black orator and journalist almost foreshadows the New Journalism of the 1960s, when under competition from television the print medium became more literary. In an age before television, and even before many had seen photographs, Douglass focused on the delineation of character by painting a word picture based on revealing detail. The simplicity of the language suits his purpose well.

Douglass had been born into slavery in Maryland about 1817 but escaped to the North in 1838, where he became a showpiece of the Massachusetts and New England Anti-Slavery Societies and raised enough money on a two-year lecture tour of Great Britain to buy his own freedom, an action criticized by some as condoning slavery. His journalistic background is summarized at the beginning of the selection below by another distinguished black journalist, W. E. B. Du Bois (see Chapter 8). Later, Douglass was named U.S. minister to Haiti, but at the time of the incident at Harper's Ferry he had to flee again—to Canada and a six-month lecture tour of England and Scotland—because the governor of Virginia sought to arrest him as a conspirator in the Harper's Ferry raid. The historic interview with John Brown presented here took place in Springfield, Massachusetts, in 1847. Brown was already making a reputation for himself as an unswerving opponent of slavery and an agent of the Underground Railroad, a network of hiding places used to spirit runaway slaves north to freedom. After his death and martyrdom, John Brown's fame partly fueled the hostilities that eventually were to engulf the nation.

The first national Negro leader, Frederick Douglass, had delivered his wonderful salutatory in New Bedford in 1844. After publishing his biography, he went to England for safety, but returned in 1847, ransomed from slavery and ready to launch his paper, *The North Star*. No sooner had he landed than the black Wise Men of New York told him of the new Star in the East, whispering of the strange determined man of Springfield who flitted silently here and there among the groups of black folk and whose life was devoted to eternal war upon slavery. Both were eager to meet each other—John Brown to become acquainted with the greatest leader of the race which he aimed to free; Frederick Douglass to know an intense foe of slavery. The historic meeting took place in Springfield and is best told in Douglass' own words: . . .

"I was not long in company with the master of this house [John Brown] before I discovered that he was indeed the master of it, and was likely to become mine too if I stayed long enough with him. His wife believed in him, and his children observed him with reverence. Whenever he spoke his words commanded earnest attention. His arguments, which I ventured at some points to oppose, seemed to convince all; his appeals touched all, and his will impressed all. Certainly I never felt myself in the presence of a stronger religious influence than while in this man's house.

"In person he was lean, strong, and sinewy, of the best New England mold, built for times of trouble and fitted to grapple with the flintiest hardships. Clad in plain American woolen, shod in boots of cowhide leather, and wearing a cravat of the same substantial material, under six feet high, less than 150 pounds in weight, aged about fifty, he presented a figure straight and symmetrical as a mountain pine. His bearing was singularly impressive. His head was not large, but compact and high. His hair was coarse, strong, slightly gray and closely trimmed, and grew low on his forehead. His face was smoothly shaved, and revealed a strong, square mouth, supported by a broad and prominent chin. His eyes were bluish gray, and in conversation they were full of light and fire. When on the street, he moved with a long, springing, racehorse step, absorbed by his own reflections, neither seeking nor shunning observation. Such was the man whose name I had heard in whispers; such was the spirit of his house and family; such was the house in which he lived; and such was Captain John Brown, whose name has now passed into history, as that of one of the most marked characters and greatest known to American fame.

"After the strong meal already described, Captain Brown cautiously approached the subject which he wished to bring to my attention; for he seemed to apprehend opposition to his views. He denounced slavery in look and language fierce and bitter; thought that slaveholders had forfeited their right to live; that the slaves had the right to gain their liberty in any way they could; did not believe that moral suasion would ever liberate the slave, or that political action would abolish the system. He said that he had long had a plan which could accomplish this end, and he had invited me to his house to lay that plan before me. He said he had been for some time looking for colored men to whom he could safely reveal his secret, and at times he had almost despaired of finding such men; but that now he was encouraged, for he saw heads of such rising up in all directions. He had observed my course at home and abroad, and he wanted my coöperation. His plan as it then lay in his mind had much to commend it. It did not, as some suppose, contemplate a general rising among the slaves, and a general slaughter of the slavemasters. An insurrection, he thought, would only defeat the object; but his plan did contemplate the creating of an armed force which should act in the very heart of the South. He was not averse to the shedding of blood, and thought the practice of carrying arms would be a good one for the colored people to adopt, as it would give them a sense of their manhood. No people, he said, could have self-respect, or be respected, who would not fight for their freedom."[4]

Elijah Lovejoy, Abolitionist Editor

Among all the abolitionist editors, Elijah Lovejoy, a former Presbyterian minister, was not at first the most noteworthy. Benjamin Lundy had established the first influential abolitionist newspaper, *Genius of Universal Emancipation*, as early as 1821. Theodore Dwight Weld, according to Dumas Malone, "more than any other single man . . . was the heart and the brains of the effective abolitionist movement."[5] And others, such as James G. Birney, were threatened and persecuted, Birney's press being destroyed by a mob. But Elijah Lovejoy's presses were destroyed four times, and the tragic outcome of his perseverance makes him unique among this group—he became the only abolitionist editor who was killed defending his press and his right to speak his mind. Thus, as with John Brown later, Lovejoy became a martyr, achieving in death what he could not in life. In 1867, Wendell Phillips, the Boston abolitionist, wrote, "I can never forget the quick, sharp agony of that hour which brought us news of Lovejoy's death. . . . The gun fired at Lovejoy was like that of Sumter—it scattered a world of dreams."[6]

Elijah Parish Lovejoy was born in 1802 the son of a clergyman, and he taught school briefly before attending the seminary at Princeton and later being licensed to preach in 1833 by the Philadelphia Presbytery. He then went to Missouri, a slave state, to edit the Presbyterian weekly for the West, the *St. Louis Observer*. When he drifted from religious themes and criticism of intemperance to the immorality of slavery, a mob ransacked his print shop. Lovejoy moved twenty-five miles upriver to Alton, Illinois, a border city in a free state. But when his press was shipped from St. Louis, it was dumped in the river by a few ruffians. The citizens of Alton in a town meeting unanimously condemned this lawlessness and pledged money for a new press. On his part Lovejoy said that he was not an abolitionist but that he was against slavery. And he also declared, "I shall hold myself at liberty to speak, to write, and to publish whatever I please on any subject."[7]

That he did. Two more presses—sent by the Ohio Anti-Slavery Society—were wrecked by mobs on August 21 and September 21, 1837. It was while defending his fourth press on November 7 of that year that Lovejoy was shot five times and died at the age of thirty-five. A witness recalled that those who later smashed the press did so in an "orderly . . . quiet sort of way. They seemed to be happy while engaged in breaking it in pieces."[8] The letter to his brother Joseph, presented here, written on July 30, 1836, from Alton, Illinois, nine days after his print shop had been destroyed in St. Louis, reveals a courageous journalist who anticipated—and perhaps even welcomed—the trials to come.

By the Alton Telegraph, which I send you today, you [Joseph] will learn that I have had the honour of being *mobbed* at last. I have been expecting the catastrophe for some time, and now it has come.

The "Observer" will have informed you of the immediate cause of the outrage. Because I dared to comment upon the charge of Judge Lawless—an article so fraught with mischief and falsehood; the mob, which I chose to call his *officials*, tore down my office. What a comment upon the freedom of our institutions!

The act was the more mean and dastardly, inasmuch as I had previously determined to remove the office of the "Observer" to this place [Alton, Illinois] and had made all my arrangements accordingly, and had so stated in the number of the paper issued previous to the act of the mob.

You will also see that on my arrival here, a few miscreants undertook to follow the example of St. Louis, and so demolished what was left of the printing office. However, they met with but little countenance here. Thus the *whole* of the "St. Louis Observer" is destroyed. Not, however, until by the influence it has exerted, it has paid for itself, as I think. It has kindled up a fire in Missouri, that will never go out, until Popery and Slavery are extinct. And, moreover, I hope its very death will tell with effect upon the cause of human rights and religious liberty.

Tell my dear mother, that I am no whit discouraged. I feel myself standing on the broad basis of eternal justice, and so long as I stand there, full well do I know, that all the hosts of hell cannot prevail against me. I have found God a very present help in this my time of need. He has gloriously fulfilled his promises, and held me up, so that I have been astonished at the little effect produced upon my feelings by these outrages. But I determined when He carried me through last fall, that I would never again distrust Him.

Though cast down, I am not destroyed, nor in the least discouraged; and am now busily engaged in endeavouring to make arrangements for starting the "Observer" again. I think I shall succeed. I do believe the Lord has yet a work for me to do in contending with his enemies, and the enemies of humanity. I have got the harness on, and I do not intend to lay it off, except at His command.

What is said in the resolutions at the public meeting here about *Abolitionism*, and all that, is all for effect. I told them, and told the truth, that I did not come here to establish an Abolition paper, and that in the sense they understood it, I was no Abolitionist, but that I was the uncompromising enemy of Slavery, and so expected to live, and so to die.

My health is good, and so is John's [another brother]. My dear wife is sick with a fever, but I think she is recovering. The babe is well. Give my love to all. Tell sister Sarah I wish she would write to me. Tell all to write. I am so very busy that I can write no more.

Your affectionate brother,

Elijah P. Lovejoy[9]

William Lloyd Garrison Defends the Abolitionists

The actual effectiveness of the abolitionists has long been debated. With the cool eye resulting from the passage of time, some historians minimize their impact, citing their small audiences. The circulation of the *Liberator* of William Lloyd Garrison, the most aggressive and durable of the abolitionist newspapers, never exceeded three thousand, and that was entirely in the nonslaveholding North. These historians add that the abolitionists were preaching to an already committed group, and if anything they stiffened resistance against freeing the slaves. On the other hand, defenders point out that the small circulations reached the "opinion makers"— ministers, professors, and community leaders who spread the word. At least the abolitionist journalists kept the issue of slavery alive—as the underground press of the twentieth century did with its agenda—until a major political party, the newly formed Republicans, took up the task. Russell B. Nye makes a convincing case that the major contribution of the abolitionists was in the area of freedom of the press, as Northern editors who perhaps disagreed with the abolitionists' extreme stand on slavery nevertheless upheld their right to speak out. This was at a time when it was a crime in some Southern states even to have a copy of an abolitionist journal, and these publications were barred from mail going to the South by Postmaster General Amos Kendall, the former Jacksonian reformer.

In 1831, the same year that Garrison founded the *Liberator*, Nat Turner, a slave, led a revolt in Virginia, killing some sixty whites, mainly women and children, which sent shock waves throughout the South. Despite this inauspicious climate of opinion, however, Garrison managed to issue the *Liberator* for thirty-five years, until the Civil War ended. In his first issue of January 1, 1831, Garrison threw down the gauntlet: "I am in earnest—I will not equivocate—I will not excuse—I will not retreat a single inch—and *I will be heard.*" In 1831 in Boston he helped form the New England Anti-Slavery Society and two years later in Philadelphia the American Anti-Slavery Society. But he refused to attend the World's Anti-Slavery Convention in London in 1840 when he found out that women were excluded.

Garrison, like many other abolitionists, was a fiery orator who could electrify a crowd. He would burn copies of the U.S. Constitution on the platform because of its provision allocating three-fifths electoral representation of blacks in slave states, tacitly condoning the institution of slavery. One of the "ears" on the front page of the *Liberator* proclaimed that the Constitution was "a covenant with death and an agreement with hell." Georgia offered a reward of $5,000 for the arrest and conviction of Garrison for treason.

The South had no equivalent to the abolitionist press because the mainstream newspapers there were almost unanimous in their support of slavery and the states' rights philosophy to protect that institution. In a landmark study of Southern editorials, Donald E. Reynolds found: "The isolation of the Southern press from any influences that might have restored to it a national perspective and its intensely partisan nature helped make Southern newspapers the perfect vehicles to emotionalize both real and imaginary sectional differences."[10]

This is not to suggest that there were no reasoned defenses of the South's stance in some major newspapers in the region. See, for example, Dwight Lowell Dumond, *Southern Editorials on Secession* (1964). But extremist newspapers such as the *Charleston Mercury*, under the editorship of Robert Barnwell Rhett, carried the day. The close relationship between government and the press in the South was evidenced in at least one instance by the fact that Rhett was the first signer of the Confederacy Constitution of six seceding states (later eleven altogether) at Richmond in 1861. The war was doubly hard on Southern editors who saw not only their presses but also their ideals vanquished. Of the forty-three daily newspapers published in the Confederacy at the outset of hostilities, only twenty survived at the time Gen. Robert E. Lee surrendered at the McLean house in Appomattox Courthouse on Palm Sunday, April 9, 1865.

How much of a role had the abolitionist journalists played in this drama? In the following lecture given at the Cooper Institute in New York on January 14, 1862, as the fighting was under way, William Lloyd Garrison in a speech taken down by stenographers and later printed as a pamphlet answers the charges most commonly leveled at himself and his fellow abolitionists and fires off a few salvos of his own.

It is said, again, "There was no trouble in the land until the Abolitionists appeared." Well, the more is the pity! . . .

No, my friends, this fearful state of things is not of men; it is of Heaven. As we have sowed, we are reaping. The whole cause of it is declared in the memorable verse of the prophet: "Ye have not hearkened unto me in proclaiming liberty, every man to his brother, and every man to his neighbor: behold, I proclaim a liberty for you, saith the Lord, to the sword, to the pestilence, and to the famine." That is the whole story. This is the settlement day of God Almighty for the unparalleled guilt of our nation; and if we desire to be saved, we must see to it that we put away our sins, "break every yoke, and let the oppressed go free," and thus save our land from ruin. (Applause.)

Be not deceived; this rebellion is not only to eternize the enslavement of the African race, but it is also to overturn the free institutions of the North.

The slaveholders of the South are not only opposed to Northern Abolition-ists, but to Northern ideas and Northern institutions. . . .

You see, men of the North, it is a war against freedom—your freedom as well as that of the slave—against the freedom of mankind. It is to establish an oligarchic, slaveholding despotism, to the extinction of all free institu-tions. The Southern rebellion is in full blast; and if they can work their will against us, there will be for us no liberty of speech or of the press—no right to assemble as we assemble here tonight, and our manhood will be trampled in the dust. (Applause.) I say, therefore, under these circumstances, treason consists in giving aid or countenance to the slave system of the South—not merely to Jeff Davis, as president of the Southern Confederacy, or to this rebel movement in special. Every man who gives any countenance or sup-port to slavery is a traitor to liberty. (Enthusiastic applause.) I say he is a dangerous and unsafe man. (Renewed cheers.) He carries within him the seeds of despotism, and no one can tell how soon a harvest of blood and treason may spring up. Liberty goes with Union and for Union, based on judgment and equality. Slavery is utter disunion and disorganization in God's universe. (Cheers.)

But, we are told, "hang the Secessionists on the one hand, and the Abo-litionists on the other, and then we shall have peace." (Laughter.) How very discriminating! Now, I say, if any hanging is to be done (though I do not believe in capital punishment—that is one of my heresies)—if any hanging is to be done, I am for hanging these sneaking, two-faced, pseudo-loyal go-betweens immediately. (Loud and enthusiastic applause. A voice, "That's the talk!") Why, as to this matter of loyalty, I maintain that the most loyal people to a free government who walk on the American soil, are the uncom-promising Abolitionists. (Cheers.) It is not freedom that arises in rebellion against free government. It is not the love of liberty that endangers it. It is not those who will not make any compromise with tyranny who threaten it. It is those who strike hands with the oppressors. Yes, I maintain the Abolition-ists are more loyal to free government and free institutions than President Lincoln himself; because, while I want to say everything good of him that I can, I must say I think he is lacking somewhat in backbone, and is disposed, at least, to make some compromise with slavery, in order to bring back the old state of things; and, therefore, he is nearer Jeff Davis than I am. Still, we are both so bad, that I suppose if we should go amicably together down South, we never should come back again.

"Hang the Abolitionists, and then hang the Secessionists!" Why, in the name of common sense, wherein are these parties agreed? Their principles and purposes are totally dissimilar. *We* believe in the inalienable rights of man—in "liberty, equality, fraternity." *They* disbelieve in all these. *We* believe in making the law of God paramount to all human codes, compacts, and enactments. *They* believe in trampling it under their feet, to gratify their lust of dominion, and in "exalting themselves above all that is called God." *We* believe in the duty of liberating all who are pining in bondage. *They* are for extending and perpetuating slavery to the latest posterity. *We* believe in free government and free institutions. *They* believe in the overthrow of all these, and have made chattel bondage the corner-stone of their new confederacy. Where is there any agreement of similarity between these parties?

But it may be said you are for the dissolution of the Union. I was. Did I have any sympathy with the spirit of Southern secession when I took that position? No. My issue was a moral one—a Christian one. It was because of the pro-slavery nature of the compact itself that I said I could not, as a Christian man, as a friend of liberty, swear to uphold such a Union or Constitution.[11]

Covering the War: The Blue and the Gray

While the war of words waged by abolitionist and Southern editors unfolded, the painful reality of the real war took center stage. Although there had been a few correspondents who had accompanied the troops and reported the War with Mexico (1846–1848), the war correspondent, or "special" as he was called, came into his own during the Civil War. At first, the situation was unreal. Society families with their picnic baskets and parasols came out in their carriages from Washington, DC, to watch the first battle of Bull Run in the nearby Virginia countryside, the first major engagement of the war, on July 21, 1861. At first it appeared that Union forces (armed mobs, really) had won, which was the news that Henry J. Raymond flashed by telegraph to his newspaper, the *New York Times*. But the tide turned into a rout by the Southern forces, stampeding the socialites back to the capital and leaving Raymond with egg on his face.

Actually, there were no star reporters covering the Civil War on either side. Despite the dangers and risks to the newsmen in the field, accounts of great battles were signed only "By a Correspondent" or "Correspondent's Account." By-lines did not begin to appear until 1865. It was more of a group enterprise, as correspondents were assigned to cover the triumphs or failures of individual generals. James Gordon Bennett of the *New York Herald* fielded as many as forty "specials" at one time in an all-out effort to obtain comprehensive news coverage. How accurate was this news, gathered under incredibly difficult conditions, as seen in the selection below? George Alfred Townsend, one of Bennett's reporters, found his visiting newspaper's agent quite cynical. "The Federal Government was, to his eye," wrote Townsend, "merely an adjunct of the paper. Battles and sieges were simply occurrences for its columns. Good men, brave men, bad men, died to give it obituaries. The whole world was to him a reporter's district, and all human mutations plain matters of news."[12]

Civil rights did not suffer greatly during the Civil War, remarkable for a nation in convulsion. Lincoln did suspend habeas corpus, which forbids detention without charges being filed, and several of his generals did close a few newspapers in the West. But, all in all, democratic leniency prevailed except when military information was concerned.

Journalism historians Edwin Emery and Michael Emery have succinctly traced the evolution of Northern censorship policy. The first period of "fumbling" was marked by a press conference called by Gen. George B. McClellan, commanding the Army of the Potomac, in August 1861, in which correspondents signed written pledges that they would send no dispatches that could contain military information helpful to the enemy, but this unrealistic voluntary censorship broke down. In the second phase, General William Tecumseh Sherman pushed through the understanding that all correspondents must be accredited journalists and acceptable to commanders in the field—two stipulations still observed today. Although some politically appointed officers preened for the press, the third period, from 1864, was more successful. Sherman marched all the way from Atlanta to the sea in hostile country, for example, without his plans once being disclosed by the correspondents.

The South warned members of the Press Association of the Confederate States of America to be wary of rumors and offer no information that might aid the enemy. This excellent Southern press organization monitored censorship until defeat resulted in a breakdown of that function. Meanwhile, wider and more rapid communication was bringing about a journalistic revolution in both camps.

Technologically, the Civil War changed the face and content of the American newspaper. The telegraph was invented in 1844, and a spotty network had aided the transmission of news during the War with Mexico. But the device came into its own during the Civil War. Because a flood of news flowed from the telegraph each hour, the larger newspapers began using one-column "bulletins" for readers eager for the latest news. One story in the *New York Times* of May 10, 1864, for example, had nineteen crossline bulletins, filling most of the column. These were one-column labels that presaged the modern headline. On the other hand, the printing of relatively large maps of military engagements broke the tyranny of the one-column rule.

The telegraph also changed writing styles. Before it, news stories had usually been chronological or narrative, with the climax saved for the end. But with the uncertainties of telegraph transmission—the lines might be damaged or destroyed, or the correspondent might be preempted by the military at any moment—reporters quickly learned to send the most important facts first so that they would be sure to get them through. This was the beginning of the inverted-pyramid style of writing, with the climax given first and supporting details given in order of descending importance. Since transmission by telegraph was also expensive, it cut down on wordy or flowery writing.

One further impact of the Civil War on news reporting must be stressed. Greater objectivity in news stories appeared in dispatches issued by the fledgling news association, the Associated Press of New York. The early AP managers realized that they served editors across the entire political spectrum and did not want to offend clients at either extreme. Thus, political comments in wire stories became more subdued.

The trials of Civil War journalists are captured in the diary, excerpted below, of Junius Henri Browne, special war correspondent to the *New York Tribune*, who was captured at Vicksburg on May 3, 1863, and was interned in five Confederate prisons before escaping and rejoining the Union lines at Knoxville. Here, in his account of *Four Years in Secessia* (1865), was the reality faced every day by reporters on the battlefield.

During the few days I have passed in the Free States since the breaking out of the Rebellion, I have been so often questioned about the province, purpose, and habits of a War Correspondent, that I deem it well, in the initial chapter of this volume, to state what manner of animal he is, and what are his peculiarities.

That the War Correspondent is a hybrid, neither a soldier nor a citizen; with the Army, but not of it; is present at battles, and often participating in them, yet without any rank or recognized existence, has mystified not a few, and rendered his position as anomalous as undesirable.

"Do you belong to the Army?" inquiried a bumpkin, riding up beside myself and a couple of journalistic companions, as we were moving toward Fayetteville during the Bragg-Buell campaign in Kentucky, in the autumn of 1862. "Yes," was the answer. "Are you soldiers?" "No." "Are you officers?" "No." "Are you sutlers [provisioners]?" "No." "What are you, then?" "War Correspondents." "Oh, that's what you are, is it?" and after this comment on our response, he seemed lost in reflection the most profound. Fully a minute must have passed, when his face brightened, and he seemed to have solved some mental problem. "Oh, well, boys, you're all right. War Correspondents [confusing them with the Committees of Correspondence], eh? Why, they're the fellows that fought in the Revolution!". . .

Since the first gun discharged at Fort Sumter awoke the American world to arms, War Correspondence on this side of the Atlantic has been as much an avocation as practising law or selling dry goods. Every newspaper, of prominence in the metropolitan cities, has had its Correspondents in the field and with the Navy. No army in the East or West but has had a journalistic representative. No expedition of importance has set out without its writing medium between it and New York, Philadelphia, Boston, Cincinnati, Chicago, and St. Louis.

The War Correspondent is the proper and natural medium between the Army and Navy and the people at home, and ought to be, and is generally, the purest, because the only unprejudiced medium between the military and civil phases of existence. He only has, as a general thing—and there should be no exceptions—no friends to reward, and no foes to punish. He is at his post to relate what he sees; to applaud valor and merit wherever found; to point out abuses and blunders that would not otherwise be reached, save through the endless duration of military investigations and courts-martial. His duty is to illustrate the situation so far as is prudent; to describe the movements, actions, and combinations of the forces; in a word, to photograph the life and spirit of the combatants for the benefit of the great Public, united to them by blood and sympathy, and who thrill and suffer with the gallant warriors, and mourn over and honor the heroic dead.

Such being the duty and obligation—and it should be a solemn one—of the Correspondent, he has as much place and fitness in the field as the Commander-in-Chief; and is as much entitled to consideration. That he is not what he should be often, is true of him, as it is of every other class; and that many of his profession have, by unworthy conduct, reflected discredit upon its members, is equally true. The misfortune is, that the unworthy, by their assurance, carelessness, and lack of principle, give such false impressions of the entire tribe, that I marvel not a most wholesome prejudice exists against them on the part of many officers. . . .

The worst feature of [the correspondents'] profession is—and they deplore it as much as any one—they are compelled, from the great competition in respect to news, to write up their accounts so rapidly, and forward them so early, that correctness of statement and excellence of style are often precluded. When they write their letters, as I have seen them in the midst of action; on their knee and upon the ground; in crowded railway cars and on thronged transports; under every variety of adverse circumstance, I have wondered, and still wonder, at their fluency, propriety, and exactness. They certainly accomplish marvels, considering their surroundings and facilities, and at least suggest what they might do if leisure and opportunity were given them. . . .

If they have any fondness—and many of them have—for fighting, they can always be accommodated. I have more than once seen them in the field, musket in hand, and frequently trying their skill as sharpshooters. They very often act as voluntary aides on the staff of General Officers, and have, in numerous instances, played a conspicuous and important part in engagements. They have again and again joined hazardous expeditions for which volunteers have been called; have gone on perilous raids and scouts; run batteries, and taken risks purely from a love of adventure—to have the experience—which is a very natural desire with the poetico-philosophic temperament. They have done a number of what many would call very foolish and reckless, though certainly courageous, acts—all the more courageous because they had no inducement of glory, and would not at all have been honored as an officer or a soldier would if they had fallen, as they sometimes have, in what would be considered obedience to a freak of feeling, instead of a conviction of duty.[13]

Notes

1. April 23, 1861. Quoted in Charles Carleton Coffin, *Four Years of Fighting: A Volume of Personal Observation with the Army and Navy, from the First Battle of Bull Run to the Fall of Richmond* (Boston: Ticknor and Fields, 1866).

2. Dumas Malone and Basil Rauch, *Empire for Liberty: The Genesis and Growth of the United States of America*, vol. 1 (New York: Appleton-Century-Crofts, 1960), 579.

3. Coffin, *Four Years of Fighting*, 557.

4. W. E. B. Du Bois, *John Brown* (Millwood, NY: Kraus-Thomson Organization, 1973), 101–2, 104–6.

5. Malone and Rauch, *Empire for Liberty*, 1:483.

6. Quoted in Merton L. Dillon, *Elijah P. Lovejoy, Abolitionist Editor* (Westport, CT: Greenwood Press, 1961), 178.

7. Quoted in Dillon, *Elijah P. Lovejoy*, 92.

8. Ibid., 170.

9. Joseph C. and Owen Lovejoy, *Memoir of the Rev. Elijah P. Lovejoy: Who Was Murdered in Defence of the Liberty of the Press, at Alton, Illinois, Nov. 7, 1837* (New York: John S. Taylor, 1838), 181–83.

10. Donald E. Reynolds, *Editors Make War: Southern Newspapers in the Secession Crisis* (Nashville, TN: Vanderbilt University Press, 1966), 217.

11. William Lloyd Garrison, *The Abolitionists, and Their Relations to the War* (New York: E. D. Barker, 1862), 43–45.

12. George Alfred Townsend, *Rustics in Rebellion: A Yankee Reporter on the Road to Richmond, 1861–65* (Chapel Hill: University of North Carolina Press, 1950), 71.

13. Junius Henri Browne, *Four Years in Secessia: Adventures within and beyond the Union Lines* (Hartford, CT: O. D. Case and Company, 1865), 13–19.

4

The Frontier Press

On a calm April morning of 1875, a group of U.S. soldiers under the command of Austin Henely, second lieutenant in the Sixth U.S. Cavalry, raided the sleeping encampment of a group of about seventy-five Northern Cheyennes in northwest Kansas and killed them all. This encounter, thought to be the grounds for a retaliatory Indian raid against white settlers on the Kansas frontier three years later, was totally without cause. The Northern Cheyennes, who had been shoved onto the arid reservation of Indian Territory (Oklahoma), wanted only to return to their homeland in the Dakotas. They were proceeding northward peacefully when the massacre occurred. Trapped in a horseshoe loop of the Middle Sappa creek, surrounded on three sides by clay and limestone bluffs, the Indians had no chance. In fact, according to the diary of an officer who participated in the slaughter, after all of the tepees had been burned and all the Indians were presumed dead, they heard the cry of a baby. The cavalrymen threw the child into a burning tepee because, as the officer wrote, "Nits make gnats."[1]

Unfortunately, there was no reporter who dug out these facts at the time, as Seymour Hersh did with the My Lai massacre in the Vietnam War, but the reactions of the cavalrymen—full of bravado—as recorded in the Kansas State Historical Society, sealed their place in history. The frontier press minimized these violent confrontations in the Indian Wars (1867–1881) in order to attract settlers and bring business into their bustling prairie towns. As Hill P. Wilson, then sutler (provisioner) of nearby Fort Hays, said in a letter to the Kansas State Historical Society, at that time it was "understood that the least said about the affair [the massacre] the better for all concerned." And as Ruth Laird, professor emerita of journalism at South Dakota State University, adds, "The white man lives, in the microfilmed pages of old South Dakota weeklies. It is to be regretted that the red man does not."

This is not to paint an idyllic picture of innocent American Indian life shattered by the violence of land-hungry whites. On the contrary, there were wars among native American tribes and nations long before Columbus. But the near eradication of the American Indian by the whites can only be described as racial genocide in the view of historian James Malen. The slogan of the day was "The only good Indian is a dead Indian." That attitude was driven by a sense of Manifest Destiny, a phrase coined by John Louis O'Sullivan, editor of the *United States Magazine and Democratic Review*, when Texas was annexed in 1845. The concept was that God had ordained that Anglo-Saxons should occupy all the land between the Atlantic and Pacific oceans, and by inference displace the peoples thereon.

As the edge of settlement moved ever westward, the printing press moved with it. No frontier town could aspire to respectability without a newspaper, sometimes several. At first, some newspapers were handwritten, and "exchanges" (printed newspapers from neighboring towns) were read to an illiterate audience who paid admission. But frontier printers came to use small hand-operated presses that could be transported in a horse-drawn wagon if printer-editors felt civilization closing in on them. Capable of producing 250 impressions an hour, one such press was patented by Samuel Rust of New York in 1821.

Then in 1891 a momentous thing happened, little noticed at the time—the frontier was closed. There was no more free land to be distributed under the Homestead Act of 1862, whereby settlers had been able to obtain title to 160 acres by occupying it for five years. The closing of the frontier stirred a historian, Frederick Jackson Turner, to give a paper on "The Frontier in American History" before the American Historical Association in 1893; it was to influence generations of U.S. historians. More than just a place, a line of settlement, Turner found the frontier to be a historical concept that fostered egalitarian ideals.

Revisionists maintain that the West has been romanticized beyond all recognition. Hollywood movies, particularly those of director John Ford, raised the westerns to an art form as stylistic as Greek drama but distorted reality by creating stereotypes—Indians were all bloodthirsty savages, the cavalry was pristine pure. Late in his career Ford sought to make amends with *Cheyenne Autumn*, but the first movie to recognize Indian culture in any depth was Kevin Costner's award-winning *Dances with Wolves*.

With the frontier closed, U.S. aggressiveness in a sense jumped overseas with the war with Spain in 1898. But before looking at that war, a brief review of the American experience is in order. The "frontier" had symbolically opened when the first Pilgrims set foot on Plymouth Rock. The result of population pressures in the East, expansionist tendencies manifested themselves early. Settlers were first prohibited from going west of the Appalachian Mountains by establishment by the British of the Proclamation Line in 1763. In the early national period, Thomas Jefferson—in what was to be the crowning achievement of his administration—doubled the young nation's size by acquiring the Louisiana Purchase in 1803 for seven cents an acre from France, which desperately needed the money to prosecute the Napoleonic Wars. The immensity of the Purchase, which extended from the present states of Louisiana to Montana, fired the imaginations of people seeking a new life—and they brought their journalism with them. Texas was annexed in 1845, and we obtained half of Mexico—our present Southwest—in the war with Mexico of 1846-1848. The contours of the present continental United States were rounded out when Spain ceded Florida in 1821 and Britain yielded to U.S. claims to the Oregon territory in 1846.

During all this, frontier editors minimized the dangers and hardships to attract settlers. Every little town had at least one newspaper. Rexford, Kansas, for example, a village of scarcely more than three hundred people, had a weekly newspaper until the 1930s. One might well ask the reason for a newspaper in such a small community, where everyone knew what was going on anyway. For one thing, people liked to see their names in print. Also, the obituaries were the most popular part of the weekly, in which hardened frontier men and women sought the meaning of life.

Although there were scattered bilingual Spanish-language newspapers in the Southwest and a very few American Indian papers, the tidal wave of white settlement and English-language papers swept all before it. Hometown newspapers became boosters for their communities, exaggerating the possibilities to attract new settlers. They were optimistic, vying for railroad service to relieve their isolation and get their goods to market. Thus, they downplayed what was perceived as the Indian threat and the ever-present violence. According to historian William E. Huntzicker, six lynchings occurred at one time near an early newspaper office in Albuquerque that the editor did not consider newsworthy enough to mention in print.

The editors offered hope and stability for the booming towns of the West, although they also were the last gasps of politically partisan journalism. The newspaper usually was simply an adjunct to job printing, but editors also indulged their editorial spleen on partisan figures such as Ulysses S. Grant, as in this extreme example: "Grant, the whisky bloated, squaw ravishing adulterer, monkey ridden, nigger worshipping mogul is rejoicing over his election to the presidency. . . . The road to the White House which Grant has traveled over during our last campaign is paved with the skeletons of many thousand soldiers whom he slaughtered uselessly during his western and southern career."[2]

Many frontier editors sought to help build decent and law-abiding communities, although many obstacles stood in their way—not the least of which often was financing. Frontier editors at times were forced to accept barter rather than cash on the barrelhead, and they were constantly chiding their delinquent subscribers to pay up. At the same time, the romantic figure of the self-contained cowboy hides the reality of an unwashed, lice-ridden, hard-drinking drifter who worked the great cattle drives from Texas to the railheads of Dodge City, Abilene, and Hays. At the end of these drives were saloons, gambling halls, prostitutes, corrupt sheriffs, and, of lesser interest, a church or two. One may marvel at the cowboys' sense of independence and freedom, but one must also salute the newspaper trying to weld a community out of disparate elements.

Bret Harte Reports a Massacre of Indians

The raw life of the far West, particularly the mining frontier of Nevada and California, spawned a trio of writers—Mark Twain, Bret Harte, and Ambrose Bierce—who thrived on the tall tales of the region. They all got their literary starts on frontier newspapers, perhaps the lasting legacy of the American West. They and others played fast and easy with the "facts" in the days before Joseph Pulitzer and his New York *World* began to stress accuracy and objectivity. These latter two qualities are at the barricades today, particularly in television news, where every segment ends with a veiled editorial comment.

Consider, for example, the early work of Francis Brett Harte, who changed his pen name to Bret Harte and got his start on the *Northern Californian*, later writing for the San Francisco *Golden Era*, which was first issued in 1852 and lasted thirty years. Harte's view of newspapering was encapsulated in a little sketch of those who wrote, and typeset by hand, their own stories: " 'Wanted—a printer,' says a contemporary [newspaper]. Wanted, a mechanical curiosity, with brain and fingers—a thing that will set so many type in a day—a machine that will think and act, but still a machine—a being who undertakes the most systematic and monotonous drudgery, yet one the ingenuity of man has never supplanted mechanically—that's a printer."[3] (Actually, the ingenuity of man did relieve the tedious task of setting type by hand when Ottmar Mergenthaler revolutionized printing in 1886 by inventing the Linotype, which cast lines, or slugs, of hot-metal type for an operator punching a keyboard.)

Bret Harte, always a maverick, burst on the newspaper scene in a swirl of controversy in reporting the Gunther's Island massacre, in which about sixty peaceful Indians were slaughtered on February 26, 1860. Unlike the Sappa massacre in Kansas, the Indians in California had a spokesman in Bret Harte. His boss was on a trip, having left Harte in charge, and he recounted the incident with seething indignation and relish in a hostile white community. Using the largest type available, Harte headlined his news column "Indiscriminate Massacre of Indians, Women and Children Butchered." The story read in part:

> Little children and old women were mercilessly stabbed and their skulls crushed with axes. When the bodies were landed at Union, a more shocking and revolting spectacle never was exhibited to the eyes of a Christian and civilized people. Old women, wrinkled and decrepit, lay weltering in blood, their brains dashed out and dabbled with their long gray hair. Infants scarce a span long, with their faces cloven with hatchets and their bodies ghastly with wounds. . . . No resistance was made, it is said, to the butchers who did the work, but as they ran or huddled together for protection like sheep, they were struck down with hatchets.[4]

Harte conceded that there was an Indian problem. "But we can conceive of no palliation for woman and child slaughter. We can conceive of no wrong that a babe's blood can atone for."

Harte became persona non grata in the community for telling the truth, however embellished, and left town a month later. He went on to give us the delightful short stories "The Luck of Roaring Camp" and "The Outcasts of Poker Flat." Perhaps his newspapering had some effect, as the townspeople he left behind passed this resolution: "*Resolved*, That as it is the white man who pays and supports Government, their lives and property should be the first to receive protection from that Government. But as white men and human beings of a superior race—from principles of humanity—we are sensible that the Indians should have protection also."[5]

Ambrose Bierce: "Corrupting the Press"

Ambrose Bierce was also a product of the rough-and-tumble frontier journalism in which rival editors frequently resorted to verbal abuse, fisticuffs, and canings in the street—not to mention more sordid forms of retaliation. The caustic comments of Ambrose Bierce earned him the nickname of "Bitter Bierce" for tongue-in-cheek satire, long before H. L. Mencken came on the scene. Bierce hardly endeared himself to generations of journalists with his definition of a reporter in his *Devil's Dictionary* (1906): "A writer who guesses his way to the truth and dispels it with a tempest of words."[6] The sardonic *Dictionary*, a collection of earlier work, was dedicated to "enlightened souls who prefer dry wines to sweet, sense to sentiment, wit to humor, and clean English to slang." He left his newspaper jobs on the *Argonaut* and *News Letter* in San Francisco to seek "obscurity in the writing and publishing of books." He unfortunately picked the forces of conservative chief Venustiano Carranza in covering the Mexican Revolution, which began in 1910, and disappeared, probably at the wrong end of a firing squad. In one of his final letters, Bierce wrote, "Goodbye, if you hear of my being stood up against a Mexican stone wall and shot to rags please know that I think it a pretty good way to depart this life. It beats old age, disease, or falling down the cellar stairs."[7] So ended the career of Ambrose Bierce, whose literary trajectory was prolific if uneven, but who left us, among other things, the classic short story "Occurrence at Owl Creek Bridge" and the following fictional vignette of frontier journalism.

A TALE OF FRONTIER PRESS ETHICS

When Joel Bird was up for Governor of Missouri, Sam Henly was editing the Berrywood *Bugle*; and no sooner was the nomination made by the State Convention than he came out hot against the party. He was an able writer, was Sam, and the lies he invented about our candidate were shocking! That, however, we endured very well, but presently Sam turned squarely about and began telling the truth. *This* was a little too much; the County Commitee held a hasty meeting, and decided that it must be stopped; so I, Henry Barber, was sent for to make arrangements to that end. I knew something of Sam: had purchased him several times, and I estimated his present value at about one thousand dollars. This seemed to the committee a reasonable figure, and on my mentioning it to Sam he said "he thought that about the fair thing; it should never be said that the *Bugle* was a hard paper to deal with." There was, however, some delay in raising the money; the candidates for the local offices had not disposed of their autumn hogs yet, and were in financial straits. Some of them contributed a pig each, one gave twenty bushels of corn, another a flock of chickens; and the man who aspired to the distinction of County Judge paid his assessment with a wagon. These things had to be converted into cash at a ruinous sacrifice, and in the meantime

Sam kept pouring an incessant stream of hot shot into our political camp. Nothing I could say would make him stay his hand; he invariably replied that it was no bargain until he had the money. The committeemen were furious; it required all my eloquence to prevent their declaring the contract null and void; but at last a new, clean one thousand-dollar note was passed over to me, which in hot haste I transferred to Sam at his residence.

That evening there was a meeting of the committee: all seemed in high spirits again, except Hooker of Jayhawk. This old wretch sat back and shook his head during the entire session, and just before adjournment said, as he took his hat to go, that p'r'aps 'twas orl right and on the squar'; maybe thar war'n't any shenannigan, but he war dubersome—yes, he war dubersome. The old curmudgeon repeated this until I was exasperated beyond restraint.

"Mr. Hooker," said I, "I've known Sam Henly ever since he was so high, and there isn't an honester man in old Missouri, Sam Henly's word is as good as his note! What's more, if any gentleman thinks he would enjoy a first-class funeral, and if he will supply the sable accessories, I'll supply the corpse. And he can take it home with him from this meeting."

At this point Mr. Hooker was troubled with leaving.

Having got this business off my conscience I slept late next day. When I stepped into the street I saw at once that something was "up." There were knots of people gathered at the corners, some reading eagerly that morning's issue of the *Bugle*, some gesticulating, and others stalking moodily about muttering curses, not loud but deep. Suddenly I heard an excited clamor—a confused roar of many lungs, and the trampling of innumerable feet. In this babel of noises I could distinguish the words "Kill him!" "Wa'm his hide!" and so forth; and, looking up the street, I saw what seemed to be the whole male population racing down it. I am very excitable, and, though I did not know whose hide was to be warmed, nor why anyone was to be killed, I shot off in front of the howling masses, shouting "Kill him!" and "Warm his hide!" as loudly as the loudest, all the time looking out for the victim. Down the street we flew like a storm; then I turned a corner, thinking the scoundrel must have gone up that street; then bolted through a public square; over a bridge; under an arch; finally back into the main street; yelling like a panther, and resolved to slaughter the first human being I should overtake. The crowd followed my lead, turning as I turned, shrieking as I shrieked, and—all at once it came to me that I was the man whose hide was to be warmed!

It is needless to dwell upon the sensation this discovery gave me; happily I was within a few yards of the committee rooms, and into these I dashed, closing and bolting the doors behind me, and mounting the stairs like a flash. The committee was in solemn session, sitting in a nice, even row on the front benches, each man his elbows on his knees, and his chin resting in the palms of his hands—thinking. At each man's feet lay a neglected copy of the *Bugle*. Every member fixed his eyes on me, but no one stirred, none uttered a sound. There was something awful in this preternatural silence, made more impressive by the hoarse murmur of the crowd outside, breaking down the door. I could endure it no longer, but strode forward and snatched up the paper lying at the feet of the chairman. At the head of the editorial columns, in letters half an inch long, were the following amazing head-lines:

"Dastardly Outrage! Corruption Rampant in Our Midst! The Vampires Foiled! Henry Barber at his Old Game! The Rat Gnaws a File! The Democratic Hordes Attempt to Ride Roughshod Over a Free People! Base Endeavor to Bribe the Editor of this Paper with *a Twenty-Dollar Note*! The Money Given to the Orphan Asylum."

I read no farther, but stood stockstill in the center of the floor, and fell into a reverie. Twenty dollars! Somehow it seemed a mere trifle. Nine hundred and eighty dollars! I did not know there was so much money in the world. Twenty—no, eighty—one thousand dollars! There were big, black figures floating all over the floor. Incessant cataracts of them poured down the walls, stopped, and shied off as I looked at them, and began to go it again when I lowered my eyes. Occasionally the figures 20 would take shape somewhere about the floor, and then the figures 980 would slide up and overlay them. Then, like the lean kine of Pharoah's dream, they would all march away and devour the fat naughts of the number 1,000. And dancing like gnats in the air were myriads of little caduceus-like phantoms, thus—$$$$$. I could not at all make it out, but began to comprehend my position. Directly Old Hooker, without moving from his seat, began to drown the noise of countless feet on the stairs by elevating his thin falsetto:

"P'r'aps, Mr. Cheerman, it's orl on the squar'. We know Mr. Henly can't tell a lie; but I'm powerful dubersome that thar's a balyance dyue this yer committee from the gent who hez the flo'—if he ain't done gone laid it yout fo' sable ac—ac—fo'fyirst-class funerals."

I felt at that moment as if I should like to play the leading character in a first-class funeral myself. I felt that every man in my position ought to have a nice, comfortable coffin, with a silver doorplate, a foot-warmer, and bay-windows for his ears. How do you suppose you would have felt?

My leap from the window of that committee room, my speed in streaking it for the adjacent forest, my self-denial in ever afterward resisting the impulse to return to Berrywood and look after my political and material interests there—these I have always considered things to be justly proud of, and I hope I am proud of them.[8]

Mark Twain Comments on Newspapering

The giant literary figure to come out of the prints of the West, however, was Samuel Langhorne Clemens, better known to the world as Mark Twain, who could embellish or invent a "fact" without batting an eyelash. As George Bernard Shaw once said, "Mark Twain and I are in very much the same position. We have to put things in such a way as to make people, who would otherwise hang us, believe that we are joking."[9] Such shenanigans would not be tolerated in a newspaper today—witness the fate of Janet Cooke, who was fired from her *Washington Post* job for inventing a story about an eight-year-old heroin addict—but one must remember that Twain was writing at a time when a premium was placed on entertainment: There were no movies, radio, or television. Readers seemed to expect to be joshed by their newspapers, and later they flocked to the Chautauqua lecture circuit to see and hear Twain and others in person.

After gold was discovered at Sutter's Mill in California in 1848, prospecting fever gripped many, including Mark Twain, who sought silver in Nevada in 1861–62. Without any luck in that field of endeavor, he became a "reporter" on the *Territorial Enterprise* in Virginia City, Nevada, for the following two years. During that time he published two accounts of massacres of whites by Indians, one with a thousand victims—and both hoaxes. Yet Twain could be a straightforward reporter, as when he covered the legislature at Carson City and signed his dispatches "Clemens."

More than any other journalistic figure, Mark Twain had the ability to laugh at himself, as when he once declared, "I have been an author for 20 years and an ass for 55."[10] Again, he said of himself, "My books are water; those of the great geniuses are wine. Everybody drinks water."[11] Below is a rare glimpse of a serious Mark Twain assessing the journalism of his day in a talk before the Monday Evening Club in Hartford, Connecticut, in 1873. But it should be pointed out that in defending Bret Harte from his critics, Twain seemed conveniently unaware of the right of "fair comment and criticism" whenever anyone places artistic or literary productions before the public.

MARK TWAIN: "LICENSE OF THE PRESS"

It (the press) has scoffed at religion till it has made scoffing popular. It has defended official criminals, on party pretexts, until it has created a United States Senate whose members are incapable of determining what crime against law and the dignity of their own body is, they are so morally blind, and it has made light of dishonesty till we have as a result a Congress which contracts to work for a certain sum and then deliberately steals additional wages out of the public pocket and is pained and surprised that anybody should worry about a little thing like that.

I am putting all this odious state of things upon the newspaper, and I believe it belongs there—chiefly, at any rate. It is a free press—a press that is more than free—a press which is licensed to say any infamous thing it chooses about a private or a public man, or advocate any outrageous doctrine it pleases. It is tied in no way. The public opinion which should hold it in bounds it has itself degraded to its own level. There are laws to protect the freedom of the press's speech, but none that are worth anything to protect the people from the press. A libel suit simply brings the plaintiff before a vast newspaper court to be tried before the law tries him, and reviled and ridiculed without mercy. The touchy Charles Reade can sue English newspapers and get verdicts; he would soon change his tactics here; the papers (backed by a public well taught by themselves) would soon teach him that it is better to suffer any amount of misrepresentation than go into our courts with a libel suit and make himself the laughing stock of the community.

It seems to me that just in the ratio that our newspapers increase, our morals decay. The more newspapers the worse morals. Where we have one newspaper that does good, I think we have fifty that do harm. We ought to look upon the establishment of a newspaper of the average pattern in a virtuous village as a calamity.

The difference between the tone and conduct of newspapers to-day and those of thirty or forty years ago is very noteworthy and very sad—I mean the average newspaper (for they had bad ones then, too). In those days the average newspaper was the champion of right and morals, and it dealt conscientiously in the truth. It is not the case now. The other day a reputable New York daily had an editorial defending the salary steal and justifying it on the ground that Congressmen were not paid enough—as if that were an all-sufficient excuse for stealing. That editorial put the matter in a new and perfectly satisfactory light with many a leather-headed reader, without a doubt. It has become a sarcastic proverb that a thing must be true if you saw it in a newspaper. That is the opinion intelligent people have of that lying vehicle in a nutshell. But the trouble is that the stupid people—who constitute the grand overwhelming majority of this and all other nations—do believe and are moulded and convinced by what they get out of a newspaper, and there is where the harm lies.

Among us, the newspaper is a tremendous power. It can make or mar any man's reputation. It has a perfect freedom to call the best man in the land a fraud and a thief, and he is destroyed beyond help. Whether Mr. Colfax is a liar or not can never be ascertained now—but he will rank as one till the day of his death—for the newspapers have so doomed him. Our newspapers—all of them, without exception—glorify the "Black Crook" and make it an opulent success—they could have killed it dead with one broadside of contemptuous silence if they had wanted to. *Days Doings* and *Police Gazettes* flourish in the land unmolested by the law, because the *virtuous* newspapers long ago nurtured up a public laxity that loves indecency and never cares whether laws are administered or not.

In the newspapers of the West you can use the editorial voice in the editorial columns to defend any wretched and injurious dogma you please by paying a dollar a line for it.

Nearly all newspapers foster Rozensweigs and kindred criminals and send victims to them by opening their columns to their advertisements. You all know that.

In the Foster murder case the New York papers made a weak pretense of upholding the hands of the Governor and urging the people to sustain him in standing firmly by the law; but they printed a whole page of sickly, maudlin appeals to his clemency as a paid advertisement. And I suppose they would have published enough pages of abuse of the Governor to destroy his efficiency as a public official to the end of his term if anybody had come forward and paid them for it—as an advertisement. The newspaper that obstructs the law on a trivial pretext, for money's sake, is a dangerous enemy to the public weal.

That awful power, the public opinion of a nation, is created in America by a horde of ignorant, self-complacent simpletons who failed at ditching and shoemaking and fetched up in journalism on their way to the poorhouse. I am personally acquainted with hundreds of journalists, and the opinion of the majority of them would not be worth tuppence in private, but when they speak in print it is the newspaper that is talking (the pygmy scribe is not visible) and then their utterances shake the community like the thunders of prophecy.

I know from personal experience the proneness of journalists to lie. I once started a peculiar and picturesque fashion of lying myself on the Pacific coast, and it is not dead there to this day. Whenever I hear of a shower of blood and frogs combined, in California, or a sea serpent found in some desert, there, or a cave frescoed with diamonds and emeralds (always found by an Injun who died before he could finish telling where it was), I say to myself I am the father of this child—I have got to answer for this lie. And habit is everything—to this day I am liable to lie if I don't watch all the time.

The license of the press has scorched every individual of us in our time, I make no doubt. Poor [Henry Morton] Stanley was a very god, in England, his praises in every man's mouth. But nobody said anything about his lectures—they were charitably quiet on that head, and were content to praise his higher virtues. But our papers tore the poor creature limb from limb and scattered the fragments from Maine to California—merely because he couldn't lecture well. His prodigious achievement in Africa goes for naught—the man is pulled down and utterly destroyed—but still the persecution follows him as relentlessly from city to city and from village to village as if he had committed some bloody and detestable crime. Bret Harte was suddenly snatched out of obscurity by our papers and throned in the clouds—all the editors in the land stood out in the inclement weather and adored him through their telescopes and swung their hats till they wore them out and then borrowed more; and the first time his family fell sick, and in his trouble and harassment he ground out a rather flat article in place of another heathen Chinee, that hurrahing host said, "Why, this man's a fraud," and they began to reach up there for him. And they got him, too, and fetched him down, and walked over him, and rolled him in the mud, and tarred and feathered him, and then set him up for a target and have been heaving dirt at him ever since. The result is that the man had had only just nineteen engagements to lecture this year, and the audience have been so scattering, too, that he has never discharged a sentence yet that hit two people at the same time. The man is ruined—never can get up again. And yet he is a person who had great capabilities, and might have accomplished great things for our literature and for himself if he had had a happier chance. And he made the mistake, too, of doing a pecuniary kindness for a starving beggar of our guild—one of the journalistic shoemaker class—and that beggar made it his business as soon as he got back to San Francisco to publish four columns of exposures of crimes committed by his benefactor, the least of which ought to make any decent man blush. The press that admitted that stuff to its columns had too much license.

In a town in Michigan I declined to dine with an editor who was drunk, and he said, in his paper, that my lecture was profane, indecent, and calculated to encourage intemperance. And yet that man never heard it. It might have reformed him if he had.

A Detroit paper once said that I was in the constant habit of beating my wife and that I still kept this recreation up, although I had crippled her for life and she was no longer able to keep out of my way when I came home in my usual frantic frame of mind. Now scarcely the half of that was true. Perhaps I ought to have sued that man for libel—but I knew better. All the papers in America—with a few creditable exceptions—would have found out then, to their satisfaction, that I was a wife beater, and they would have given it a pretty general airing, too.

Why I have published vicious libels upon people myself—and ought to have been hanged before my time for it, too—I do say it myself, that shouldn't.

But I will continue these remarks. I have a sort of vague general idea that there is too much liberty of the press in this country, and that through the absence of all wholesome restraint the newspaper has become in a large degree a national curse, and will probably damn the Republic yet.

There are some excellent virtues in newspapers, some powers that wield vast influences for good; and I could have told all about these things, and glorified them exhaustively—but that would have left you gentlemen nothing to say.[12]

Woes of Frontier Editors: Eastern Correspondents

The wave of settlement pushed inexorably toward the Pacific Ocean after the Union Pacific and Central Pacific railroads were joined by the golden spike at Promontory, Utah, in 1869. The coming of the railroad brought not only settlers but also the decimation of the thundering herds of buffalo on the plains, which were split into northern and southern herds. The rails also brought hunters and traders in buffalo hides and bones—used for fertilizer—while the meat was left to rot. Thomas Jefferson's vision of an agrarian democracy faded in the name of "progress." Whereas in 1900 some 70 percent of Americans were farmers, today, in the era of large-scale mechanized agribusiness, less than 3 percent are. The West was dotted with mining ghost towns after the veins of metal played out, and settlements on the high plains (from the Dakotas to Texas, an area once described on one-room country schoolroom maps as the Great American Desert) also withered and died. At times railroad construction bypassed budding towns, sealing their doom. The coming of the automobile and graveled or paved roads spurred farmers to do their trading on Saturdays at county seat towns, which were the only ones to survive. Today even their downtown sections are imperiled, by encircling shopping malls and fast-food and merchandise chains. At the time of the frontier, however, the optimism was almost palpable, as hometown boosterism held sway. The motto was "bigger is better," as delineated later by Sinclair Lewis in *Main Street*, wherein the town of Zenith liked to refer to itself as Zip City.

When towns on the frontier were first being founded, one of the jobs of the newspaper editor was to paint a favorable picture of life on the prairie or, more accurately, short-grass country. The wars with the Indians between 1867 and 1881 left editors jittery about renewed violence, which would have discouraged European immigrants and others from homesteading, denying them business. This fear surfaced in a kind of hysteria fanned by Eastern reporters when the ceremonial and nonbelligerent "ghost dancing" swept the Indian communities in the late nineteenth century. Ruth Laird has intensively examined South Dakota weeklies of that period, and following are a few of her findings, from the *Hot Springs* (South Dakota) *Star*. Each of these five selections speaks for itself.

"UNRELIABLE CORRESPONDENTS" (DECEMBER 5, 1890)

Now, as the intense excitement of the past week has subsided to a great extent, the exaggerated reports sent into eastern papers by the excited correspondents are beginning to have their damaging effects on South Dakota, and especially the Black Hills country. The damage done this country by such papers as the Omaha Bee, St. Paul Globe and kindred sheets cannot be estimated by dollars and cents. The people living in the immediate vicinity were not so excited as the people farther east, and those intending to come out here in the spring, will now be deterred on account of those wild rumors emanating from over ambitious newspaper correspondents. The most reliable, and the reports we depended upon for the most part in forming an opinion of the extent of the Indian news we found in the Sioux City Journal. These accounts were sent into that paper by correspondents who had some little conscience left, and were edited by a man who undoubtedly must have thoroughly understood the situation. While it might have been a good thing, financially, for the Bee, in the way of enabling them to sell more papers, it was doing so at the expense of South Dakota. The [Sioux City] Journal exhibited as much enterprise and sold as many papers and yet did not go out of its way to damage our country. Even the telegrams from here were baseless rumors and no doubt, many others had as little to support them. In excitement like the present, conservatism in a journal is to be commended, and instead of giving currency to all telegraphic reports, it would be much wiser to allay, rather than add to the excited imaginations of the masses.

Farmer and Reporter (REPRINTED IN *Hot Springs Star*, DECEMBER 12, 1890)

If a few of the fools who are wont to breed murderous Indian rumors, for the purpose of enjoying a joke on some timid acquaintance were treated to a good and thorough booting there would be a good deal less Indian talk. If the joke affected only the "rounder" the ploy might be innocent enough, but they go further, and like a wild prairie fire which takes on added fury as it advances, so do Indian rumors gather force as they go and their tendency is to unnecessarily frighten women and children. Intelligent people will cheerfully abstain from lending aid to false alarm, while wilful news mongers should be made to taste the folly of their wanton "friks" in a manner which they would long remember.

Hot Springs Star (DECEMBER 20, 1890)

Rapid City has begun to draw in its horns. It was glorious to be the seat of war and blood-curdling messages flashed over the wires from that precinct, while the war lasted, but now with its business paralized [*sic*], the settlers scared away and travel abandoned, it begins to feel the effects of aiding and abbetting [*sic*] an uncalled for and altogether damaging newspaper war. Nothing could have so hurt this country as the wild and unreliable reports sent east by blood thirsty tenderfoot correspondents. At no time has there been any serious danger of an outbreak, and it now comes to light that the Indians in the Bad Lands were hiding in fear of being punished for stealing horses and cattle. How history will glisten with the exciting incidents of this bloodless Indian War.

Hot Springs Star (MARCH 7, 1890)

A strolling squad of Indians from the reservation have been filling with terror the lives of our women and children for a few days back. They were entirely friendly however and went from house to house begging. Nevertheless our women dislike to see them come and this begging propensity should be nipped. They are fed and clothed by the nation and there is no reason why they should be permitted to annoy our people particularly our women by being permitted to go from house to house begging.

"A RIDICULOUS FARCE" (*Hot Springs Star*, DECEMBER 19, 1890)

For the past month or six weeks the whole country has been in the throes of agony over one of the most gigantic newspaper fakes ever perpetrated upon the citizens of the United States. Since the election, the columns of the eastern papers have been filled with sanguine hued reports of excited and irresponsible correspondents, describing an imaginary Indian outbreak in South Dakota. Troops have been hustled around from one post to another, and one could almost believe that he was in the midst of an intercine [sic] war. The reports as energetically circulated by such papers as the Omaha Bee, and its ilk, have been read throughout the country, and as a result South Dakota and the Black Hills especially, have suffered untold damage. Hot Springs and its sister cities all tell the same tale of injury. Our hotels are depopulated, business ventures are abandoned or held in abeyance, travel on the railroad has been almost entirely suspended, investment companies have become diffident about loaning money, settlers have abandoned their claims and thousands who had made every preparation to emigrate to this state in the spring have abandoned the idea. All this and much more damage of as serious nature has befallen us, all on account of the intentional misrepresentations published in the Bee and similar daily papers.

While there has been ghost dances and some local disturbances about the agencies and in the reservation, there never has been any cause for serious alarm. There have been no cattle stolen by the Indians, they were hungry and killed what they wanted to eat out of the government herd; they did not wantonly destroy any buildings or property, and the wild rumors printed day after day by the eastern papers, for the sake of a few nickels to be gained by selling extras, have proved disastrous to our country.

The people of South Dakota should unite in one emphatic protest against this journalistic attempt to sacrifice our interests to the miserly greed of quasi enterprising eastern papers. Even the more truthful dispatches are so garbled in the central offices that the senders hardly recognize them in the morning papers. As a newspaper fake the Indian scare has been a decided success.[13]

The Old West: Myth and Reality

The epitome of the early Western newspaper was the *Tombstone Epitaph*, which served that mining center in Arizona, about fifty miles southeast of Tucson. It was founded in 1880 by a former Apache Indian agent named John Clum. It has perhaps the most distinctive name in American journalism history, displaying the final words for the desperados and others buried in nearby Boot Hill. Clum gave the newspaper its name because, he said, "Every tombstone needs an epitaph." Still publishing as a monthly for aficionados of the Old West, it has not missed an issue in 115 years, since 1974 being under the editorship of Wallace Clayton. The *Epitaph* is the oldest continuously published newspaper in Arizona and has been the distillation of Western lore for many enthusiastic readers. In the early days, Tombstone had 110 saloons, and the town was once so raucous and unruly that President Chester Arthur threatened to impose martial law. Most famous of the early stories the newspaper covered was the celebrated gunfight at the O.K. Corral on October 21, 1881. The newspaper's front-page headline read "Yesterday's Tragedy: Three Men Hurled into Eternity in the Duration of a Moment." According to David Lamb of the *Los Angeles Times*, sixty-four books and more than two dozen movies have mythologized the story, in whole or in part. The 1950s television series *Tombstone Territory* claimed to draw its material "from the files of the Tombstone Epitaph," but actually the writers never got within three hundred miles of the town and simply made up the stories.

Myth and reality mix in other areas of the frontier as well. Some accounts of life on the fringes of civilization were realistic, such as those portrayed by Willa Cather, gifted writer and editor from Nebraska, in *Pioneers, Oh Pioneers!* and other works, or by Ole Rolvaag of Minnesota in *Giants in the Earth*. The newspapers also told a story of hopes and shattered dreams. The late economist John Ise of the University of Kansas, who grew up on the frontier, exploded some myths about it in his book *Sod and Stubble*. Ise challenged assertions such as that the pioneers were neighborly, generous, and cooperative. Barn-raisings and quilting bees aside, Ise found that frontier families were parsimonious, husbanding what meager resources they had. There was no largesse for the wayfaring stranger, as depicted in the stories by Laura Ingalls Wilder in her series *Little House on the Prairie*.

Romantic notions aside, the last of the Old West was found in the mining centers such as Denver, Colorado, where in 1895 two men—known simply as Bonfils and Tammen—bought the *Denver Post* and turned it into one of the most sensational newspapers in the history of American journalism. The linkage between the western environment and gaudy press sensationalism has gone largely unnoticed, but there is a correlation. Life on the frontier—and especially in mining towns—was so flamboyant, violent, and confrontational that newspapers like the *Denver Post*, known as the "Bucket of Blood" because of its early sensationalism and the fact that the walls of the editorial offices were painted a brilliant red, seemed to feel that they had to exaggerate to top events in the streets. At its height the *Post* was making more than one million dollars a year in uninflated and untaxed money. The raw journalistic flavor of the newspaper abounds in Gene Fowler's delightful book *Timber Line* (the timber line is the line above which trees cannot grow at high altitudes in the mountains). For years the *Denver Post* published on reddish pink newsprint, a final salute to a fading past.

Notes

1. George W. Martin, ed., *Transactions of the Kansas State Historical Society, 1907-1908*, vol. X (Topeka: State Printing Office, 1908), 368–73.

2. Quoted in William E. Huntzicker, "The Frontier Press, 1800–1900," in *The Media in America, a History*, 2nd ed., ed. William David Sloan, James G. Stovall, and James D. Startt (Scottsdale, AZ: Publishing Horizons, 1993), 202.

3. Quoted in George R. Stewart, Jr., *Bret Harte: Argonaut and Exile* (Boston: Houghton Mifflin Company, 1931), 98.

4. Quoted in Stewart, *Bret Harte*, 87–88.

5. Ibid., 84.

6. Ambrose Bierce, *The Devil's Dictionary* (New York: Dover Publications, 1958), 110.

7. Bertha Clark Pope, ed., *Letters of Ambrose Bierce* (San Francisco: Book Club of California, 1922), 196–97.

8. Ernest Jerome Hopkins, ed., *The Complete Short Stories of Ambrose Bierce* (Garden City, NY: Doubleday and Company, 1970), 471–74.

9. James Charlton, ed., *Fighting Words: Writers Lambast other Writers— From Aristotle to Anne Rice* (Chapel Hill, NC: Algonquin Books, 1994), 41.

10. Quoted in Charles Neider, *The Selected Letters of Mark Twain* (New York: Harper and Row, 1982), 209.

11. Quoted in Charlton, *Fighting Words*, 42.

12. Charles Neider, ed., *The Complete Essays of Mark Twain* (Garden City, NY: Doubleday and Company, 1963), 10–14.

13. Ruth Laird, "Examination of Newspaper Accounts of Indian Activities in Selected South Dakota Weeklies, 1887–1920" (unpublished paper, Library of South Dakota State University, n.d.), n.p.

5

The Age of Consolidation

———⟨◆⟩———

The period between the end of the Civil War and the close of the nineteenth century has been described in various ways—from the Gilded Age, when a few enjoyed ostentatious wealth, to the politically nondescript Brown Decades. It was a time of great change in American life, including rapid industrialization, urbanization, and an influx of immigrants. Those who amassed huge fortunes in an era of unregulated capitalism, such as John D. Rockefeller in oil and Andrew Carnegie in steel, were regarded by some historians as "robber barons" because of their ruthless tactics in squeezing out competition, and by others as "captains of industry" for laying the foundations for our present economic system.

Profound changes occurred in journalism as well, as the focus shifted from the individual editor of the nineteenth century to the impersonal, machine-tooled newspapers of today. In less than a decade (between 1869 and 1878) five giants of the preceding era died: Henry J. Raymond of the *New York Times*, James Gordon Bennett of the *New York Herald*, Horace Greeley of the *New York Tribune*, Samuel Bowles of the *Springfield* (Massachusetts) *Republican,* and poet William Cullen Bryant, who edited the *New York Evening Post* for half a century. The nineteenth century had been the era of hands-on publisher/editors; the emphasis in the twentieth century shifted to the reporter and the writer, from Richard Harding Davis to Bob Woodward and Carl Bernstein.

Newspapers had become big business. Colonial printer Hugh Gaine had set up his shop with two thousand dollars from his savings as an apprentice, whereas Charles A. Dana, who rejuvenated the *New York Sun* after purchasing it in 1868, estimated at the close of the century that it would require a million dollars to start a major journal from scratch. Under such conditions, newspaper stockholders and owners alike tended to look more at profits than quality. Like their compatriots in railroads and financing, they did not relish competition and sought to eliminate it whenever possible, so they could set their own prices for advertising space based on monopoly circulation. And if one newspaper was profitable, why not double the profits by having two or more? The number of newspapers shrank as journalism moved from the editorial office to the counting house. In 1890, New York City had fifteen general-circulation, English-language daily newspapers; today it has three, if one does not include the national *Wall Street Journal*. Sometimes newspapers were bought for their Associated Press franchise (one to a city) until the Supreme Court judged the AP practice to be in restraint of trade, but generally opposition newspapers were bought and then simply killed off. In Philadelphia, Cyrus H. K. Curtis, who founded the *Ladies' Home Journal* in 1883 and bought the *Saturday Evening Post* in 1897, spied profits in the newspaper field as well, but of the seven Philadelphia newspapers he owned, only one remains.

Frank A. Munsey, who applied the penny-press success formula to the magazine field by selling *Munsey's* for ten cents, a move that brought in a circulation of 650,000 by 1900, once said, "There is no business that cries so loud for organization and combination, as that of newspaper publishing. For one thing, the number of newspapers is at least 60 percent greater than we need." Thus, Munsey proceeded to eliminate them, without the slightest regard for the diversity of viewpoints that should be available to readers in Thomas Jefferson's "marketplace of ideas." When Munsey died in 1925, Kansas editor William Allen White wrote his famous obituary of "the butcher of New York," presented here in its entirety:

> Frank A. Munsey contributed to the journalism of his day the talent of a meatpacker, the morals of a money-changer and the manners of an undertaker. He and his kind have about succeeded in transforming a once-noble profession into an eight percent security. May he rest in trust![1]

The toll of fallen newspapers was felt nationwide. According to the Bureau of the Census, the number of daily papers in the United States reached a peak of 2,600 in 1909, before the inroads of radio and television and the expensive technological advances that smaller papers simply could not afford. For some time it was thought that the number of dailies would hold steady at around 1,700 (the figure for 1970 was 1,748), but it continues to decline (in 1995 it was 1,533). Coupled with this alarming trend is the sharply diminishing number of cities with competing newspapers. One-newspaper towns limit the access by their citizens to varied news reporting and opinion. In 1991 only forty-one U.S. cities had separately owned, competing newspapers, and that figure declined to thirty-seven by 1997. Seventeen of those had joint printing arrangements.

Where have all the newspapers gone? Many have been absorbed by group ownership, and we now witness the phenomenon of chains being gobbled up by chains. According to the American Newspaper Publishers Association, in 1991 a total of 1,233 newspapers in the United States, or 82 percent of the total, were owned by chains. Largest in number was the British-owned Thomson Newspapers, Inc., with 125 newspapers, and the highest in circulation was Gannett with 82 newspapers representing a readership of 5,943,792. Second largest in circulation was Knight-Ridder, followed by Newhouse, New York Times, Scripps-Howard, and Hearst. As is true of one-newspaper cities, chain ownership with central editorial control tends to limit the way that the news is presented and commented upon, particularly when cross-ownership with television stations is included.

When commercial radio first appeared on the scene in the late 1920s, doomsayers sounded a premature death knell for newspapers. Much the same was said when television arrived in the late 1940s. Yet we remain a nation of newspaper readers. According to the American Newspaper Publishers Association, in 1991 more than 113 million American adults read a daily newspaper on an average weekday. That is 62.4 percent of the total adult population, and we further have the spectacle of prominent print journalists being called upon to comment about the news on both radio and television.

Joseph Pulitzer and the New Journalism

The beginnings of a mass press can be traced to the penny papers, but the fruition came at the end of the nineteenth century, when newspaper giants Joseph Pulitzer and William Randolph Hearst locked horns in combat for the New York market. Before Hearst appeared on the scene in 1895, however, Pulitzer had set the tone for the mass press with devices that so boosted circulation that they became known as the New Journalism. These techniques included large headlines, lavish illustrations, and simple, lively writing about interesting persons and events. These devices were deliberately fashioned to capture the attention of semiliterate immigrant New Yorkers whose education in the new language came largely from the daily papers. Despite the sensationalism inherent in the New Journalism formula, however, the news policy of Pulitzer's *World* stressed accuracy above all else, to ensure credibility—and therefore sales.

Joseph Pulitzer, who always took an active interest in his newspapers, understood the difficulties facing immigrants because he had been one himself. Son of a Hungarian-Jewish father and an Austro-German mother and without speaking any English when he first came to the United States during the Civil War (in which he served briefly), Pulitzer bought the *St. Louis Dispatch* at a sheriff's sale in 1878 and merged it with the *Post* three days later. So successful were the editorial crusades of the *St. Louis Post-Dispatch*, together with its human-interest stories—another integral part of the New Journalism—that in 1883 Pulitzer was able to invade the Mecca of all journalists, New York City, by buying the ailing *New York World* for $346,000.

It has sometimes been wondered why a publisher who exploited sensationalism, always latent in American journalism and rising to the fore with cyclical regularity, should be honored by the prizes for excellence in journalism he established at Columbia University. Pulitzer regarded sensationalism—appealing to all the senses—as a means to an end—namely, to draw semiliterate readers into the editorial page, which he considered the heart of the newspaper. He also established the first separate sports section of any American newspaper.

Mott likens Pulitzer to a hula dancer performing on the steps of a cathedral, to entice people to enter. Julius Chambers, managing editor of the *World*, put it this way: "In every case, the successful American journal has been built upon sensationalism; but it has been found that, once established, absolute accuracy and truth are the only bases for enduring success."[2] One can see a reflection of this in popular magazines of the twentieth century such as *Esquire* and *Playboy*, which began by catering to the prurient but, once established, included social commentary and interviews as well.

With all its stunts, promotions, and political cartoons, including social services such as medical care for the poor of New York, Pulitzer's *World* personified liberal ideas in America. That he struck a chord in seemingly uncaring New Yorkers at the close of the century can be seen by his booming circulation—booming enough for him to build the $2,500,000 *World* building as a symbol of his ideas about the role of journalism. The newspaper's building was to dominate the cityscape just as the cathedral had dominated the medieval town. Pulitzer was nearly blind for twenty years after he bought the *World*, and totally blind for the last few years before his death in 1911, but to the very end he maintained direction of both the *World* and the *Post-Dispatch*. Here are excerpts from the tribute by Frank I. Cobb, the brilliant managing editor of the *World*, published two days after the death of his boss.

Practically all the newspaper estimates of Mr. Pulitzer's work and service agree in their recognition of him as the creator of "a new kind of journalism. . . ."

This is true. Mr. Pulitzer did create a new kind of journalism. By means of it he became the great emancipator of the American press. He found it shackled to tradition, to systems and to parties. He struck off its shackles and showed it the way to freedom.

He was not the first of the great editors to regard a newspaper not as private property but as public property—not merely as affected with a public interest but animated and inspired by public interest; independent of everything except public interest—independent even of its own proprietor when occasion required.

Mr. Pulitzer's theory of journalism was so simple that it often bewildered friends and opponents alike. His aim was to make a newspaper that would print all the news that ought to be printed without fear or favor; that would present this news in such a manner as to appeal to the widest circle of readers; that would fearlessly attack all forms of wrong and injustice; that would safeguard the weak, restrain the strong and be a great forum of popular self-government; that would hold itself beyond every form of influence except that of the public welfare.

To this end he concentrated all his energy and all his genius. Although he was the owner of *The World* and the *St. Louis Post-Dispatch*, he was in no sense a newspaper publisher. Practically, all his knowledge of counting-room affairs was second-hand. He once told the writer of this article that in all the years of his journalistic career he never spent an hour at any one time in the business office.

Nothing connected with *The World* appealed to him less than its income and profits. There was nothing about which he worried less or to which he devoted less thought. Its prosperity was a means, never an end. When business questions were presented to him he was inclined to be resentful. He disliked to waste time and energy on them which could be devoted to the newspaper itself. To him journalism was never a business; it was the most powerful and responsible profession in which any man could engage.

His chief concern centered in the editorial page as the expression of the paper's conscience, courage and convictions. To that he devoted infinite care and attention. Sick or well, it was never wholly absent from his thoughts. When he was well he had it read to him every day and expressed his opinion about every editorial article, the style in which it was written, the manner in which the thought was expressed, whether the editorial was strong or weak, whether it served any useful public purpose, whether it said the thing that a great newspaper ought to have said.

When ill-health made it impossible for him to have the editorial page read every day he would keep the files for weeks, and then when his condition permitted, he would go over them with painstaking care, always from the point of view of a detached critic, seeking only to determine whether the page was taking the fullest advantage of its opportunities for public service and whether it was measuring up to the high standards that he had set for it.

Nothing was ever allowed to interfere with its independence and its freedom of expression. There were certain questions about which he became convinced that in spite of all his efforts he was possibly prejudiced. In these matters he exacted a pledge that no suggestions or instructions or even commands from him would ever be followed, but that the paper would always say what an independent, untrammelled newspaper ought to say in performing its duties to the people. This pledge was never violated, and nobody respected it more tenaciously than he himself, even when he was aggressively unsympathetic with the attitude the page sometimes assumed toward the issues in question. . . .

He keenly appreciated the fact that it was necessary to interest people greatly in order to get a hearing for the things that he wished to say. That is why he dressed up the news with pictures. That is why he employed effective stage management in presenting it. That is why he reached out for every kind of news that appealed to human nature. Through that he built up the great editorial power that was the creative pride of his life; for back of everything he did was this dominating motive.[3]

Lincoln Steffens Interviews William Randolph Hearst

The success of the New Journalism bred competitors for Pulitzer, a very formidable one in the person of William Randolph Hearst. Born in 1863 and expelled from Harvard, where he had observed closely the New Journalism of nearby New York, Hearst persuaded his father, a wealthy silver miner, into letting him put these new techniques to work on the *San Francisco Examiner*, which his father had bought to further his political ambitions. Young Hearst proved that Pulitzer's innovations in journalism could be as successful on the west coast as the east. A few years after his father died in 1891, William Randolph Hearst's mother made available to him $7,500,000 to buy his entrance into the New York journalistic sweepstakes. In 1895 he acquired the *Morning Journal* for $180,000, which marked the second step toward the establishment of a newspaper empire and precipitated the well-known press war of the 1890s between Hearst and Pulitzer.

Both hired the finest talent available, and the *Journal* and *World* raided each other's staffs mercilessly. Both indulged in extreme sensationalism—exploiting news of crime, disasters, sex, and scandals—but Hearst did not share the higher purpose of luring readers into the editorial page. On the other hand, as the only Democratic newspaper in New York, he recognized the circulation-building effect of crusades, and in his early liberal career he championed the popular election of

U.S. senators, the initiative and referendum, graduated income and inheritance taxes, and widespread public ownership of utilities, including nationalization of railroads, telegraph lines, and coal mines. Hearst came to build the world's largest publishing empire to that time. A conglomerate itself, Hearst's far-flung holdings attacked trusts and monopolies after the passage of the Sherman Anti-Trust Act of 1890. At its peak in 1935, his empire included twenty-six daily newspapers in nineteen cities, various syndicates, the International News Service, thirteen magazines, eight radio stations, and two motion picture companies. Before overextension and the Depression wiped out all but twelve newspapers, some regarded Hearst—commanding all that power to sway public opinion—as a powerful menace to a democratic society. Books attacking him began to appear, such as Ferdinand Lundberg's *Imperial Hearst* and Oliver Carlson's and Ernest Sutherland Bates's *Hearst, Lord of San Simeon* (both 1936). Orson Welles's movie *Citizen Kane*, a thinly veiled account of Hearst's life, captured the attention of critics and public alike, although it was never reviewed or advertised in any Hearst newspaper.

Pulitzer, apparently uninterested in establishing a chain of papers, made the *World* and *Post-Dispatch* pay-as-you-go, whereas Hearst kept pumping the family fortune into his ventures. In the interview between famed muckraker Lincoln Steffens and Hearst presented below, Hearst is quoted as saying, "I didn't care about making money; at least not just to make money. If money was what I was after, I could get that—now—more easily, more surely, and with less trouble and less labor, in some other way." Hearst wanted power—political power—but how successful was he in that endeavor? He ran for governor of New York and lost. He ran for mayor of New York City and lost. He was elected representative to Congress for one term but seldom showed up. Pulitzer, on the other hand, seemed to have no personal political ambitions. Also, the Hearst newspapers did not support a single winning presidential candidate. One wonders about the vaunted power of the press when one considers that these were the men Hearst supported for President: William Jennings Bryan, Champ Clark, Hiram W. Johnson, William Gibbs McAdoo, John Nance

Garner, Alf Landon, Gen. Douglas MacArthur, and William Randolph Hearst.

The press war in the New York arena between Hearst and Pulitzer has been called "yellow journalism" because of the tug-and-pull efforts to obtain or retain the services of Richard F. Outcault, whose comic strip "The Yellow Kid" was immensely popular. Hearst did not like the word "sensational," preferring "striking." But call it what you will, when William McKinley was elected president in the bitter campaign of 1896, both the *World* and the *Journal* passed the million mark in circulation. Later, Hearst's *Evening Journal* attacked McKinley with such reckless statements as this: "If bad institutions and bad men can be got rid of only by killing, then the killing must be done."[4] When McKinley was in fact assassinated shortly thereafter, the public was outraged. Circulation fell off, and Hearst was forced to change the name of the *Journal* to the *American*, but as circulation continued to decline, wags referred to it as "the vanishing American."

Lincoln Steffens, who conducted this interview with Hearst in 1906, had become a towering figure in the muckraking movement (see Chapter 6) largely through his series "The Shame of the Cities" in *McClure's Magazine*. But simply uncovering corruption, he discovered, did not lead to its reform. And he found that corruption was omnipresent in American life, a many-headed Hydra that defied being slain. Later he sought a solution in revolution—both in Mexico after 1910 and Russia after 1917, but he returned to join the ranks of his fellow disillusioned muckrakers. His *Autobiography*, published in two volumes in 1931, has become a classic. In an interview on a train ride in 1906, the powerful reporter Steffens confronts the powerful publisher Hearst in a rare moment of candor. Following are pertinent excerpts from that historic interview.

All over the country all sorts and conditions of men are asking "What about Hearst?" and, if they think you should be able to answer, they put the question with an eagerness—or an anxiety—which denotes a very real desire to know. And nobody seems to know. They have read his "yellow" newspapers, heard some yellow gossip about him, and "that's enough."

Some of those who say that Hearst's newspapers are enough to judge the man by, say also that Hearst's newspapers are not Hearst's; that he did not make them. A rich young man, Hearst was able to buy brains, and the talented men he hired, having put themselves into his newspapers, are putting him into politics. Almost his very existence is denied. The *New York Evening Post* declared last August that "William Randolph Hearst" was a myth, a syndicate, a trade-mark, an empty name.

Is there such a man? Somebody must be back of the papers and the politics that bear his name. If it isn't Hearst himself, who is it? And whether "Hearst" is Hearst or somebody else, what manner of man is it that moved in silence behind all the noise he was making, arousing in some people dread, in others hope, but compelling in all an interest which of itself is significant? For, suppose the worst of Hearst: suppose him to be a yellow millionaire, without a mind of his own or the morals of other people; suppose his inherited millions have fallen under the control of an unscrupulous group of able men who, by pandering in journalism to the love of the vices, and by playing in politics with the hatred of the riches of the rich, propose to bring on a class war and destroy the U.S. Government—what does it mean of the American people that so many of them read the Hearst newspapers and look to such a political leadership with at least half a mind to follow it? Why should a myth be a "menace" in this land of prosperity and liberty? We approach, in more senses than one, a national question when we ask who, what, where is the reality behind the mystery of William Randolph Hearst, the unknown? . . .

He lives nowhere. He has residences, but no home. He has many businesses: mines, ranches and, in five cities—San Francisco, New York, Chicago, Boston and Los Angeles—he has one or two newspapers; also he has two magazines; but he has no place of business; no office. In each of the five cities where he has newspapers, he has a career, and in others besides; for he is busy everywhere politically. And yet he goes rarely to Boston; he has visited Los Angeles but once since his paper was started there; and in none of these other places has he either many friends or many enemies who know him. You can learn all about his agents, but of Mr. Hearst—nothing. . . .

In the first place he has no intimates, apparently. He has employees; he has lieutenants; he has relatives; and most of these are his friends. What is more, these friends of his admire him beyond all reason; at any rate no two of them admire him for the same reason. Indeed, as they describe him, no two seem to be talking about the same man. They all relate anecdotes to illustrate their conception of their chief, but their stories are principally of what they said to him; there is very little of what he said to them. All they all agreed upon was that, even to them, "Mr. Hearst does not say much.". . .

That crimes are tragedies, and that they are, if properly done, legitimate material for journalism as well as fiction and poetry, are undeniable propositions. That the problem of getting such things written with understanding and decent feeling is one of the most difficult in the newspaper offices will not be disputed. But the problem is not unsolvable. It amounts to getting news editors who understand the difference between tragedies and crimes, and reporters with feelings fine enough, and an imagination sympathetic enough, to grasp and to tell such stories. And Mr. Hearst, inexpressive himself, has few, if any, news editors who know what he is talking about.

"I think," he said, "that part of the fault for the failure is mine. If I had stuck to one newspaper, I might by personal direction in detail have made a newspaper to suit me exactly. But I went off starting other papers in widely separated places, and, of course, I can supervise all of them only in a general way. I can't give myself up to any one. . . ."

The local reform movements where, in states and cities, the new national spirit is breeding are all, at bottom, moral. Mr. Hearst is political. The watchword everywhere is "representative government," and that is the same as Mr. Hearst's cry "Democracy," but back of the people's demand there is a sentiment which is not only moral but, in a suppressed way, emotional. Mr. Hearst knows nothing of this. It will take a man of some fervor to express this feeling. Mr. Hearst has no fervor. Cold, isolated, hard, he is distinctly unmoral.[5]

Yellow Journalism Defended

Sensationalism ebbs and flows in American journalism history with tidal regularity, beginning with the penny press of the 1830s, continuing with the yellow press of the 1890s, resurfacing with the "Jazz Journalism" of the 1920s, and culminating with the present cycle. The sheer volume of coverage of the O. J. Simpson murder trial, which dragged on seemingly forever, with television cameras in the courtroom, will stagger the future analyst of press performance. Again, the allegations of sexual misconduct and obstruction of justice leveled against President Bill Clinton in the 1990s were blown out of all proportion by the press, blurring the line between gossip and fact. Yet a century earlier a few observers, such as Lydia Kingsmill Commander, writing in 1905 in the magazine

Arena, defended yellow journalism. A forerunner of those who study popular culture today, she spoke up for what interested the common people.

Yellow journalism is outwardly distinguished by the flaring makeup of the paper, the striking headlines in startling type and the free use of illustrations; by the attention given to crime, sports, divorces and the tragic aspects of life in general; and by the constant appeal to the emotions in the presentation of the news. Human interest goes into every column; everything is a story and is told as such.

No papers were ever before, no others are now, so execrated and so beloved as are the yellow journals. But whether approved or condemned they must be considered, because of their tremendous influence. Their circulation figures are staggering. Not merely thousands, nor even hundreds of thousands, but millions of Americans read the yellow papers regularly. Therefore they cannot be ignored by anyone who would understand his age and his people.

The harshest criticism of yellow journalism is passed upon its method of obtaining circulation by indulging the low tastes of its readers. This is most reprehensible in the eyes of people of refined nature, who revolt at the details of crimes, despise prize-fights or horse-racing and loathe the exposure of family scandals.

But, after all, is not the difference between the readers and the critics of the yellow press one of cultivation, rather than of kind? The latter simply prefer scandal, crime and combat that deal with imaginary or historical characters. They are indifferent to the tragedy enacted yesterday in a slum tenement; but they follow with vivid interest the investigations of Sherlock Holmes; and thrill with the horror of Poe's tales or Balzac's gruesome stories or Stevenson's morbid, ghoulish, dual creature, Dr. Jekyll and Mr. Hyde. Is not the biography which stands preëminent in the opinion of the world—Boswell's *Life of Johnson*—a mass of petty, personal detail, a bundle of gossip? The high literary skill of the masterwriters makes yellow-journal subjects acceptable to the cultured few who turn with disgust from the crude newspaper of the multitude.[6]

E. W. Scripps and a Press for Workers

Hearst was not the first to build a chain of newspapers in the United States. That journalistic practice was introduced by Edward Wyllis Scripps, that rarest of all rare species—a capitalist entrepreneur who through noblesse oblige saw some value in socialism. Scripps began his newspaper career as an office boy at the age of eighteen on the *Detroit Tribune*. In 1878 on a shoestring he started his first newspaper, the *Cleveland Penny Press*, supplemented two years later with what became the *Cincinnati Post*. These two cheap evening newspapers, along with the *Detroit Evening News*, constituted the first chain of daily newspapers in the United States. By the efforts of Scripps and his partner, Milton Alexander McRae, after 1889 the chain would mushroom into the Scripps-McRae League of Newspapers. Later, in his famous "Disquisitions," Scripps acknowledged that he owned "twenty or thirty" newspapers—as if he had lost track.

Like Greeley and Bennett before him, Scripps viewed himself as a man with a mission and his newspapers as vessels of trust. True to his own humble origins, he believed that his newspapers were "classrooms" for the working man and woman, who had no other avenue or means of advancement. The self-described "damned old crank" declared that "whatever is, is wrong," meaning that anything can stand improvement, and newspapers entrusted to his stewardship were there to make things right for those he called the "95 percent," the common people. His optimistic belief that society could be changed presaged that of the muckrakers, but at the same time the partners launched capitalist journalistic structures such as the Newspaper Enterprise Association in 1902 and the United Press in 1907. If Scripps could not have socialism, however, he seemed to settle for participatory capitalism, because at the time of his death in 1926, two-fifths of the stock of his papers was owned by the employees. He also staked editors in profit-sharing arrangements, but in 1908 he asked the nagging question, "Is honest journalism possible?" in a capitalist society. Here are excerpts from his completely frank answer.

There is not only a community of interest but a community of social feeling between the capitalists of any locality, section, or country. The successful journalist, that is to say, when he owns his newspaper, is a wealthy man, a capitalist by necessity. His associates are necessarily other capitalists. The greater this association of capitalists is, the more completely does it minister to and give satisfaction to the natural, normal, human social instincts. A social capitalistic class quickly crystallizes and solidifies into a social caste, and the journalist who has become a capitalist is inevitably estranged from the larger community. . . .

What would one think of a poor man who had a case in court against a rich man, who allowed his rich antagonist to employ the lawyers on both sides—who would allow his rich antagonist to employ and pay his, the poor man's, lawyer fees?

Yet, this is just what the poorer people of the United States do in every case that is tried between labor and capital before the bar of public opinion. A modern, up-to-date great newspaper is published in the form of a great and bulky document. The white paper used by the publisher in many cases costs at the paper mills more money than the reader pays for it. This being the case, all the other expenses, the employment of great staffs of writing journalists, of printers, of other mechanics, the cost of rent, machinery, and the wear and tear on the same, the telegraph tolls, and all the profit of the business of making a great newspaper, is borne, not by the readers of a newspaper, but by the advertisers, men in business, men who are capitalists. . . .

What does the great mass of the people in the United States know that they do not learn from the newspapers? In this day and age, the public gets 99 percent, at least, of all its information concerning public affairs from the daily newspaper press. If the whole press is bearing false witness on a large number of important facts, the possession of which is the right of the public, how can the public know that it is the victim of false testimony? Has not one got to prove first to the public mind that the press, as it stands today, is false and dishonest, before that public can demand an honest and truthful press? What other means can exist in these times for conveying to the public this proof, than the press?[7]

Voices from the Heartland

While Hearst and Scripps were creating their newspaper empires, Pulitzer became less sensational, and Adolph S. Ochs and his staff after 1896 were building one of the great newspapers of the world, the *New York Times*. But there also were voices from the hinterlands that achieved national and even international recognition. Among the first of the country editors to do this was Edgar Watson Howe of Kansas, who founded the *Atchison Globe* in 1877 with two hundred dollars' capital and reputedly became the most-quoted editor of his time. An iconoclast, he ridiculed feminist aspirations and religion. Concerning the latter, for example, he commented, "In Missouri, the other day, a mule deliberately committed suicide. He put his head through a post-and-rail fence, slipped his neck down to a narrow place, pulled back, and choked himself. The cause of the suicide is not known. He had not been drinking, and there was no trouble with his family. It is thought by some to have been the result of religious excitement." Howe preceded William Allen White (see Chapter 7), but both were part of a vanishing breed. The only modern counterpart who comes to mind is Harry Golden of the late *North Carolina Israelite*, who joshed his readers into more rational race relations. But small-town editors like Howe looked askance at the growing encroachment of "corporate America" and urban sprawl. His ideas are more fully presented in Calder M. Pickett's *Ed Howe: Country Town Philosopher*, but here was his response to the accelerating consolidation in the newspaper business.

Editors formerly poor are now rich and powerful; and instead of being dishonest men, they reek with virtue. They are not only good men; they are too good; they demand a perfection in business that they do not equal in their own business offices. It is absurd to say that these powerful, rich and intelligent editors are corrupt. They are as honorable in their dealings as other business men; but their greatness and power have turned their heads, and they have become insolent in demanding that the people dance attendance on their excessive virtue measures, and give freely to their too-liberal plans for community and social betterment.

Probably the most insolent American is the big editor who has acquired a big circulation, a big advertising patronage, a big building, and a big fortune. Being rich himself, he advocates all sorts of public improvements, that they may become monuments to his memory; as the preacher insists on building a new and unnecessary church as evidence of his activity. The big editor is more insolent with his power than the rich are with their money, and pursues his enemies with a viciousness that will in time, I hope, be prohibited. He is the patron of all other visionary ladies and gents, and joins them in private consultations about the slowness of the people, and their lack of proper enthusiasm. Although always praising The People in print, the big editor really feels superior to them, and harshly criticizes them in his private conferences with fellow uplifters.[8]

Newspapers without Ads?

The mass press, whether chain-owned or not, would not have been possible without advertising income, but there have been some highly vocal nay-sayers. Bill Moyers once asked historian Barbara Tuchman on PBS what she thought was the most "insidious" development of the twentieth century, and she replied without hesitation, "Advertising. It packages our political candidates and reduces us all to the lowest common denominator." The other side of the coin is that advertising also fuels the economy and helps make possible, for some, the highest standard of living in human history. Another historian, Frank Tannenbaum, maintained that the true revolutionary of modern times was not Karl Marx or Vladimir Lenin but Henry Ford, who through mass production and lower prices launched the consumer revolution.

In the early years of the century, however, people feared that advertisers controlled the content of the press. As an antidote, E. W. Scripps published *The Day Book* in Chicago without any ads between 1911 and 1917. It is thought to have been the first sustained daily of its kind, and boasted poet-biographer Carl Sandburg as its chief reporter. Ralph Ingersoll published *PM*, another paper without ads, in New York City between 1940 and 1948, although it did offer its readers a "Digest of Advertisements" from New York's nine major newspapers at that time, stating only what was available, where to get it, and how much it cost.

Both experimental efforts ultimately failed, but *PM* is also worthy of note for having questioned traditional news values. Crime news was reported, for example, but from a sociological viewpoint—what caused the crime and how could it have been prevented? Even the traditional editorial page, under the direction of Louis Kronenberger, came under scrutiny and revision, as indicated in the following salutatory editorial.

We have long known that newspaper editorials are written by people, be-cause every so often we have met people who wrote them. But because we have never seen them at work, we are left guessing how they manage to soar out of sight of the human family, and from some solar perch relay their utterances to a grimy composing room in time to catch the first edition.

For some reason that we have never understood, the editorial page of most daily papers speaks in an Olympian falsetto. It never uses its natural voice. It never fumbles for a word. It never coughs. It never lights a cigarette. It never sits with its feet on a desk. It sits behind a screen, and if you should knock over the screen, you still would get only a rear view of a lordly high-backed chair. Nobody has ever discovered what you'd see if you peaked over the chair.

We have no idea why the editorial page of a paper is always, in both style and tone, the least personal thing about it. It's not quite so pompous as it used to be, or so pontifical; it even discreetly dallies in slang, or throws in a few jovial lines about Shirley Temple's retirement or the sale of Joe Medwick to the Dodgers. But it never tackles the job of providing real communication between the paper and its readers. It never has the welcome sign out. It's always saying things like "For Shame!" It never says things like "Nuts to you."

Our idea of an editorial page worth its salt is something as chummy as an English pub, as scrappy as a Down East town meeting, as informal as the men's bath-houses at Coney Island. That's what this page is going to work for. That and a little humor. For that's the way people, in real life, are serious about the things that mean most to them; and this is a serious page.[9]

Rupert Murdoch and the Lords of the Global Village

Before turning to the muckraking effort to expose excesses in the press and society in the first decade of the twentieth century, it is necessary to include here a brief profile of Rupert Murdoch, who, at the pinnacle of consolidation, has capital-ized on trends long evident. Press critic Ben H. Bagdikian includes Murdoch in his gallery of the "Lords of the Global Village," published in a special issue of *The Nation* in 1989 and updated in 1997 by Ted Koppel on ABC's *Nightline*, which periodically evaluates press performance. Since the original article, reproduced below, was printed, Rupert Murdoch's News Corporation has produced an annual turnover (the volume of shares traded on the stock exchange) of $12 billion. He bought Pat Robertson's Family Channel for $2 billion, adding to his Fox network of twenty-two television stations, and he owns a Hollywood studio, 20th Century Fox, with its film library. He has also acquired a major book publishing house along the way, controls Star TV, a satellite system that covers most of Asia, and owns 36 percent of the British press, in addition to his native Australian holdings. In short, Rupert Murdoch, who became an American citizen to skirt regulations for the acquisition of a television station, makes William Randolph Hearst look like small potatoes, alarming many who fear a near global press monopoly within a few years. Such a monopoly would include the likes of Bagdikian's other "Lords of the Global Village"—Reinhard Mohn of Germany, the late Robert Maxwell of Czechoslovakia, and Jean-Luc Lagardère of France. In view of such powerful, overwhelming transnational holdings, one can no longer talk of a single country's press. The global village is here, but who is running the show? Here is Bagdikian's profile in its entirety of one of those who call the tune.

Rupert Murdoch may or may not be the most voracious media baron of them all, but he probably is the only one who ever prompted his critics to convene an entire conference devoted to dissecting him. This gathering of journalists and sundry others took place earlier this year in Sydney, Australia, where for three days various damning papers were presented, and the mood can best be summed up by the observation that Murdoch has become "the Magellan of the Information Age, splashing ashore on one continent after another."

Murdoch started his media voyage Down Under in 1954, after his father died and left him *The News* in Adelaide. He was content to toil there until 1960, when, at age 29, he began his empire-building by taking over the Norton newspapers in Sydney, Melbourne and Brisbane. In those days Murdoch was a vocal socialist, supported the Labor Party and professed high journalistic ideals: "Unless we can return to the principles of public service," he said about that time, "we will lose our claim to be the Fourth Estate. What right have we to speak in the public interest when, too often, we are motivated by personal gain?"

In 1964, Murdoch appeared to be acting on those sentiments when he founded the continent's first national newspaper, a quality daily named *The*

Australian. The country's journalists rejoiced, but not for long. For soon Murdoch was bending the paper to his increasingly conservative views. Betty Riddell, a poet and one of Australia's leading journalists, recalls that in the beginning Murdoch was always in the newsroom, could always be talked to and argued with. "Now it's all gone," she says. "Why? Power, not money."

Murdoch soon had plenty of both. In 1969 he splashed ashore in England and outbid Robert Maxwell for *News of the World*, befriending its chair, Sir William Carr, and then forcing him out soon after the deal was done, a standard Murdoch tactic. Stafford Somerfield, the paper's editor, was next. "I did not come all this way," Magellan said, "not to interfere."

Nor to settle for merely one newspaper. He bought the ailing *Sun* in 1969, and by 1977 it was the biggest-selling daily in the English-speaking world (circulation now 4 million). Murdoch lured readers into his tent by perfecting the prurient journalism that by now has become the standard at almost all his publications, a mix of lurid crime tales under souped-up headlines and pinups with their bare breasts pushing out of page three. Even the august *Times* and *Sunday Times of London* were not immune. After Murdoch acquired them in 1981 and they were too slow to introduce the titillation formula, a memorandum appeared demanding more sex. The next day *The Times* carried the headline, "How I Sold Myself to a Sex Club."

Murdoch unabashedly used his British papers to help Margaret Thatcher into power. The late Charles Douglas-Home, while editor of *The Times* under Murdoch, told the press lord's biographer, Thomas Kiernan: "Rupert and Mrs. Thatcher consult regularly on every important matter of policy. . . . Around here he's often jokingly referred to as Mr. Prime Minister." Murdoch wielded the same conservative clout in the United States, putting the editorial page and news columns of his sex-and-crime crazed *New York Post* (sold in 1988) in the slavish service of the Reagan Administration.

One payoff was that Reagan's Federal Communications Commission permitted him to do what it had never allowed any other broadcaster in the country to do: acquire a new television station in a city where he also owned a daily newspaper, and keep both. That paved the way for Fox Broadcasting, Murdoch's chain of television stations in the United States. Not surprisingly, this so-called fourth network offers a steady diet of sex, violence and peeping-Tom programming.

Murdoch is a master at weaving his way through the complex laws that permit multinational corporations to escape taxes. He and his family own less than 50 percent of News Corporation Ltd., the Australian firm that is his base. The rest of the stock is safely in the hands of docile shareholders. Murdoch makes sure *not* to own 50 percent or more probably because, under U.S. tax regulations, that would increase his income taxes in this coun-try. *Forbes* has calculated that in 1985, News Corporation profits were $101 million but were set at only $30 million in the United States because of U.S. tax accounting loopholes. Murdoch has built up a debt in the hundreds of millions in acquiring his empire. But this enormous obligation has its tax advantages, too, providing large deductions for interest paid to help offset the extraordinary profit levels and cash flows typical of the mass media.

Murdoch's acquisition technique is shrewd if informal. David Davis Jr., a publisher involved in one takeover, said it all happened so fast "I didn't know whether I'd made a deal or not. . . . They do everything on the phone or in hallways." A London *Times* staff member is less bewildered: "One minute he's swimming along with a smile, then snap! There's blood in the water. Your head's gone."[10]

Notes

1. Quoted in Michael Emery and Edwin Emery, *The Press and America: An Interpretive History of the Mass Media*, 7th ed. (Englewood Cliffs, NJ: Prentice-Hall, 1992), 291.

2. Quoted in Mott, *American Journalism*, 443.

3. Quoted in John L. Heaton, *Cobb of "The World," A Leader in Liberal-ism* (New York: E. P. Dutton and Company, 1924), 239–42.

4. *New York Evening Journal*, April 10, 1901.

5. Lincoln Steffens, "Hearst, the Man of Mystery," *American Magazine* 63, no. 1 (November 1906): 3–4, 12, 20.

6. Lydia Kingsmill Commander, "The Significance of Yellow Journal-ism," *Arena* 34 (August 1905): 150.

7. Oliver Knight, ed., *I Protest: Selected Disquisitions of E. W. Scripps* (Madison: University of Wisconsin Press, 1966), 243–45.

8. E. W. Howe, *Ventures in Common Sense* (New York: Alfred A. Knopf, 1919), 134–35.

9. *PM*, June 19, 1940.

10. Ben H. Bagdikian, "Rupert Murdoch," *The Nation* (June 12, 1989): 806.

6

Muckrakers and
the American Dream

<‹◆›>

The "American Dream" is almost always couched in terms of economic opportunity—owning one's own house with two cars in the garage—with little attention given to our political freedoms and promise of social fulfillment. That dreary stretch of political ineptness and corruption in the Gilded Age of unbridled capitalism after the Civil War spawned a generation of journalists determined to resurrect the American dream and mend a flawed society. As the heyday of the muckrakers (1902–1912) recedes into the distant past, however, this dedicated band is relegated to fewer and fewer pages in journalism history textbooks, eclipsed as they are by two world wars, the Great Depression, Korea, Vietnam, and sundry contemporary crises and scandals. Yet muckraking was a watershed as important in shaping modern journalism as the penny press or the New Journalism. The connection between the muckrakers, who accomplished much social good, and those reporters who unraveled Watergate, for example, an effort that restored faith in the governmental process, goes largely unnoticed. And it does not take a leap of faith to see the relationship between Upton Sinclair's *The Jungle* (1906), clearly a novel but based on solid, on-the-scene observations in the Chicago stockyards, and Truman Capote's meticulously researched "non-fiction novel," *In Cold Blood* (1965).

Some even still hold the muckrakers in derision, their sobriquet an epithet applied to them by President Theodore Roosevelt; yet perhaps it was American journalism's finest hour. They bore the epithet as a badge of honor in their quest to bring reality to the American dream. Their persistent hammering away—sensationalism with a purpose, if you will—at the pervasive ills of society played a large part in major reforms such as pure food and drug legislation, the meat inspection act, reorganization of the railroads, employers' liability, and the prohibition against transporting women across state lines for purposes of prostitution.

In short, muckraking was the dawn of investigative reporting, which has reappeared in cycles since then—partly in response to the competition of television, with its visual impact and open-ended deadlines (any program can be interrupted with important news, consigning the newspaper "extras" to the archives). The print medium could not follow that act, so it assumed another mantle after World War II, when television came into its own. Doomsayers predicted that first radio and then television would mean the slow death of newspapers, but fresh approaches to the news saved the day. Editors realized that they could offer readers more detail than that skimmed over in a fifteen-minute or half-hour telecast. A new way of looking at the news emerged under a succession of labels—backgrounding the news, in-depth and interpretative reporting, precision and investigative journalism: in short, the grandchild of muckraking.

Television, which like radio had been slow to develop its own news staffs, relying instead on newspapers and wire services, countered with muckraking "news magazines" such as *60 Minutes*—which *The New Yorker* claimed prosecuted rather than presented the news—and its spin-offs. Unlike the original muckrakers, however, this "tabloid television" seems designed mainly for entertainment. At least, one is hard-pressed to think of a single lasting reform to come out of it. But let us define our terms and let the readers decide for themselves.

When David Graham Phillips claimed in his *Cosmopolitan* series "The Treason of the Senate" that Chauncey Mitchell Depew, one of the senators from Massachusetts, had bilked the country out of one billion dollars, President Theodore Roosevelt was infuriated at this attack upon his friend. In a speech to the Washington Correspondents at the Gridiron Club on March 17, 1906, the president likened such reporters as Phillips to the man in John Bunyan's *Pilgrim's Progress*:

There was a man that could look no way but downwards,
with a muck-rake in his hand. There stood also one over his
head, with a celestial crown in his hand, and proffered to
give him that crown for his muck-rake; but the man did neither look up nor regard, but raked to himself the straws, the
small sticks, and dust of the floor.[1]

As Judson A. Grenier has pointed out, "It was no accident that
Bunyan's diligent stick-sweeper used a rake usually reserved
for the dung of the barnyard to collect his earthly riches."[2]

There had been earlier newspaper crusades, such as those
launched by Joseph Pulitzer on the *New York World*, and William Randolph Hearst on his *New York Journal*, but it fell to
magazines to unfurl the banner of full-blown muckraking.
The November 1902 issue of *McClure's Magazine* contained
the opening salvo on Standard Oil by Ida M. Tarbell; the first
of Lincoln Steffens's series, "The Shame of the Cities"; and
Ray Stannard Baker's hard look at the plight of American labor. Other magazines, notably *Collier's* and *Ladies' Home Journal*, took up the gauntlet, but the original impetus came from
the dynamic S. S. McClure. Will Irwin, who had served as
McClure's managing editor before going over to *Collier's*,
where he wrote a fifteen-part series published in 1911 on "The
American Newspaper," once said that asking McClure for
ideas was like praying for rain in the Amazon jungle. William Allen White, who temporarily left the *Emporia* (Kansas)
Gazette to join McClure's staff, added that his boss had three
hundred ideas a minute, but his managing editor, John S.
Phillips, was the only man around the shop who knew which
one was not crazy. Irwin, an acute observer of the American
journalism scene, noted that even the mainstream magazines
were touched by muckraking:

Contemporaneously with the rise of *McClure's*, George
Horace Lorimer had taken over the *Saturday Evening Post*, a
local weekly of meager circulation, and turned it into a veritable national institution—as American as a baseball game
or a Rotary luncheon. He too had perceived the great areas
of current life hitherto ignored by both fiction and the larger
journalism. In pouring the plastic American mind into

certain grooves he had a minor part in the literature of exposure.[3]

In October 1906, five of McClure's top writers left to gain control of their own magazine, *The American*, and continue muckraking with greater independence. Why were magazines the outlet for this outpouring of protest literature? First of all, these magazines built national circulations and thus were less vulnerable to local pressures. Secondly, they had the time, beyond the tyranny of daily deadlines, to develop a story in great depth. Ida Tarbell spent two years researching and writing *The History of Standard Oil*, which ran in eighteen installments. Thirdly, magazines had greater resources for investigative reporting. S. S. McClure invested almost $50,000 in Tarbell's series. Economics also played another part: In 1893 three new popular magazines—*McClure's*, *Cosmopolitan*, and *Munsey's*—had applied the old penny press formula by cutting their price to a dime, increasing circulation and thus attracting more advertising. And, finally, there is that inexplicable confluence of history that brought together such talented men and women at one time and in one place.

Ray Stannard Baker, who began his journalistic career on the Chicago newspaper *The Record* and covered the bloody Pullman strike of 1894, became a muckraking partisan of labor and the first white journalist to write about the problems of blacks (see Chapter 8). Baker was a kindred spirit with Ida M. Tarbell because both were of that rare breed, scholar-journalists. He criticized Woodrow Wilson's inaugural speech in 1912, when the first phase of muckraking was coming to an end, but went on (1927–1939) to write an eight-volume biography, *Life and Letters of Woodrow Wilson*, that won the Pulitzer Prize for history. In his autobiography, *American Chronicle*, Baker described the heady atmosphere of working in the *McClure's* editorial offices:

But what a boon to the writer! To be able really to take his time, saturate himself with his subject, assure accuracy by studying the subject at first hand and by consulting every possible expert, and then, above all, to be able to write and rewrite until the presentation should not only be clear to any reader of reasonable intelligence, but be interesting. *Interesting! Interesting!* For everything, at *McClure's*, given thorough knowledge of the subject, turned upon the quality of the writing. We maintained no society of mutual admiration in those good days. We were friends indeed, but we were also uncompromising critics of one another. I have always regarded John S. Phillips as the most creative editor I ever knew. He could tell wherein an article failed and why; he could usually make fertile suggestions for improving it; he was willing to give the writer all the precious time he needed for rewriting his story or his essay or his article. One of the warmest satisfactions, and to the writer certainly the most valuable reward of this method of striving for dependability and thoroughness, was the criticism or commendation that came in, not from casual readers but from men who were themselves experts in the field, and whose comments had especial value in further establishing the truth of the author's report.[4]

Publishers and editors are frequently the unsung heroes of journalism, the best of them prodding, wheedling, and cajoling those towering egos entrusted to their care into producing something worth saying (Steffens left *The American* because someone dared to edit his copy). Sam McClure made sure his contribution was known by putting his name on the cover of his publication—as did Frank A. Munsey. As newspaper and magazine staffs became more specialized, some editors rose to greatness—such as Sarah Josephus Hale of *Godey's Lady's Book* of the middle and late nineteenth century, who became a respected and admired national figure. And Edward W. Bok, editor of the *Ladies' Home Journal*, became a household word as his magazine unmasked the patent medicine fraud, a theme first broached by Samuel Hopkins Adams in *Collier's* (1905-6). But it was the indefatigable S. S. McClure who led the way in muckraking. He maintained a stable of thoroughbred writers whom he jealously guarded, including Willa Cather and Finley Peter Dunne.

The muckraking phenomenon was clearly part of the Progressive political movement, which sought to change the face of America at the turn of the century. It was relegated to the back burner by readers who became tired of social problems, and by the outbreak of war in Europe in 1914, which took center stage.

Ms. Tarbell, Meet Mr. Rockefeller

Of all the torrent of words that cascaded from the muckrakers, probably no work will stand up longer than Ida M. Tarbell's *History of Standard Oil*, an ambitious undertaking that required five years of research, ran to eighteen installments in *McClure's*, and was published in two volumes in 1904. Tarbell's father and brother, independent oil producers, born and raised in the oil country of Pennsylvania, were squeezed out by the unfair business practices of the John D. Rockefeller Standard Oil interests, but there was not a hint of vindictiveness in her exhaustive work. In her autobiography, *All in the Day's Work*, Tarbell summarized some of her findings: "In studying the testimony of independents over a period of some thirty years I had found repeated complaints that their oil shipments were interfered with, their [railroad] cars side-tracked en route while pressure was brought on buyers to cancel orders. There were frequent charges that freight clerks were [informing on] independent shipments."[5]

Rockefeller did interest her as a person, however, as she seemed drawn to strong figures, at one time or another preparing biographies of Louis Pasteur, Napoleon Bonaparte, Abraham Lincoln, and Madame Roland. Previously, after a two-year teaching stint and work on the *Chautauquan*, a monthly that complemented the lecture circuit, Ida Tarbell had gone to Paris on her own to study the role of women in the French Revolution; it was there that S. S. McClure had recruited her. Her diligence in researching *The History of Standard Oil* was so convincing that in 1907 the federal government brought an antitrust suit against Standard Oil that resulted in a conviction upheld by the Supreme Court four years later. It had been an uphill battle. Tarbell found that Standard Oil's publicity agents had contracted with at least 110 Ohio newspapers to run editorials and canned news favorable to the company during this confrontation.

Ida Tarbell then turned her attention to the deleterious effects of high protective tariffs, a subject she also mastered, but she declined a seat on the newly created federal Tariff Commission in 1916. Curiously, she did not actively support the suffragist movement, perhaps choosing to devote herself totally to her work, and in later life she wrote favorable biographies of two "ethical capitalists." But the decisive moments in her life came not only with the publication and wide circulation of *The History of the Standard Oil Company* but also at that fleeting instant in history when she came face to face with John D. Rockefeller. She recounts the meeting in her autobiography, *All in the Day's Work*:

Everybody in the office interested in the work began to say, "After the book is done you must do a character sketch of Mr. Rockefeller." I was not keen for it. It would have to be done like the book, from documents; that is, I had no inclination to use the extraordinary gossip which came to me from many sources. If I were to do it I wanted only that of which I felt I had sure proof, only those things which seemed to me to help explain the public life of this powerful, patient, secretive, calculating man of so peculiar and special a genius.

"You must at least look at Mr. Rockefeller," my associates insisted. "But how?" Mr. Rogers himself had suggested that I see him. I had consented. I had returned to the suggestion several times, but at last was made to understand that it could not be done. I had dropped his name from my list. It was John Siddall who then took the matter in hand.

"You must see him," was Siddall's judgment.

To arrange it became almost an obsession. And then what seemed to him like a providential opening came. It was announced that on a certain Sunday of October 1903 Mr. Rockefeller before leaving Cleveland, where he had spent his summer, for his home in New York would say good-bye in a little talk to the Sunday school of his church—a rally, it was called. As soon as Siddall learned of this he begged me to come on. "We can go to Sunday school; we can stay to church. I will see that we have seats where we will have a full view of the man. You will get him in action."

Of course I went, feeling a little mean about it too. He had not wanted to be seen apparently. It was taking him unaware.

Siddall's plan worked to perfection, worked so well from the start that again and again he seemed ready to burst from excitement in the two hours we spent in the church.

We had gone early to the Sunday-school room where the rally was to open—a dismal room with a barbaric dark green paper with big gold designs, cheap stained-glass windows, awkward gas fixtures. Comfortable, of course, but so stupidly ugly. We were sitting meekly at one side when I was suddenly aware of a striking figure standing in the doorway. There was an awful age in his face—the oldest man I had ever seen, I thought, but what power! At that moment Siddall poked me violently in the ribs and hissed, "There he is."

The impression of power deepened when Mr. Rockefeller took off his coat and hat, put on a skullcap, and took a seat commanding the entire room, his back to the wall. It was the head which riveted attention. It was big, great breadth from back to front, high broad forehead, big bumps behind the ears, not a shiny head but with a wet look. The skin was as fresh as that of any healthy man about us. The thin sharp nose was like a thorn. There were no lips; the mouth looked as if the teeth were all shut hard. Deep furrows ran down each side of the mouth from the nose. There were no puffs under the little colorless eyes with creases running from them.

Wonder over the head was almost at once diverted to wonder over the man's uneasiness. His eyes were never quiet but darted from face to face, even peering around the jog at the audience close to the wall.

When he rose to speak, the impression of power that the first look at him had given increased, and the impression of age passed. I expected quavering voice, but the voice was not even old, if a little fatigued, a little thin. It was clear and utterly sincere. He meant what he was saying. He was on his own ground talking about dividends, dividends of righteousness. "If you would take something out," he said, clenching the hand of his outstretched right arm, "you must put something in"—emphasizing "put something in" with a long outstretched forefinger.

The talk over, we slipped out to get a good seat in the gallery, a seat where we could look full on what we knew to be the Rockefeller pew.

Mr. Rockefeller came into the auditorium of the church as soon as Sunday school was out. He sat a little bent in his pew, pitifully uneasy, his head constantly turning to the farthest right or left, his eyes searching the faces almost invariably turned towards him. It was plain that he, and not the minister, was the pivot on which that audience swung. Probably he knew practically everybody in the congregation; but now and then he lingered on a face, peering at it intently as if he were seeking what was in the mind behind it. He looked frequently at the gallery. Was it at Siddall and me?

The services over, he became the friendly patron saint of the flock. Coming down the aisle where people were passing out, he shook hands with everyone who stopped, saying, "A good sermon." "The Doctor gave us a good sermon." "A good sermon." "The Doctor gave us a good sermon." "It was a very good sermon, wasn't it?"

My two hours' study of Mr. Rockefeller aroused a feeling I had not expected, which time has intensified. I was sorry for him. I know no companion so terrible as fear. Mr. Rockefeller, for all the conscious power written in face and voice and figure, was afraid, I told myself, afraid of his own kind. My friend Lewis Emery, Jr., priding himself on being a victim, was free and happy. Not gold enough in the world to tempt him to exchange his love of defiance for a power which carried with it a head as uneasy as that on Mr. Rockefeller's shoulders. . . .

The plan I had taken to Mr. McClure in the fall of 1899, which we had talked over in Salsomaggiore, Italy—I still have notes of our talk on a yellow piece of the stationery of the Hôtel des Thermes—called for three papers, possibly twenty-five thousand words. But before we actually began publication Mr. Phillips and Mr. McClure decided we might venture on six. We went through the six, and the series was stretched to twelve. Before we were through we had [eighteen] articles, and when the [eighteen] were off my hands I asked nothing in the world but to get them into a book and escape into the safe retreat of a library where I could study people long dead, and if they did things of which I did not approve it would be all between me and the books. There would be none of these harrowing human beings confronting me, tearing me between contempt and pity, admiration and anger, baffling me with their futile and misdirected power or their equally futile and misdirected weakness. I was willing to study human beings in the library but no longer, for a time at least, in flesh and blood, so I thought.

The book was published in the fall of 1904—two fat volumes with generous appendices of what I considered essential documents. I was curious about the reception it would have from the Standard Oil Company. I had been told repeatedly they were preparing an answer to flatten me out; but if this was under way it was not with Mr. Rockefeller's consent, I imagined. To a mutual friend who had told him the articles should be answered Mr. Rockefeller was said to have replied: "Not a word. Not a word about that misguided woman." To another who asked him about my charges he was reported as answering: "All without foundation. The idea of the Standard forcing anyone to sell his refinery is absurd. The refineries wanted to sell to us, and nobody that sold or worked with us but has made money, is glad he did so.

"I thought once of having an answer made to the McClure articles but you know it has always been the policy of the Standard to keep silent under attack and let their acts speak for themselves.". . .

I had hoped that the book might be received as a legitimate historical study, but to my chagrin I found myself included in a new school, that of the muckrakers. Theodore Roosevelt, then President of the United States, had become uneasy at the effect on the public of the periodical press's increasing criticisms and investigations of business and political abuses. He was afraid that they were adding to the not inconsiderable revolutionary fever abroad, driving people into socialism. Something must be done, and in a typically violent speech he accused the school of being concerned only with the "vile and debasing." Its members were like the man in John Bunyan's "Pilgrim's Progress" who with eyes on the ground raked incessantly "the straws, the small sticks, and dust on the floor." They were muckrakers. The conservative public joyfully seized the name.

Roosevelt had of course misread his Bunyan. The man to whom the Interpreter called the attention of the Pilgrim was raking riches which the Interpreter contemptuously called "straws" and "sticks" and "dust." The president would have been nearer Bunyan's meaning if he had named the rich sinners of the times who in his effort to keep his political balance he called "malefactors of great wealth"—if he had called them, "muckrakers of great wealth" and applied the word "malefactors" to the noisy and persistent writers who so disturbed him.[6]

"The Treason of the Senate"

One lesson that the muckrakers and their editors learned from Joseph Pulitzer's *New York World* crusades was continuity—he urged his writers to keep pounding away on a topic until it engrained itself in the popular mind. As we have seen, Ida M. Tarbell's series on *The History of the Standard Oil Company* ran to nineteen installments over a two-year period in *McClure's*. Lincoln Steffens, another scholar-journalist (see Chapter 4) in "The Shame of the Cities" did not examine municipal corruption in just one place, but in St. Louis (twice), Minneapolis, Pittsburgh, Philadelphia, Chicago, and New York.

Another famous series, more intemperate in tone than the others, was David Graham Phillips's "The Treason of the Senate," which appeared as nine articles between March and November of 1906 in *Cosmopolitan*, which William Randolph Hearst had bought the year before. Senators were elected by state legislatures before the Seventeenth Amendment, providing for their direct election by the people, was ratified in 1913; Phillips was taking on a two-layered power structure of wealthy and powerful men accountable only to their cronies. The framers of the Constitution, in a bow to the Federalists and Alexander Hamilton's fears of a "mobocracy" if there were not a buffer between the people and the upper house of their government, had created this mechanism, but it was fraught with possible abuse.

Phillips had gleaned solid newspaper experience on Cincinnati dailies before moving on to the *New York Sun*, purchased by Charles A. Dana in 1868 and under him built into "the newspaperman's newspaper." Phillips also reported briefly for the *New York World*, as London correspondent, before turning his talents to muckraking. For his *Cosmopolitan* series, "The Treason of the Senate," Phillips dealt in length and detail with the careers of twenty-one senators selected primarily for their private wealth and key committee posts in the 59th Congress of 1905. In the age of the "robber barons" just past, Phillips wanted to know how they got their own money and how they were spending the public's money. His main theme, which produced a firestorm on the political landscape, was that "the interests," the wealthy power brokers in American life, controlled the Senate for their own ends.

It is difficult to determine the exact extent of the influence of Phillips's angry denunciations on the final ratification of the Seventeenth Amendment authorizing the direct election of U.S. senators. But it is known that in the next elections only four of those twenty-one senators Phillips had targeted were reelected. The muckraker did not live to see ratification of the amendment, however. On January 23, 1911, he was assassinated by a man who believed that his sister had been the prototype for a prostitute in one of Phillips's novels. Here is his introduction to the first installment of "The Treason of the Senate."

One morning, during this session of the Congress, the Senate blundered into a discussion of two of its minor disreputables, Burton and Mitchell, who had been caught with their fingers sliding about in the change pocket of the people. The discussion on these change-pocket thieves was a fine exhibition of "senatorial dignity and courtesy," which means, nowadays, regard for the honor and dignity of the American people smugly sacrificed to the Senate's craftily convenient worship of the Mumbo-Jumbo mask and mantle of its own high respectability. In closing the brief debate over his fellow senators who had been so unluckily caught, Senator Lodge said:

"There is too much tendency to remember the senators, and to forget the Senate."

A profound criticism—profounder far than was intended, or realized, by the senator from the "interests" that center in Massachusetts.

Let us take Mr. Lodge's hint. Let us disregard the senators as individuals; let us for the moment "remember the Senate."

The treason of the Senate!

Politics does not determine prosperity. But in this day of concentrations, politics does determine the distribution of prosperity. Because the people have neglected politics, have not educated themselves out of credulity to flimsily plausible political lies and liars, because they will not realize that it is not enough to work, it is also necessary to think, they remain poor, or deprived of their fair share of the products, though they have produced an incredible prosperity. The people have been careless and unwise enough in electing every kind of public administrator. When it comes to the election of the Senate, how describe their stupidity, how measure its melancholy consequences? The Senate is the most powerful part of our public administration. It has vast power in the making of the laws. It has still vaster power through its ability to forbid the making of laws and in its control over the appointment of the judges who say what the laws mean. It is, in fact, the final arbiter of the sharing of prosperity. The laws it permits or compels, the laws it refuses to permit, the interpreters of laws it permits to be appointed—these factors determine whether the great forces which modern concentration has produced shall operate to distribute prosperity equally or with shameful inequality and cruel and destructive injustice. The United States Senate is a larger factor than your labor or your intelligence, you average American, in determining your income. And the Senate is a traitor to you.

The treason of the Senate! Treason is a strong word, but not too strong, rather too weak, to characterize the situation in which the Senate is the eager, resourceful, indefatigable agent of interests as hostile to the American people as any invading army could be, and vastly more dangerous; interests that manipulate the prosperity produced by all, so that it heaps up riches for the few; interests whose growth and power can only mean the degradation of the people, of the educated into sycophants, of the masses toward serfdom.

A man cannot serve two masters. The senators are not elected by the people; they are elected by the "interests." A servant obeys him who can punish and dismiss. Except in extreme and rare and negligible instances, can the people either elect or dismiss a senator? The senator, in the dilemma which the careless ignorance of the people thrusts upon him, chooses to be comfortable, placid and honored, and a traitor to oath and people rather than to be true to his oath and poor and ejected into private life.[7]

Upton Sinclair Muckrakes the Press

Upton Sinclair wrote more than eighty books but will always be remembered for his exposé of the horrid, unsanitary conditions in the Chicago meat-packing plants, and the blighted lives of those who worked there. *The Jungle* (1906) first appeared in the Socialist weekly *Appeal to Reason* because no mainstream publisher would touch it, although it later appeared in seventeen languages in thirty-two countries. Still, Sinclair was somewhat disappointed in the reaction to his work. After seven weeks of research in the Chicago stockyards and packing plants, he wanted the public to focus on the deplorable working and living conditions there, but instead readers latched onto the contaminated meat issue. "I aimed at the public's heart," Sinclair said, "and by accident hit it in the stomach."

The writer recounts his trials and tribulations in getting *The Jungle* into print, in the selection which follows, extracted from his muckraking look at the press itself, *The Brass Check: A Study of American Journalism*, privately printed in 1920. The title referred to the brass token a man bought upon entering a brothel, which he later gave to his sexual partner, thus maintaining the fiction that no money had passed between them. In other words, Sinclair was saying that the American press was hypocritically prostituting itself, bowing before powerful advertisers and special political interests. The public's lack of access to the press also came under his fire, especially the "concrete wall" of the Associated Press, which he claimed filtered the news and shunned outsiders.

Perhaps exaggerated at the time, this indictment of the press was certainly true of the media in general when Sinclair, a member of the Socialist party from 1902 to 1917, ran for governor of California on the Democratic ticket in 1934, a campaign called "the birth of media politics" by Greg Mitchell. For the first time negative political advertising appeared on the American scene, such as radio soap operas and comedy shows tailored to frighten Californians out of electing the

"Red" candidate. Previously, radio had simply broadcast campaign speeches. And there were dirty tricks. Hundreds of thousands of *"SincLiar"* dollar bills, printed in red ink and imprinted "Good only in California or Russia" circulated in the state. Opponents also ridiculed the End Poverty in California campaign, and fake Communist posters endorsed Sinclair. Nevertheless, the muckraking politician came within 200,000 votes of winning, out of a total of 2,300,000 votes cast.

This was not the first time Sinclair had lost a political race, but perhaps he drew sustenance from his earlier muckraking efforts, particularly the writing of *The Jungle*, which had spurred President Theodore Roosevelt to establish a commission that soon led to passage of the Meat Inspection Act of 1906. Some of the reforms urged by the muckrakers may have seemed radical at the time, but they are commonplace today. Like third political parties the muckrakers goaded the major parties into action. Until he died at the age of ninety, Sinclair refused to become disillusioned with the muckraking movement, even as widespread new corruption sprang up. He felt, according to a newspaper interview, that his position on social issues had been right, and he would not have changed anything. Here is Sinclair's account of his perseverance against seemingly insurmountable odds to get *The Jungle* published. It is "The Condemned Meat Industry," from *The Brass Check*.

"The Jungle" had been accepted in advance by the Macmillan Company. Mr. Brett, president of the company, read the manuscript, and asked me to cut out some of the more shocking and bloody details, assuring me that he could sell ten times as many copies of the book if I would do this. So here again I had to choose between my financial interest and my duty. I took the proposition to Lincoln Steffens, who said: "The things you tell are unbelievable. I have a rule in my own work—I don't tell things that are unbelievable, even when they are true."

Nevertheless, I was unwilling to make the changes. I offered the book to four other publishers, whose names I do not now remember; then I began preparations to publish it myself. I wrote to Jack London, who came to my help with his usual impetuous generosity, writing a resounding call to the Socialists of the country, which was published in the "Appeal to Reason." The result was that in a couple of months I took in four thousand dollars.

The Socialists had been reading the story in the "Appeal," and were thoroughly aroused.

I had the book set up and the plates made, when some one suggested Doubleday, Page and Company, so I showed the work to them. Walter H. Page sent for me. He was a dear old man, the best among business-men I have met. There were several hustling young money-makers in his firm, who saw a fortune in "The Jungle," and desperately wanted to publish it. But Page was anxious; he must be sure that every word was true. We had a luncheon conference, and I was cross-questioned on every point. A week or two passed, and I was summoned again, and Herbert S. Houston of the firm explained that he had a friend, James Keeley, editor of the "Chicago Tribune," to whom he had taken the liberty of submitting my book. Here was a letter from Keeley—I read the letter—saying that he had sent his best reporter, a trusted man, to make a thorough report upon "The Jungle." And here was the report, thirty-two typewritten pages, taking up every statement about conditions in the yards, and denying one after another.

I read the report, and recall one amusing detail. On page one hundred and sixteen of "The Jungle" is a description of the old packing-houses, their walls covered with grease and soaked with warm moist steam. "In these rooms the germs of tuberculosis might live for two years." The comment upon this statement was: "Unproven theory." So it was necessary for me to consult the text-books on bacteriology, and demonstrate to Doubleday, Page and Company that unicellular parasitic organisms are sometimes endowed with immortality!

I said: "This is not an honest report. The thing you have to do, if you really wish to know, is to send an investigator of your own, somebody in whom you have confidence." They decided this must be done, and picked a young lawyer, McKee by name, and sent him to Chicago. He spent some time there, and when he came back his verdict was that I had told the truth. I went to dinner at McKee's home and spent the evening hearing his story—incidentally getting one of the shocks of my life.

McKee had done what I had urged him not to do: he had gone first to the packers, to see what they had officially to show him. They had placed him in charge of a man—I do not recall the name, but we will say Jones—their publicity agent, a former newspaper man, who served as host and entertainer to inquiring visitors. He had taken McKee in charge and shown him around, and in the course of their conversation McKee mentioned that he was looking into the charges made in a novel called "The Jungle." "Oh, yes!" said Jones. "I know that book. I read it from beginning to end. I prepared a thirty-two page report on it for Keeley of the 'Tribune.' "

So here was a little glimpse behind the curtain of the newspaper world of Chicago! James Keeley was, and still is the *beau ideal* of American newspaper men; I have never met him, but I have read articles about him, the kind of "write-ups" which the capitalist system gives to its heroes. He had begun life as a poor boy and risen from the ranks by sheer ability and force of character—you know the "dope." Now he was one of the high gods of newspaperdom; and when it was a question of protecting the great predatory interest which subsidizes all the newspapers of Chicago and holds the government of the city in the hollow of its hand, this high god sent to Armour and Company and had a report prepared by their publicity-agent, and sent this report to a friend in New York as the result of a confidential investigation by a trusted reporter of the "Chicago Tribune" staff! . . .

Doubleday, Page and Company published "The Jungle," and it became the best-selling book, not only in America, but also in Great Britain and its colonies, and was translated into seventeen languages. It became also the subject of a terrific political controversy.

The packers, fighting for their profits, brought all their batteries to bear. To begin with, there appeared in the "Saturday Evening Post" a series of articles signed by J. Ogden Armour, but written, I was informed, by Forrest Crissey, one of the staff of the "Post." The editor of this paper, George Horace Lorimer, was for nine years an employee of the Armours; he is author of "The Letters of a Self-Made Merchant to His Son," a text-book of American business depravity. From first to last his paper was at the service of the packers, as it has always been at the service of every great financial interest.

Some of the statements made under Armour's signature made me boil, and I sat down to write an answer, "The Condemned Meat Industry." I had the facts at my fingers ends, and wrote the article in a few hours, and jumped on the train and came up to New York with it. I took it to the office of "Everybody's Magazine" and asked to see E. J. Ridgway, the publisher. I was wise enough by this time to understand that it is the publisher, not the editor, you need to see. I read the article to Ridgway, and he stopped the presses on which "Everybody's Magazine" was being printed, and took out a short story and shoved in "The Condemned Meat Industry."

"Everybody's Magazine" at this time was on the crest of a wave of popularity. It had finished Tom Lawson's exposé of Wall Street upon the strength of which it had built up a circulation of half a million. Its publishers, Ridgway and Thayer, were advertising men who had bought a broken-down magazine from John Wanamaker, and had made the discovery that there was a fortune to be made by the simple process of letting the people have the truth. They wanted to go on making fortunes, and so they welcomed my article. It gave the affidavits of men whom the Armours had employed to take condemned meat out of the destructors and sell it in Chicago. It told the story of how the Armours had bribed these men to retract their confessions. It gave the reports of State health authorities, who showed how the Armours had pleaded guilty to adulterating foods. It was a mass of such facts fused in a white heat of indignation. United States Senator Beveridge told me that he considered the article the greatest piece of controversial writing he had every read.

You may find it in the library, "Everybody's" for May, 1906. Whatever you think of its literary style, you will see that it is definite and specific, and revealed a most frightful condition in the country's meat supply, an unquestionable danger to the public health. It was therefore a challenge to every public service agency in the country; above all, it was a challenge to the newspapers, through which the social body is supposed to learn of its dangers and its needs.

It was my first complete test of American Journalism. Hitherto I had tried the newspapers as a young poet, clamoring for recognition; they had called me a self-seeker, and although I felt that the charge was untrue, I was powerless to disprove it to others. But now I tried them in a matter that was obviously in the public interest—too obviously so for dispute. I was still naïve enough to be shocked by the result. I had expected that every newspaper which boasted of public spirit would take up these charges, and at least report them; but instead of that, there was silence—silence almost complete! I employed two clipping-bureaus on this story, and received a few brief items from scattered papers here and there. Of all the newspapers in America, not one in two hundred went so far as to mention "The Condemned Meat Industry."

Meantime "The Jungle" had been published in book form. I will say of "The Jungle" just what I said of the magazine article—whatever you may think of it as literature, you must admit that it was packed with facts which constituted an appeal to the American conscience. The book was sent to all American newspapers; also it was widely advertised, it was boosted by one of the most efficient publicity men in the country. And what were the results? I will give a few illustrations.

The most widely read newspaper editor in America is Arthur Brisbane. Brisbane poses as a liberal, sometimes even as a radical; he told me that he drank in Socialism with his mother's milk. And Brisbane now took me up, just as Robbie Collier had done; he invited me to his home, and wrote one of his famous two-column editorials about "The Jungle"—a rare compliment to a young author. This editorial treated me personally with kindness; I was a sensitive young poet who had visited the stockyards for the first time, and had been horrified by the discovery that animals had blood inside them. With a fatherly pat on the shoulder, Brisbane informed me that a slaughter-house is not an opera-house, or words to that effect.

I remember talking about this editorial with Adolph Smith, representative of the "London Lancet." He remarked with dry sarcasm that in a court of justice Brisbane would be entirely safe; his statement that a slaughter-house is not an opera-house was strictly and literally accurate. But if you took what the statement was meant to convey to the reader—that a slaughter-house is necessarily filthy, then the statement was false. "If you go to the municipal slaughter-houses of Germany, you find them as free from odor as an opera-house," said Adolph Smith; and five or six years later, when I visited Germany, I took the opportunity to verify this statement. But because of the kindness of American editorial writers to the interests which contribute full-page advertisements to newspapers, the American people still have their meat prepared in filth.[8]

The Rebirth of Muckraking

Leonard Downie, Jr., in his book *The New Muckrakers* (1976) credited *The Nation*, a weekly journal of opinion and ideas still being published, with keeping the muckraking tradition alive in the decade from 1955 to 1965. This was largely due to the leadership of Carey McWilliams, a specialist on the problems of migrant farm workers, who wrote *Factories in the Field* in 1939, the same year that John Steinbeck's *Grapes of Wrath* came out. The *New York Times* reviewer called both books "equally masterful." McWilliams gave up a law career to head the California Division of Immigration and Housing for four years, and within the next decade he produced seven major sociological works. In 1945 he became West Coast contributing editor to *The Nation*, associate editor in 1951, and editor in 1955. Always the champion of the underdog, he opposed relocation of Japanese-Americans in World War II in internment camps in the interior, and vigorously denounced the anti-Communist hysteria exploited by Senator Joseph McCarthy in the early 1950s. Jack Anderson, a latter-day muckraker himself and well known to an older generation for his Washington Merry-Go-Round column, offered this assessment and caveat in 1976 in the wake of Watergate: "Muckraking, like depressions and above-the-knee hemlines, is a creature of cycles. The youngsters who today flock to college classes on investigative reporting should understand one thing clearly: those who pursue muckraking for a lifetime are destined to spend part of their span as anachronisms, part as unsung precursors and only a fraction as the temporary lions of the hour."[9]

In one of these cycles, *The Nation* took on such thorny issues as J. Edgar Hoover and the FBI at a time when, in McWilliams's words, "in general the press had been inattentive and slothful as well as timid." Contrary to Anderson's pessimistic view, Carey McWilliams saw a more permanent legacy of muckraking: "A function of good investigative reporting, as the original muckrakers demonstrated, is to make known what is already known but to do it in a way that makes sense and leaves a lasting impact." In this selection from *The Education of Carey McWilliams*, the editor further places the revival of muckraking in its historical perspective.

In 1956 James Playsted Wood, the historian of American magazines, announced without qualification that the muckraking tradition was dead, and, indeed, that seemed to be the case. In the years from 1902 to 1912 the original muckrakers—Lincoln Steffens, Ida Tarbell, Ray Stannard Baker, and the rest—had conducted a highly successful postmortem on the excesses of the Gilded Age. But World War I brought this first phase to a close. A revival of a sort took place after the war, with some fine investigative reporting on the scandals of the [Warren G.] Harding Administration, but the mood of the 1920s was too buoyant for exposé journalism. One might have expected the 1929 stock market crash to usher in a great decade of investigative reporting, but it did not. With the press so nearly unanimous in its opposition to Roosevelt, most of the muckraking of the 1930s took the form of books based on the superb congressional investigations of those years.

As in World War I, the muckraking impulse was held in abeyance during World War II, and the decade from 1945 to 1955 did not yield much in the way of good investigative journalism. A large section of the press promptly joined Joe McCarthy's cheering section, and the papers that did not were so preoccupied with his antics and fending off his attacks they had little time for exposés. Thus the list of prime subjects that cried aloud for in-depth investigation kept extending; by the middle 1950s it was a mile long. So after I became editor I decided to see what could be done to revive the muckraking tradition, which by then had been dormant for nearly four decades. I knew the timing was right—too many inviting subjects had been too long neglected—but there were some difficult practical problems. *The Nation* lacked the resources to indulge in investigative reporting, which tends to be expensive. Nor did it have the space; exposé articles are often lengthy, and serialization presents special problems for a weekly. Somewhat reluctantly I decided to devote an entire issue now and then to in-depth investigations, even doubling or quadrupling the number of pages if necessary. . . .

So to some extent the increased emphasis on muckraking journalism in the years after 1955 reflected my personal interest in this type of reporting.

But by the late 1960s, after *Newsday* and the Associated Press had set up the first teams of investigative reporters, the revival of muckraking was well under way and *The Nation* was rapidly outdistanced. We could not compete once muckraking had become the new radical chic in American journalism, nor was there any reason why we should. During a long arid season we had kept the tradition alive by demonstrating the need for investigative journalism and the interest in it. At the same time we had lifted taboos on subjects long regarded as sacrosanct and called attention to a wealth of new subjects in urgent need of critical media attention.[10]

Notes

1. John Bunyan, *Pilgrim's Progress* (New York: Macmillan, 1948), 206.

2. Judson A. Grenier, "Muckraking and the Muckrakers: An Historical Definition," *Journalism Quarterly* 37 (1960): 553.

3. Will Irwin, *The American Newspaper* (Ames: Iowa State University Press, 1969), 153.

4. Ray Stannard Baker, *American Chronicle: The Autobiography of Ray Stannard Baker* (New York: Charles Scribner's Sons, 1945), 94–95.

5. Ida M. Tarbell, *All in the Day's Work: An Autobiography* (New York: Macmillan, 1939), 225.

6. Tarbell, *All in the Day's Work*, 234–37, 239–42.

7. David Graham Phillips, "The Treason of the Senate," *Cosmopolitan Magazine* 40, no. 5 (March 1906): 487–88.

8. Upton Sinclair, *The Brass Check: A Study of American Journalism* (Pasadena, CA: Privately printed, 1920), 32–36.

9. Jack Anderson, "Muckrakers' Day Is Passing but They Always Come Back," *Philadelphia Bulletin*, February 8, 1976.

10. Carey McWilliams, *The Education of Carey McWilliams* (New York: Simon and Schuster, 1978), 213–14, 220–21.

7

War Correspondence in the Twentieth Century

———⟨◆⟩———

Within the short time span from 1914 to 1945, the world twice was wracked with global conflict, followed by an uneasy Cold War in which the Soviet Union and the United States avoided mutual annihilation by nuclear weapons through a "balance of terror." Never was the role of the journalist more crucial in unraveling the complex political and socioeconomic causes of worldwide dislocations and making them understandable to the people at home, whose national soil was largely untouched by the conflagrations abroad.

At the same time, some of these journalists became disillusioned with the power of the printed or broadcast word to alter the course of events. As Civil War general William Tecumseh Sherman, famous for his scorched-earth march from Atlanta to the sea, said in a public speech in 1880, "There is many a boy here who looks on war as all glory, but, boys, it is all hell."[1] This sentiment was shared by William Howard Russell, reputed during the Crimean War of 1853–1856 to have been the first foreign war correspondent, who declared when it was all over, "Cursed is he that delighteth in war."[2] (Actually, the first war correspondent seems to have been George W. Kendall of the *New Orleans Picayune*, who followed Zachary Taylor's northern campaign in the war with Mexico of 1846–1848.)

The feelings against war expressed by Sherman and Russell found an echo in the twentieth century in Quentin Reynolds, radio commentator and writer, who summed up World War II as "a surfeit of carnage."[3] That war saw the beginnings of "herd journalism," when at times it seemed that the correspondents—ten thousand worldwide by 1945—outnumbered the combatants. As David Collier has pointed out, "This was to be the most reported war . . . in the history of the world."[4] As noncombatants, these correspondents were forbidden to carry arms, and the Geneva Convention ranked them as captains if taken as prisoners of war.

How does one become a foreign correspondent? Traditionally, it has been up-the-ladder training—unless you have an area specialty acquired by education and on-the-scene experience to offer to a wide-circulation publication. Al Ravenholt, East Asian correspondent who later worked for American Universities Field Staff, once said that foreign correspondents tended to interview each other in hotel bars or English-speaking taxi drivers rather than digging out the story. At any rate, it seems unlikely that any one person has the expertise to cover events intelligently in all parts of the globe. Yet Phil Foisie, late foreign editor of the *Washington Post*, believed that reporters and foreign correspondents were essentially "interchangeable," stating that "any good street reporter" could do a creditable job anywhere in the world. Georgie Anne Geyer, once a foreign correspondent for the *Chicago Daily News* and now a syndicated columnist, also points out that, through newspaper mergers and technological changes, the number of full-time foreign correspondents on major newspapers has dropped from more than four hundred to only sixty or seventy.[5] Some publications and wire services rely on professional resident nationals, who certainly know the history, language, and culture of their countries but may be unconsciously biased in covering events there.

One of the many severe problems that has faced war correspondents has been getting their dispatches through military censors. World War II however was regarded as a just and popular war, fighting German and Italian fascism and Japanese imperialism, and most participants cooperated fully with the authorities. During World War I, a time when many civil liberties were eroded, the government created the Committee on Public Information headed by George Creel for censorship and propaganda purposes. Those functions were separated during World War II, with the creation of the Office of Censorship under Byron Price and the Office of War Information under Elmer Davis.

To what degree should military security override the people's right to know? A military censor in Washington was reported as saying, "I wouldn't tell the people anything until the war is over, and then I'd tell them who won."[6] Alan Moorehead of the *London Daily Express* declared ironically, "You must always give the public good news."[7] But, he added, "what the public disliked intensely was having its hopes raised high only to be plunged into the disappointment of reality later on." And there was early distrust by the military of the press, a distrust that later became acute in Vietnam. One brigade major in World War II told Moorehead, "The only time I want to see anything about my men in print is when the honours list comes out."[8] Josef Goebbels, minister of propaganda in Adolf Hitler's Third Reich, put it more bluntly: "News policy is a weapon of war. Its purpose is to wage war and not to give out information."[9]

Actually, the more lenient restraints used by the forces of democracy proved more effective in the long run. When the armada of troops crossed the English Channel and landed on the beaches of France on June 6, 1944—the largest single military operation in human history—General Dwight D. Eisenhower, Supreme Allied Commander, allowed correspondents to report anything except that which directly affected military security. Compare that with U.S. military policy during the invasion of the tiny Caribbean island of Grenada in 1989. Still smarting from criticism by the press during the Vietnam War, military commanders there ordered a news blackout for two days, not allowing any correspondent—even pool representatives—to accompany the landing at Grenada, claiming it was "too dangerous." This did a profound disservice to the memory of the 37 American correspondents killed and 112 wounded in World War II.

Richard Harding Davis and the End of an Era

In many respects, the twentieth century began for the United States not in the year 1900 but rather in 1898, when the war with Spain, fought largely in Cuba, propelled us into the position of world power with an empire stretching from Puerto Rico to the Philippines. Stemming from the Cubans' struggle for independence—which actually began with their abortive Ten Years' War (1868–1878) and resurfaced in 1895—our intervention was fanned by the yellow press of William Randolph Hearst's *New York Journal* and Joseph Pulitzer's *New York World*. Although Spain capitulated on all demands by the United States, President William McKinley caved in to public pressure—especially after the sinking of the U.S.S. *Maine* for unknown causes on February 15, 1898—and on March 11 asked Congress for a declaration of war. The conflict, which lasted only four months, was called "a splendid little war" by John Hay, and indeed it was *The Correspondents' War* as graphically described by Charles H. Brown.[10]

Leading the pack was Richard Harding Davis, a name perhaps unknown to younger readers but undoubtedly the most famous journalist of his time. He was a prolific writer of fiction and travel articles and, by covering six foreign wars in the late nineteenth and early twentieth centuries, he came to create the swashbuckling, romantic image of the war correspondent. Nevertheless, journalism historian Frank Luther Mott calls Davis, unlike journalistic dilettantes—some of whom never got closer to the Cuban fighting than Key West— "an excellent war reporter."[11] Reporting for the *New York Herald* and other publications, Davis was not content to be a mere observer. Like others before and since, he chose also at times to be a participant in the action, about which he was supposed to be detached and objective. He led a charge in the assault on Las Guasimas in Cuba that won the praise of Col. Theodore Roosevelt. This would be unheard of in modern war reporting, although John Reed did take a few potshots at the Germans from French trenches in World War I. The nonchalance of Davis also was evident in taking along his bride of less than a year when he covered the Boer War in South Africa (1899–1902). Journalism at that time was not only fun but also an adventure, and the dashing Davis cultivated his image assiduously. Davis died shortly before World War I broke out, and he thus missed the opportunity to cover "the war to end all wars." It may have been just as well, for as he wrote shortly before his death, "The newspapers themselves, with the improved, almost miraculous methods of forwarding news have killed the man who furnished it."

In this selection, written for *Collier's* in 1911, Davis laments the passing of the traditional correspondent, with all his resourcefulness and ingenuity, a victim of technological advances and the thundering mob of reporters who descended on any event of significance—and some that had little importance. "Herd journalism" accelerated to almost incredible proportions. To cover World War II, the United Press fielded some five hundred reporters; the International News Service fielded 125; and the Associated Press, 110. And in the brief Persian Gulf War of 1991, sixteen hundred American journalists crowded to the scene. Few stood out above the crowd, and none the equal of Richard Harding Davis.

The first of the war correspondents [wrote Davis] enjoyed certain distinct advantages over those who came later. They lacked the tremendous advantage of having a telegraph wire within riding distance, and at times even the use of the army telegraph lines, but for this they were compensated by the one great asset of almost complete independence.

In those early days the expense of sending a special correspondent to the front and the difficulty of getting word from him after he got there was so great that the papers attempting to send a correspondent into the field were very few. Those papers obviously were only those of greath wealth and importance. They were either the official organs and supporters of the government that was prosecuting the war, or others in opposition equally powerful, which latter the government had no wish to offend. As a result, when the representatives of these few and powerful journals arrived at headquarters in the field they were received with mixed emotions. No general desired a civilian critic standing by to report his blunders, nor on the other hand, after William Russell had shown that one correspondent could bring about the downfall of two commanding generals, did they care to antagonize him. At home the war office was afraid of the newspapers; in the field the commanding general was afraid of the correspondents; and while the Cabinet and the "Thunderer" [Theodore Roosevelt?] and the generals were engaged in a triangular fight to determine the exact status of the war correspondent and to whom he was responsible, that gentleman was happily galloping about at his own sweet will. He was his own transport and commissary and he gave himself orders. He also was his own courier, cook, and forager. He was not hampered by orders from his paper, because his managing editor did not know where he was or how to find him. At times he disappeared for weeks. MacGahan [one correspondent] once was lost for three months.

Later, when the telegraph lines spread, the correspondent moved with a cable from the home office attached to his spinal column, jerking him this way and that. It naturally interfered with his usefulness, but not even to-day is he able to make it clear to his chief that a man dodging bullets behind a rock is in a better position to decide where there is fighting than a gentleman at a rolled-top desk in London or New York.

The war correspondent of the early days had to contend with no such long-distance instructions. If he saw the force to which he had attached himself held in reserve, he put spurs to his horse and joined one that promised him a run for his money. He was a free lance, hampered neither by the military authorities nor by his newspaper. Neither was he aided by his newspaper, and for that reason not only do the correspondents of the early days loom large as giants, but they *were* giants. . . .

The work of the war correspondent has been systematized, made easy for him, robbed of the chances it once gave for brilliant, spectacular effort. Any man can look at a battle, and many can write of what they see, but in the old days the difficult work began when the battle was decided and what was written had to be carried to the wire. That meant a lonely ride, often of several days, through a hostile territory, without pause for sleep or food, regardless of swollen streams or false trails, or whether the way lay through snow or over burning sand, or through jungle or mountain passes or among peoples to whom every white man was an enemy. . . .

What now is chiefly desired of a war correspondent is that he be able to write. The hard work, the daring, difficult work is accomplished for him by many others. He is part of a syndicate, and the collecting of news, the getting it back from the front, and transmitting it to the home office is a matter which, should he be that sort of person, need not concern him in the least. Indeed, were he to attempt to ride away to give his own ideas of a battle, he would probably be arrested. And if he succeeded in eluding the censor and defying the regulations, the story he would tell would be his swan song. . . .

In the Spanish-American War, with an army of 17,000, there were 165 correspondents! Such generosity in the bestowal of passes was absurd. Those among that large number who were responsible suffered from the misrepresentations of those who were not. Many of these remained at the coast and gathered their information from stragglers, deserters, and the wounded who in their views were more or less hysterical. And it was the hysterical, half-baked news sent north by these water-front correspondents that, of necessity, first reached the American people. That was not fair to the people at home, to the army, or to the correspondents who were actually at the front.[12]

A Kansas Editor Covers Versailles

To a recent request at a prominent used-book shop in Philadelphia for a copy of *The Autobiography of William Allen White*, the young clerk replied, "Oh, we don't handle that oddball stuff!" Whatever else the eternally optimistic White was, the Kansas editor who launched his *Emporia Gazette* to international fame was not an "oddball." (A recent survey, incidentally, showed that most journalism students today also have not heard of Lincoln Steffens.)

William Allen White, who bought his newspaper for three thousand dollars, reversed the political trajectory of many persons: He began life as a staunch conservative and ended as what was then considered a radical internationalist. An editorial of 1896, "What's the Matter with Kansas?" catapulted him to national notice by attacking the reform Populists who swept the prairie states as "shabby, wild-eyed, rattle-brained fanatics."[13] A later editorial, which won him the Pulitzer prize, "To an Anxious Young Friend," defended the rights of labor and free expression, and his touching tribute to his daughter Mary immediately after her death in a horseback-riding accident has been anthologized all over the world.

White flirted with the muckraking movement, and when he went to Paris to cover the Versailles peace conference in 1918 and to try to make some sense of the grueling trench warfare and the horrendous casualties of World War I, he was doing what every writer of note—from Isaiah Thomas at the Battle of Lexington and Concord to Mary McCarthy at the Watergate hearings—wanted to do: to be on the scene. Indeed, such literary giants as Stephen Crane (*The Red Badge of Courage*) and Frank Norris (*The Octopus*), among others, had raced to Cuba to record their impressions of the war with Spain.

William Allen White was right about the League of Nations, as detailed below, for it was powerless to stop the brutal and senseless Chaco War between Bolivia and Paraguay (1932–1935) or the Italian invasion of vulnerable Ethiopia (1935). Despite his roots in the isolationist Midwest, when World War II broke out in 1939—two years before the United States entered the conflict—White worked tirelessly for the Committee to Defend America by Aiding the Allies and was instrumental in getting President Franklin D. Roosevelt to send some fifty older warships to beleaguered England in the famous Lend-Lease program. White's thoughts on coverage of the Versailles Peace Conference presented below were written in 1942. At that time he found that war news and editorial comment had improved vastly in the quarter-century since he had gone to Versailles, and he blamed uninformed American public opinion for our refusal to join the League of Nations, which he supported but found too weak. The Kansas journalist died in 1944, only one year before the end of World War II and the creation of the United Nations, an event that William Allen White, from his perch in Emporia, Kansas, would have relished.

Just now [1942] foreign affairs are major issues in American politics [White wrote]. But twenty-five or thirty years ago foreign affairs should have been a major issue in our politics, for we were about to enter the First World War. It was not a world war. It was a European war with certain African and Asiatic annexes, sideshows, and minor commitments. But the so-called First World War did mark our country's complete abandonment of isolation. . . . Fumblingly, blindly, the American newspapers groped their way to the truth: that in a world shrunk by the airplane, the radio, the long-distance telephone, the five-day liner to Europe, and by the solidarity of world credit, centering not in London but in Wall Street, economic isolation is merely a demagogue's phrase full of sound and fury but ending in nothing.

I can no better illustrate what has happened to the American press than by a short reminiscence. I was one of the reporters who covered the Peace Conference in Paris which made the Versailles Treaty and wrote the Covenant of the League of Nations. I filed three days a week a cable story to fifty American newspapers, gathered together by a powerful syndicate in New York. In Paris I was one of nearly a hundred American reporters. Some of them filed daily stories by cable, some filed three a week as I did, some sent two a week, others filed weekly. But all of us were busy. All of us were well-trained newspapermen.

We had as our interpreter Ray Stannard Baker, who saw President Wilson every day. Press conferences were held by Colonel [Edward] House with those who filed daily cables. We all went to press conferences held by the British, two or three times a week. We met Lord Robert Cecil, Lloyd George, Philip Kerr, and others who were close to the British end of the story. We also had access to the French. They entertained us with their most adroit and obvi-

ous liars, and nobody believed anything he heard at a French press conference. Every American reporter who used the cable had access to some person of the American delegation who was fairly close to President Wilson. For
instance, I often walked in the afternoon with Colonel House, along the Seine,
when we would talk over the day's doings. I should have been informed. Ray
Stannard Baker was my dear friend. We lived at the same hotel, ate break-
fast together, and loafed and talked together. He was not reserved. Arthur
Krock, of the *New York Times*, was then in Paris for the *New York World*. He
had a better "leak" than I had, and should have been able to report the story
of the Treaty and the Covenant as it was formed.

Yet, while each of us reported the facts of the conference from day to day,
we all missed the truth. Only one man in the American reportorial galaxy
gave the world the truth, though I am sure we all honestly tried. But Frank
Simonds had been through the war, at the front. He knew the French. He
knew European politics. One day he wired his papers:—

"The Versailles treaty is wrecked. The League of Nations is doomed!"

I remember now that we all wrangled with him about it—we reporters who
met around the Hotel Crillon. But he held his ground. He told us that when it
was decided—as we knew that it was decided—to get along without a military arm of the League, that organization would fail by the domination of the
British-French alliance; and when they decided to keep Russia and Germany
out of the League, it was obvious that the Peace Treaty, quite apart from the
Covenant of the League, was merely an attempt at balance-of-power politics. Looking back twenty-five years, it seems obvious. Yet none of us believed it then.

Not that we hailed the League of Nations as the political savior of Western civilization. Reportorial opinion was fairly well divided about it among
the correspondents at Paris who were reporting the news that year to the
United States. But we just did not know—none of us except Frank Simonds
and possibly Oswald Garrison Villard and Lewis Gannett—what was going on
in the larger sense. We could report the facts but we could not correlate the
facts so that we could come at the truth and tell it. . . .

So when we all came home from Paris, we news gatherers, with the
government's economic, political, social, geographical experts and other four-
eyed cattle, we found the country rising in wrath against the Treaty and the
League. The funny part, looking back over those years, was that people were
wrathy at Wilson and the League for the wrong things. One real weakness of
the League was its lack of power to discipline recalcitrant members. Yet its
enemies read into the League Covenant gnashing, flashing teeth which
gleamed in fancy like those in the mouth of a tiger. As a matter of fact,

America was fooled out of the League by a set of rubber teeth that didn't and couldn't chew anything.

Editorials on the League question in the United States were sadly uninformed. Newspaper editorial writers, who on the whole represent the best elements of the American popular mind, just didn't grasp the real truth. And newspaper leadership failed. It failed because, even though it had the facts, it would not disseminate the truth. The threatening specter of those rubber teeth was too horrendous for American newspapers. . . .

My contention in this article is that, despite the handicap which our press has in printing and commenting freely upon controversial domestic matters, in the foreign field during the last ten years the people have had as much of the truth as much of the time as they could take. For, after all, truth is a medicine which must be administered in broken doses—homeopathic doses.

So I feel justified in venturing a guess that, when it comes to discussing the [World War II] treaty, American newspapers will not be without influence. The precious thing is that this time they will not be without knowledge, without some sense of the fundamental verities in the world situation. The best proof that we are going straight as we follow the path of our international opportunity is that the American newspapers today, their editors-in-chief, the editorial writers, the managing editors, the Washington reporters, their foreign correspondents, the columnists, all big ones and little ones, as a whole understand the world situation. They have had a quarter of a century of education. . . . I doubt that the people of our country will ever be fooled again by a league with rubber teeth.[14]

Martha Gellhorn Sees the Face of War

The history of women foreign correspondents goes back to 1846, when literary critic and inveterate traveler Margaret Fuller began sending reports back from Europe to Horace Greeley's *New York Tribune*, but female correspondents did not come into their own until the twentieth century. In World War I, only one woman, Peggy Hull, was accredited by the American Expeditionary Force after the United States entered the war in 1917, although others attached themselves to British and French forces. Mary Roberts Rinehart, later well known for her mystery stories, was among the first American correspondents to reach the front.

Previously, women journalists had in the nineteenth century been regarded either as shrews or as being incapable of withstanding the rigors of the job. When Elizabeth Cochrane, who adopted the pen name Nellie Bly, from a Stephen Foster song, applied for a job at Pulitzer's *World*, women were not even allowed in the newsroom. Even her feat of traveling around the world in 1889 in fewer than the eighty days logged by the fictional Phineas Fogg in Jules Verne's novel was regarded as a stunt rather than serious journalism. Recognized today as an early investigative reporter who did daring undercover exposés from snake-pit mental hospitals and other dark places of American life, Nellie Bly was described by Julia Edwards, who in 1988 did the first comprehensive history of women foreign correspondents: "As an overseas reporter, she had the shortest and most spectacular career in history."[15]

At the other end of the spectrum were such journalists as Dorothy Thompson, European correspondent for the *Philadelphia Public Ledger* and *New York Post* in the 1920s and early 1930s. From Europe, she warned incessantly and futilely of the rise of fascism, and her later column for the *New York Herald Tribune* was dropped when in 1940 she advocated a third term for President Roosevelt, in order that he guide the United States in its inevitable involvement in the European war.

Martha Gellhorn, who met and later married Ernest Hemingway before both covered the Spanish Civil War (1936–1939), was also as far removed from the women journalistic "stunt gals" of the previous century as one could get. Controlled anger and deep compassion marked everything she wrote. A tough observer, she reviewed the isolationist attitude of the United States in the years leading up to World War II: "We were guilty of the dishonest abandonment of Spain and the quick cheap betrayal of Czechoslovakia. We niggled and refused asylum to doomed Jews. We inspected and rejected anti-Fascists fleeing for their lives from Hitler. We were full of shame and ugly expediencies."[16]

Correspondents like Gellhorn, who covered World War II for *Collier's*, and Ernie Pyle, who worked for Scripps-Howard, made a great advance in war reporting by democratizing the fighting. No longer was attention focused on the officers behind the lines but on those soldiers who actually fought in the foxholes and on the unreachable ridges. True, Americans still respected men like Dwight D. Eisenhower and Douglas MacArthur and made heroes of them, but their hearts went out to the sweating, dog-tired, joking GI Joes of the hedgerows of Normandy and now forgotten islands of the Pacific. These correspondents brought the war home, and it was a salutary lesson for Americans, safely ensconced between two oceans. As Eleanor Roosevelt, who had her own newspaper column, "My Day," and traveled the globe to boost morale, said later: "We have to remember that in the future we will want to keep before our children what this war was really like. It is so easy to forget; and then, for the younger generation, the heroism and the glamour remain, while the dirt, the hardships, the horror of death and the sorrow fade somewhat from their consciousness."[17]

When I was young [Martha Gellhorn wrote in 1986] I believed in the perfectibility of man, and in progress, and thought of journalism as a guiding light. If people were told the truth, if dishonour and injustice were clearly shown to them, they would at once demand the saving action, punishment of wrongdoers, and care for the innocent. How people were to accomplish these reforms, I did not know. That was their job. A journalist's job was to bring news, to be eyes for their conscience. I think I must have imagined public opinion as a solid force, something like a tornado, always ready to blow on the side of the angels.

During the years of my energetic hope, I blamed the leaders when history regularly went wrong, when cruelty and violence were tolerated or abetted, and the innocent never got anything except the dirty end of the stick. The leaders were a vague interlocking directorate of politicians, industrialists, newspaper owners, financiers: unseen, cold, ambitious men. "People" were good, by definition; if they failed to behave well, that was because of ignorance or helplessness.

It took nine years, and a great depression, and two wars ending in defeat, and one surrender without war, to break my faith in the benign power of the press. Gradually I came to realize that people will more readily swallow lies than truth, as if the taste of lies was homey, appetizing: a habit. (There were also liars in my trade, and leaders have always used facts as relative and malleable. The supply of lies was unlimited.) Good people, those who opposed evil wherever they saw it, never increased beyond a gallant minority. The manipulated millions could be aroused or soothed by any lies. The guiding light of journalism was no stronger than a glow-worm.

I belonged to a Federation of Cassandras, my colleagues the foreign correspondents, whom I met at every disaster. They had been reporting the rise of Fascism, its horrors and its sure menace, for years. If anyone listened to them, no one acted on their warnings. The doom they had long prophesied arrived on time, bit by bit, as scheduled. In the end we became solitary stretcher-bearers, trying to pull individuals free from the wreckage. If a life could be saved from the fist of the Gestapo in Prague, or another from behind the barbed wire on the sands at Argelès, that was a comfort but it was hardly journalism. Drag, scheming, bullying and dollars occasionally preserved one human being at a time. For all the good our articles did, they might have been written in invisible ink, printed on leaves, and loosed to the wind.

After the war in Finland, I thought of journalism as a passport. You needed proper papers and a job to get a ringside seat at the spectacle of history in the making. In the Second World War, all I did was praise the good, brave and generous people I saw, knowing this to be a perfectly useless performance. When occasion presented, I reviled the devils whose mission was to deny the dignity of man; also useless. I took an absurd professional pride in getting where I intended to go and in sending my copy to New York on time; but I could not fool myself that my war correspondent's work mattered a hoot. War is a malignant disease, an idiocy, a prison, and the pain it causes is beyond telling or imagining; but war was our condition and our history, the place we had to live in. I was a special type of war profiteer; I was physically lucky, and was paid to spend my time with magnificent people. . . .

Journalism at its best and most effective is education. . . . Journalism is a means; and I now think that the act of keeping the record straight is valuable in itself. Serious, careful, honest journalism is essential, not because it is a guiding light but because it is a form of honorable behavior, involving the reporter and the reader. I am no longer a journalist; like all other private citizens, the only record I have to keep straight is my own.[18]

Ernie Pyle's Personal War

No writer of World War II captured the reality and at times poignancy of the plight of the fighting men and women more than Ernest Taylor Pyle, once called the "GIs' Boswell." Not content to rely on official handouts at rear headquarters, Ernie Pyle could be found with the troops at the front. He talked with them, ate with them, slept with them, and endured with them. He took names and addresses for items sent to hometown newspapers. Bill Mauldin also brought the war home with his ironically humorous cartoons of foxhole buddies Willie and Joe. Ernie Pyle himself followed the fighting through North Africa, Sicily, Italy, and France before going to cover "the other war" in the Pacific. There on April 18, 1945—when the war was almost over—Ernie Pyle was killed by a Japanese sniper on the tiny island of Ie Shima during the Okinawa campaign.

Feelings were running high in the United States during World War II. Americans, while fighting a war for national survival, preferred not to think of the thousands of Japanese-Americans moved from the West Coast to relocation centers inland, of the fire bombing of Dresden, of the unimaginable suffering and deaths of countless civilians at Hiroshima and Nagasaki. When the surrender came on August 14, 1945, the *Boulder Daily Camera*, where the University of Colorado is located, played the news with a banner headline: "Japan Quits." The subhead read "Frenzy of an Island Gone Mad with Hope of Conquest Saw Nipponese Threaten Supremacy of White Race." The following excerpt is Ernie Pyle's rare focus on himself and other war correspondents as the troops slogged through the Italian campaign. He once wrote that he couldn't bear to see another dead body.

Men in battle reach that stage [of fatigue] and still go on and on. As for the rest of the Army—supply troops, truck drivers, hospital men, engineers—they too become exhausted but not so inhumanly. With them and with us correspondents it's the ceaselessness, the endlessness of everything that finally worms its way through you and gradually starts to devour you.

It's the perpetual dust choking you, the hard ground wracking your muscles, the snatched food sitting ill on your stomach, the heat and the flies and dirty feet and the constant roar of engines and the perpetual moving and the never settling down and the go, go, go, night and day, and on through the night again. Eventually it all works itself into an emotional tapestry of one dull, dead pattern—yesterday is tomorrow and Troina is Randazzo and when will we ever stop and, God, I'm so tired.

I've noticed this feeling has begun to overtake the war correspondents themselves. It is true that we don't fight on and on like the infantry, that we are usually under fire only briefly and that, indeed, we live better than the average soldier. Yet our lives are strangely consuming in that we do live primitively and at the same time must delve into ourselves and do creative writing.

That statement may lay me open to wisecracks, but however it may seem to you, writing is an exhausting and tearing thing. Most of the correspondents work like slaves. Especially is this true of the press-association men. A great part of the time they go from dawn till midnight or two A.M.

I'm sure they turn in as much toil in a week as any newspaperman at home does in two weeks. We travel continuously, move camp every few days, eat out, sleep out, write wherever we can and just never catch up on sleep, rest, cleanliness, or anything else normal.

The result is that all of us who have been with the thing for more than a year have finally grown befogged. We are grimy, mentally as well as physically. We've drained our emotions until they cringe from being called out from hiding. We look at bravery and death and battlefield waste and new countries almost as blind men, seeing only faintly and not really wanting to see at all.

Just in the past month the old-timers among the correspondents have been talking for the first time about wanting to go home for a while. They want a change, something to freshen their outlook. They feel they have lost their perspective by being too close for too long.

I am not writing this to make heroes of the correspondents, because only a few look upon themselves in any dramatic light whatever. I am writing it merely to let you know that correspondents too can get damn sick of war—and deadly tired.[19]

A Vietnam Correspondent Recalls Ernie Pyle

When an "iron curtain" descended between the Soviet Union —with its Eastern European satellites—and the West after World War II, journalists found it increasingly difficult to get access to the news and report it objectively. The Cold War exacerbated nationalistic sentiments on both sides. In response, the United States adopted the policy of containment of communism, which was first severely tested when communist North Korea crossed the 38th parallel to invade South Korea in 1950. President Harry S. Truman committed American troops to stop the North Korean advance in what he called a "police action" to avoid a possible refusal by Congress to declare war. Journalists were eager to cover the fighting, but not all were allowed to do so. Gen. Walton H. Walker issued an order banning all women correspondents from Korea because "there are no facilities for ladies at the front," but Marguerite Higgins of the *New York Herald Tribune* went over his head directly to Gen. Douglas MacArthur and won the right for women correspondents to cover this conflict important to all Americans. Although there was rudimentary television coverage of the Korean War, still photography as exemplified in the work of David Douglas Duncan and Margaret Bourke-White carried greater visual impact.

The status quo was maintained in Korea, but the artificial demarcations of north and south determined by the peace settlement after World War II clashed again in former French Indo-China when Viet Cong from communist North Vietnam sought to unify their country and end colonial dependency. When President John F. Kennedy first sent military advisers to aid South Vietnam in 1961, it was the beginning of the United States' longest and most bitter war, which would claim the lives of more than fifty thousand Americans and untold Asians. Television, more refined now, covered the "living room war" vividly, bringing home its horrors to American viewers. Every evening network news showed the "body count," with little figures proportionately representing the day's casualties on both sides. Martha Gellhorn, who went to Vietnam in 1966 for the English *Guardian*, lambasted American military leaders:

> I told them they were inhuman. We were destroying a country and a whole innocent peasant population while proclaiming that we were saving them from Communism. Had they any idea how children looked and sounded when half flayed by napalm? Could they picture an old woman screaming with a piece of white phosphorous burning in her thigh? We had uprooted and turned into refugees millions of helpless people by unopposed bombing of their villages. We were hated in Vietnam and rightly.[20]

It came as no surprise when the American military denied Gellhorn permission to return to Vietnam. On the other hand, "Maggie" Higgins was an advocate of American intervention in the Vietnamese civil war and returned there ten times before contracting a tropical disease and dying at the age of forty-five.

In retrospect, in assessing the Vietnam experience, another American reporter invoked the memory of Ernie Pyle in 1995 on the fiftieth anniversary of his death. Arnold R. Isaacs was a war correspondent in Vietnam from 1972 to 1975 and is the author of *Without Honor: Defeat in Vietnam and Cambodia*. His tribute to Ernie Pyle and his lesson, reproduced here, merit preservation.

Ernie Pyle, the most famous and best-loved correspondent of World War II, wrote the memorable description of American infantrymen on the march in his column for May 2, 1943:

I am sitting among clumps of sword-grass on a steep and rocky hillside that we have just taken. We are looking out over a vast rolling country to the rear.

A narrow path comes like a ribbon over a hill miles away, down a long slope, across a creek, up a slope and over another hill.

All along the length of this ribbon there is now a thin line of men. . . .

They are 50 feet apart, for dispersal. Their walk is slow, for they are dead weary, as you can tell even when looking at them from behind. Every line and sag of their bodies speaks their inhuman exhaustion.

On their shoulders and backs they carry heavy steel tripods, machine-gun barrels, leaden boxes of ammunition. Their feet seem to sink into the ground from the overload they are bearing.

They don't slouch. It is the terrible deliberation of each step that spells out their appalling tiredness. Their faces are black and unshaven. They are young men, but the grime and whiskers and exhaustion make them look middle-aged. . . .

All afternoon men keep coming round the hill and vanishing eventually over the horizon. It is one long tired line of ant-like men. There is an agony in your heart and you feel almost ashamed to look at them. . . .

The scene happened to be Tunisia, but it could have been any of the numberless battlefields Pyle covered until on April 18, 1945—50 years ago this Tuesday—he was killed on a now-forgotten sliver of land in the Pacific called Ie Shima.

That column from Tunisia embodied all the reasons Pyle was so popular: the plainness of language, the photographic exactness of his descriptions, and above all his sympathy for the infantry soldiers who endured, as he wrote in another column later in the war, "all the war in the world."

In trying to tell his countrymen at home what the infantry went through, Pyle sometimes achieved a kind of poetry of terror. After going through a misdirected air raid by U.S. bombers, he wrote:

There is no description of the sound and fury of those bombs except to say it was chaos, and a waiting for darkness. The feeling of the blast was sensational. The air struck you in hundreds of continuing flutters. Your ears drummed and rang. You could feel quick little waves of concussion on your chest and in your eyes. At last the sound died down and we looked at each other in disbelief.

Pyle was short and slight, with gray hair and a lined face and a public image that represented him as a sort of mild, benevolent uncle to all America's sons at war.

Though not entirely inaccurate, that image was also something of a caricature. Pyle was a man with plenty of private demons, including a troubled marriage, and an inner agony at the war's violence that was much deeper and more despairing than he normally showed in his columns.

Fifty years after his death, Pyle has also come to symbolize something else: a time, now vanished, when journalists were assumed to be "on the team," supportive of American military efforts instead of carping skeptics.

The acrimony of Vietnam and later disputes over news coverage in Lebanon, Grenada, Panama and the Persian Gulf left a legacy of deep antagonism between journalists and American military professionals—who not infrequently invoke Pyle as the model war reporter whose example later generations of war correspondents regrettably failed to follow.

Pyle, in this view, would not have written destructively about the U.S. effort in Vietnam, or looked for reasons to carp and quibble about subsequent military ventures in Beirut or the skies over Baghdad.

I am not so sure. Like other World War II correspondents, Ernie Pyle certainly identified with the country's war aims in a way journalists in more recent conflicts did not. But no one who reads Pyle today could fail to see that his loyalty was to America's soldiers, not to its national leadership or their policies or patriotic mythology. Had he ever come to believe that those soldiers were being sacrificed for a bad or ambiguous policy, I think it is likely he would have written against it with all the passion and persuasive power he could muster.

A half-century after his death, Pyle's writing still has the power to make us feel something of what war is and what it does to the men who fight it. That is why he deserves to be reread.

His memory belongs to the successors of the soldiers he wrote about with such respect, affection and sympathy. But it also belongs to his successors in journalism, whose wars had the same suffering but different causes and circumstances and meanings. The last thing Ernie Pyle's memory should serve is the false value of mindlessly accepting national policy or national myths.[21]

Notes

1. Dumas Malone and Basil Rauch, *Empire for Liberty: The Genesis and Growth of the United States of America* (New York: Appleton-Century-Crofts, 1960), 789.

2. Richard Collier, *Fighting Words: The War Correspondents of World War Two* (New York: St. Martin's Press, 1989), 63.

3. Collier, *Fighting Words*, 71.

4. Ibid., 1.

5. Georgie Anne Geyer, *Who Killed the Foreign Correspondent?* (South Bend, IN: University of Notre Dame, 1996), 8–9.

6. Collier, *Fighting Words*, 118.

7. Ibid., 176.

8. Ibid., 47.

9. Ibid., 25.

10. Charles H. Brown, *The Correspondents' War: Journalists in the Spanish-American War* (New York: Charles Scribner's Sons, 1967).

11. Frank Luther Mott, *American Journalism: A History of Newspapers in the United States through 260 Years: 1690–1950* (New York: Macmillan, 1950), 534.

12. Richard Harding Davis, "The War Correspondent," *Collier's* (October 7, 1911): 21–22, 30.

13. *Emporia Gazette*, August 15, 1896.

14. William Allen White, "Editors Live and Learn," *The Atlantic Monthly* (August 1942): 56–60.

15. Julia Edwards, *Women of the World: The Great Foreign Correspondents* (Boston: Houghton Mifflin Company, 1988), 22.

16. Ibid., 128–29.

17. David Nichols, ed., *Ernie's War: The Best of Ernie Pyle's World War II Dispatches* (New York: Random House, 1986), frontispiece.

18. Martha Gellhorn, *The Face of War* (New York: Simon and Schuster, 1959), 1–4.

19. Nichols, *Ernie's War*, 153–54.

20. Edwards, *Women of the World*, 132.

21. Arnold R. Isaacs, "Ernie Pyle, Poet of the Infantry: How Would He Cover Modern War?" *Philadelphia Inquirer*, April 16, 1995.

8

The African-American Press

———⟨◆⟩———

When Ken Burns, who gave us eleven splendid hours of Civil War documentary on the Public Broadcasting System, produced another series on American baseball, he was criticized by some for being "politically correct" by giving so much attention to the all-Negro leagues before Jackie Robinson and the Brooklyn Dodgers changed baseball forever. It is unfortunate that this section on the African-American press must be segregated from the rest of the book, but the black newspapers themselves developed separately—by choice or necessity—throughout their long history.

Therefore, it is necessary to redress this historical imbalance by giving separate attention to this part of our journalism heritage. When *Freedom's Journal*, the first Negro newspaper, appeared in 1827, it was addressed primarily to the freed slaves living in the North but championed the antislavery cause in the South, along with offering religious and temperance messages. The object was to assist those who had escaped the rigors of bondage in order to build better lives for themselves in the North.

It was difficult for the black press to take root, however. There was the problem of money to finance newspapers or poor blacks to buy them, or the overwhelming problem of illiteracy common to most working-class Americans of the day. There was also the gnawing sense of futility that the abolitionist press—white or black—was simply preaching to the already converted. Reflecting short life spans because of these factors, forty struggling black newspapers appeared between 1827 and the close of the Civil War in 1865. After the war, the attrition rate accelerated. Although 45 dailies were attempted between 1850 and 1950, only five black dailies were published in the United States in 1997, with a total circulation of only

147

138,154, according to *Burrelle's Media Directory*. In addition, there are 263 black weeklies and 30 other publications to serve 33.9 million African-Americans, or 12.8 percent of the total population. Since all serve our largest minority group, they are worthy of separate attention.

The African-American press is being absorbed into the white press as blacks themselves move into the mainstream, much as foreign-language newspapers tended to disappear after immigrants were assimilated into American life. To give one striking example, Philadelphia is the country's fourth or fifth largest city, with a general population 39.9 percent black (1990). Yet the white *Philadelphia Inquirer* has a weekday circulation of 486,000, while the black *Philadelphia Tribune*, the oldest African-American newspaper in the United States, founded in 1884, has a weekday circulation of only 110,000. Some blacks moving from the inner city to the suburbs have cut off ties with the *Philadelphia Tribune* and prefer to subscribe to the *Inquirer* instead.

Indeed, the modern African-American press came into being simply because the white press was not covering events of the black community. This changed with the civil rights struggle of the 1960s, which was such a big story that it could not be ignored by the white press (which did ignore the equally important story of black migration from the rural South to Northern cities in the twentieth century, a migration that changed the demographics of America).

Economics also played a crucial role. Until the advent of the cheaper offset printing process, the cost of starting a newspaper was beyond the reach of most blacks. There was competition with the white press for the advertising dollar, so black newspapers came to rely on less lucrative circulation for revenue. (An exception is the magazine field, where the spectacularly successful *Ebony* inspired dozens of imitators, such as *Jet*.) Another problem facing black editors is that after they train young journalists, the best are siphoned off as token blacks in the white media.

On the other hand, until recently the black press in America has not received the scholarly attention it deserves. The first general history on this topic was not published until 1891. Earl Conrad in *Tomorrow* (1946) wrote, "This mass of Negro newspapers may be the most interesting footnote to contemporary national history; the journalism of a caste, the journalism of involuntary expatriates, the protest and 'community newspapers' of a people exiled on their own soil."[1] Among the foremost scholars of the African-American press is Roland E. Wolseley, whose 1990 edition of *The Black Press, U.S.A.* concluded: "It is likely, therefore, that a black press of some sort always will be available in the United States, unless fully integrated means the complete eradication of the black experience, culture, temperament, and personality. Whether it will be an important and influential press depends on the social changes occurring without respect to race."[2]

Freedom's Journal: A Brave New Voice

Racism has deep roots. As late as 1911 the *Encyclopedia Britannica* stated, "Mentally the Negro is inferior to the white." Almost a century earlier, on March 16, 1827, two African-American men attempted to breach this wall of ignorance and prejudice by launching the first black newspaper, *Freedom's Journal*, a weekly in New York City. They were John B. Russwurm, the first black graduate of an American college (Bowdoin, 1826), and the Presbyterian minister Samuel Cornish. Their newspaper had a small circulation and was aimed primarily at the freed blacks in the North but was also committed to the struggle against slavery in the South. Their prospectus or opening statement contained the ringing words, "We wish to plead our own cause. Too long have others spoken for us."

Freedom's Journal was established not only to denounce slavery, however. As with many abolitionist papers, there were strong religious and temperance allusions, along with an emphasis on education and self-improvement. It sought to improve the conditions of life for the 500,000 freed blacks in the North, a very small proportion of whom were subscribers, although it is impossible to gauge secondary circulation—more than one person reading the same copy of a newspaper.

Thus, the two African-American editors, who disagreed on the viability of colonizing former slaves in Africa, also expressed their concern for the image as well as reality of blacks.

This concern—acute and early—has been echoed today by numerous black leaders. Except for sports and entertainment celebrities, blacks today figure in the white press most prominently in crime news or in controversies about welfare or affirmative action cutbacks. As Swedish economist Gunnar Myrdal observed in 1962 after studying the black press in the United States: "No feasible widening of the reporting of Negro activities in the white press will substitute for the Negro press. What happens to Negroes will continue to have relatively low 'news value' to white people, and even the most well-meaning editor will have to stop far short of what Negroes demand if he wants to satisfy his white public."[3]

Frederick Douglass in 1891
Assesses the Future of the Black Press

Numerous scholars—black and white—have looked back on the birth and development of the African-American press from the perspective of the twentieth century, but it is perhaps more revealing to note what black participants of the preceding century thought about it. Foremost among these was the former slave and "Titan" of the black press, Frederick Douglass (see Chapter 3).

I. Garland Penn, a black school principal and former editor of the *Lynchburg* (Virginia) *Laborer*, in 1891 canvassed black journalists as to the future of their calling, in the first systematic survey, *The Afro-American Press, and Its Editors*. Penn characterized Frederick Douglass and his newspaper in this way:

> The commencement of the publication of *The North Star* [in 1847] was the beginning of a new era in the black-man's literature. Mr. Douglass' great fame gave his paper at once a place among the first journals of the country; and he drew around him a corps of contributors and correspondents from Europe, as well as from all parts of America and the West Indies, that made his columns rich with the current literature of the world. While *The North Star* became a welcome visitor to the home of the whites who had never before read a paper edited by an Afro-American, its proprietor became still more popular as a speaker in every state in the Union where Abolitionism was tolerated. Of all his labors, we re-

gard Mr. Douglass' efforts as publisher and editor the most useful to his race. For sixteen years, against much opposition, single-handed and alone, he demonstrated the fact that the Afro-American was equal to the white man in conducting a useful and popular journal.[4]

So popular was *The North Star* and so famous its editor that the name of the newspaper was changed in 1850 to *Frederick Douglass's Paper*, which was published until 1860. The early Negro scholar Penn in 1891 compiled four questions for distinguished black journalists of the century. Here are Penn's questions and Douglass's responses:

> *Question*: Do you think the Press in the hands of the Negro has been a success?
>
> *Answer* : Yes, but only as a beginning.
>
> *Question*: In your judgment, what achievements have been the result of the Afro-American editor?
>
> *Answer* : It has demonstrated, in large measure, the mental and literary possibilities of the colored race.
>
> *Question*: Do you think the Press has the proper support on the part of the Afro-American? If not, to what do you attribute the cause?
>
> *Answer* : I do not think that the Press has been properly supported, and I find the cause in the fact that the reading public, among colored people, as among all other people will spend its money for what seems to them best and cheapest. Colored papers, from their antecedents and surroundings, cost more, and give their readers less, than papers and publications by white men.
>
> *Question*: What future course do you think the Press might take in promoting good among our people?
>
> *Answer* : I think that the course to be pursued by the colored Press is to say less about race and claims to race recognition, and more about the principles of justice, liberty, and patriotism. It should say more of what we ought to do for ourselves, and less about what the Government ought to do for us; more in the interest of morality and economy, and less in the interest of office-getting; more in commending the faithful and inflexible men who stand up for our rights, and less for the celebration of balls, parties, and brilliant entertainments; more in respect to the duty of the Government to protect and defend the colored man's rights in the South, and less in puffing individual men for office; less of arrogant assumption for the colored man, and more of appreciation of his disadvantages, in comparison with those of other varieties of men whose opportunities have been broader and better than his.[5]

A Black Southern Woman Editor
Crusades against Lynching

Most white Americans have never heard of Ida B. Wells-Barnett, but her Memphis newspaper, *Free Speech and Headlight*, was from 1881 until 1892 a beacon for many African-Americans in the deteriorating South. She was not alone. Rodger Streitmatter in *Raising Her Voice: African-American Women Journalists Who Changed History* traces the careers of Wells-Barnett and ten soul-mates, previously largely ignored figures of our past.

After the Civil War more than one thousand blacks fell victim to lynch mobs in the South, when "justice" was executed by vigilantes without the accused being charged, tried, or convicted in a court of law. C. Vann Woodward in his seminal work *The Strange Career of Jim Crow* noted that discrimination and violence against blacks in the post-Civil War period resulted from the need of poor whites to put someone below their own marginal status. Others maintained that it was remarkable that the South could rebuild any society at all, good or evil, after the wrenching changes and exploitation by Northern Republicans during the harsh years of Radical Reconstruction (1867–1876).

Ida B. Wells-Barnett, born while the Civil War was under way, grew up during these later, troubled years. She was a teacher who became a full-time journalist after she was fired from her teaching position by the Memphis Board of Education for her series of articles condemning the poor condition of black schools there. She became co-owner and editor of the *Free Speech and Headlight* in 1891, whose title was soon changed simply to *Free Speech*. In 1892 she spoke out against the lynching of three black owners of a small grocery store in Memphis, a crusade that so infuriated the city that a mob destroyed her newspaper press and office while she—fortunately—was in New York attending a meeting. Her life threatened in Memphis, Wells-Barnett decided to spread her message against lynching throughout the North and abroad. She stayed in New York and wrote articles for the *New Age*, a respected black journal. Later she toured Europe, speaking out against the barbarism of lynching in America and wrote a weekly column, "Ida B. Wells Abroad," one of the rare occasions at that time that a black writer was featured in a white newspaper, the *Chicago Inter-Ocean*.

Like Ida M. Tarbell and other muckrakers slightly later, Ida B. Wells-Barnett did not simply vent her unsubstantiated opinions—she backed them up with facts. In 1894 she published *A Red Report: Tabulated Statistics and Alleged Causes of Lynchings in the U.S., 1892-1893-1894*. In 1909 she was one of those who founded the National Association for the Advancement of Colored People. She was also a journalist who became an activist, establishing the Negro Fellowship League on crime-ridden South State Street in Chicago, which provided counseling, job assistance, recreation and meeting facilities, religious services, and a temporary dormitory. It all began with the destruction of her small newspaper in Memphis by an angry mob in 1891, and here is her account of that incident.

The readers will doubtless wonder what caused the destruction of my paper after three months of constant agitation following the lynching of my friends. They were killed on the ninth of March. The *Free Speech* was destroyed 27 May 1892, nearly three months later. I thought then it was the white southerner's chivalrous defense of his womanhood which caused the mob to destroy my paper, even though it was known that the truth had been spoken. I know now that it was an excuse to do what they had wanted to do before but had not dared because they had no good reason until the appearance of that famous editorial [denouncing the lynching].

For the first time in their lives the white people of Memphis had seen earnest, united action by Negroes which upset economic and business conditions. They had thought the excitement would die down; that Negroes would forget and become again, as before, the wealth producers of the South—the hewers of wood and drawers of water, the servants of white men. But the excitement kept up, the colored people continued to leave, business remained at a standstill, and there was still a dearth of servants to cook their meals and wash their clothes and keep their homes in order, to nurse their babies and wait on their tables, to build their houses and do all classes of laborious work.

Besides, no class of people like Negroes spent their money like water, riding on streetcars and railroad trains, especially on Sundays and excursions. No other class bought clothes and food with such little haggling as they who were so easily satisfied. The whites had killed the goose that laid the golden egg of Memphis prosperity and Negro contentment; yet they were amazed that colored people continued to leave the city by scores and hundreds.

In casting about for the cause of all this restlessness and dissatisfaction the leaders concluded that the *Free Speech* was the disturbing factor. They were right. They felt that the only way to restore "harmony between the races" would be to get rid of the *Free Speech*. Yet they had to do it in such a way as not to arouse further antagonism in the Negroes themselves who were left in town, whom they wished to placate.

Months passed after the lynching before the opportunity came in which they appeared to be "defending the honor of their women" and therefore justified in destroying the paper which attacked that honor. I did not realize all this at that time, but I have come to know since that that was the moving spirit which dominated the mob in destroying my paper.

Like many another person who had read of lynching in the South, I had accepted the idea meant to be conveyed—that although lynching was irregular and contrary to law and order, unreasoning anger over the terrible crime of rape led to the lynching; that perhaps the brute deserved death anyhow and the mob was justified in taking his life.

But Thomas Moss, Calvin McDowell, and Lew Stewart had been lynched in Memphis, one of the leading cities of the South, in which no lynching had taken place before, with just as much brutality as other victims of the mob; and they had committed no crime against white women. This is what opened my eyes to what lynching really was. An excuse to get rid of Negroes who were acquiring wealth and property and thus keep the race terrorized and "keep the nigger down." I then began an investigation of every lynching I read about. I stumbled on the amazing record that every case of rape reported in that three months became such only when it became public.

Many cases were like that of the lynching which happened in Tunica County, Mississippi. The Associated Press reporter said, "The big burly brute was lynched because he had raped the seven-year-old daughter of the sheriff." I visited the place afterward and saw the girl, who was a grown woman more than seventeen years old. She had been found in the lynched Negro's cabin by her father, who had led the mob against him in order to save his daughter's reputation. That Negro was a helper on the farm.

In Natchez, Mississippi, one of the most beautiful homes of one of the leaders of society was pointed out to me. I was told the story of how the mistress of that home had given birth to a child unmistakably dark, and how her colored coachman left town on hearing the news. The *Memphis Scimi-*

tar published the story of how a young girl who had made a mistake had been awaiting confinement in the home kind-hearted women provided for such cases; how she, too, had given birth to a colored child, and because she would not tell the name of the "rapist" she was bundled out of the home to the public ward of the county hospital.

I also had the sworn statement of a mother whose son had been lynched that he had left the place where he worked because of the advances made by the beautiful daughter of the house. The boy had fallen under her spell, and met her often until they were discovered and the cry of rape was raised. A handsome young mulatto, he too had been horribly lynched for "rape." It was with these and other stories in mind in that last week in May 1892 that I wrote the following editorial:

> Eight Negroes lynched since last issue of the *Free Speech*. Three were charged with killing white men and five with raping white women. Nobody in this section believes the old thread-bare lie that Negro men assault white women. If Southern white men are not careful they will over-reach themselves and a conclusion will be reached which will be very damaging to the moral reputation of their women.

This editorial furnished at last the excuse for doing what the white leaders of Memphis had long been wanting to do: put an end to the *Free Speech*. The paper appeared the Saturday after I left home. On the following Monday morning the *Commercial Appeal* appeared, reproducing that editorial in the first column on the editorial page, and called on the chivalrous white men of Memphis to do something to avenge this insult to the honor of their women. It said, "The black wretch who had written that foul lie should be tied to a stake at the corner of Main and Madison streets, a pair of tailor's shears used on him and he should then be burned at a stake."

This editorial was written by a man named Carmack, who afterward became an editor in Nashville, Tennessee, where he pursued the same tactics against a white man and was shot down in the streets as a mad dog would have been. But the people of Memphis met in the Cotton Exchange Building the same Monday evening after the appearance of this heated editorial. There was much speech making, led by Mr. Carmack and others. As a result a committee was sent to the *Free Speech* office by this gathering of leading men. This committee destroyed our type and furnishings, and then put up a notice of warning.

Long afterward I learned that one of the leading citizens of Memphis, who had been a Union man during the Civil War, sent word to Mr. Fleming, my business manager, that this committee was coming and that he must leave town. That was why the committee did not find him.

Mr. Fleming wrote me afterward that he was through with newspapers. He had been the county clerk at Marion, Arkansas, when he first started in the newspaper business, publishing a harmless little sheet called the *Marion Headlight*. He had been run out of Marion because of politics in the overthrow of the so-called Negro domination by white Democrats in 1888. When he came to Memphis he joined forces with Rev. Taylor Nightingale and they published the *Free Speech-Headlight*, a combination of their papers.

When they invited me to join forces with them and made me the editor, the paper became simply the *Free Speech*. To lose everything the second time when prospects were so bright was almost more than Mr. Fleming could bear. He blamed me very bitterly for that editorial, and perhaps he was justified in doing so.[6]

A White Muckraker Investigates the Atlanta Race Riot of 1906

Ray Stannard Baker joined the nucleus of staff writers on *McClure's Magazine*—who were to become the muckrakers— in 1897 after doing a stint on the Chicago *Record*. His experience on both a newspaper and magazine was to stand him in good stead for the investigative reporting developed by these men and women. Baker's experience with the plight of America's working class in the age of unregulated capitalism, especially that of child labor and "wage slavery," made him realize that such abuses cut across racial lines. In 1906, Baker thus became the first prominent white writer to explore the wider conditions of black America, with his book *Following the Colour Line* and with "The Clash of the Races in a Southern City" (*American Magazine*, 1907). His stature was recognized when President Woodrow Wilson, of whom he would later write an eight-volume scholarly biography, appointed Baker to head the American news bureau in Paris during the Versailles Peace Conference following World War I.

Following the Colour Line revealed the vulnerability of blacks in the South, for example, as in the Atlanta racial disturbance of 1906. The *Atlanta Evening News* did much to foment the riot described below, which exploded into indiscriminate killings and rampaging in the streets in one of the South's most progressive cities. It editorialized, for example, after a white woman claimed she had been attacked by a black man: "No law of God or man can hold back the vengeance of our white men upon such a criminal [the Negro who attacks a white woman]. If necessary, we will double and treble and quadruple the law of Moses, and hang off-hand the criminal, or failing to find that a remedy, we will hang two, three, or four of the Negroes nearest to the crime, until the crime is no longer done or feared in all this Southern land that we inhabit and love (December 12, 1906)." The *Atlanta Journal* joined the escalating newspaper hysteria with such three-line banner headlines as this: "Angry Citizens in Pursuit of Black Brute Who Attempted Assault on Mrs. Chapin Rescued from Fiend by Passing Neighbor."

In all fairness, some Southern newspapers deplored lynching. The *Huntsville Mercury* spoke of the "deep sense of shame felt by our good citizens in being run over by a few lawless spirits." The *Birmingham News* proclaimed, "There is no justification for the mob who, in punishing one murderer, made many more." The *Birmingham Ledger* added, "This lynching is a disgrace to our state. The *Ledger* doesn't put its ear to the ground to hear from the North, nor does it care what Northern papers say. The crime is our own, and the disgrace falls on us."[7]

On the afternoon of the riot [Baker wrote] the newspapers in flaming headlines chronicled four assaults by Negroes on white women. I had a personal investigation made of each of those cases. Two of them may have been attempts at assaults, but two palpably were nothing more than fright on the part of both the white woman and the Negro. As an instance, in one case an elderly woman, Mrs. Martha Holcombe, going to close her blinds in the evening, saw a Negro on the sidewalk. In a terrible fright she screamed. The news was telephoned to the police station, but before the officials could respond, Mrs. Holcombe telephoned them not to come out. And yet this was one of the "assaults" chronicled in letters five inches high in a newspaper extra.

And finally on this hot Saturday half-holiday, when the country people had come in by hundreds, when everyone was out of doors, when the streets were crowded, when the saloons had been filled since early morning with white men and Negroes, both drinking—certain newspapers in Atlanta began to print extras with big headings announcing new assaults on white women by Negroes. The Atlanta *News* published five such extras, and newsboys cried them through the city:

"Third assault."

"Fourth assault."

The whole city, already deeply agitated, was thrown into a veritable state of panic. The news in the extras was taken as truthful; for the city was not in a mood then for cool investigation. Calls began to come in from every direction for police protection. A loafing Negro in a backyard, who in ordinary times would have not been noticed, became an object of real terror. The police force, too small at best, was thus distracted and separated.

In Atlanta the proportion of men who go armed continually is very large; the pawnshops of Decatur and Peters Streets, with windows like arsenals, furnish the low class of Negroes and whites with cheap revolvers and knives. Every possible element was here, then, for a murderous outbreak. The good citizens, white and black, were far away in their homes; the bad men had been drinking in the dives permitted to exist by the respectable people of Atlanta and here they were gathered, by night, in the heart of the city.

And, finally, a trivial incident fired the tinder. Fear and vengeance generated it: it was marked at first by a sort of rough, half-drunken horseplay, but when once blood was shed, the brute, which is none too well controlled in the best city, came out and gorged itself. Once permit the shackles of law and order to be cast off, and men, white or black, Christian or pagan, revert to primordial savagery. There is no such thing as an orderly mob.

Crime had been committed by Negroes, but this mob made no attempt to find the criminals: it expressed its blind, unreasoning, uncontrolled race hatred by attacking every man, woman, or boy it saw who had a black face. A lame boot-black, an inoffensive, industrious Negro boy, at that moment actually at work shining a man's shoes, was dragged out and cuffed, kicked and beaten to death in the street. Another young Negro was chased and stabbed to death with jack-knives in the most unspeakably horrible manner. The mob entered barber shops where respectable Negro men were at work shaving white customers, pulled them away from their chairs and beat them. Cars were stopped and inoffensive Negroes were thrown through the windows or dragged out and beaten. They did not stop with killing and maiming; they broke into hardware stores and armed themselves, they demolished not only Negro barber shops and restaurants, but they robbed stores kept by white men.

Of course the Mayor came out, and the police force and the fire department, and finally the Governor ordered out the militia—to apply that pound of cure which should have been an ounce of prevention.

It is highly significant of Southern conditions—which the North does not understand—that the first instinct of thousands of Negroes in Atlanta, when the riot broke out, was not to run away from the white people but to run to them. The white man who takes the most radical position in opposition to the Negro race will often be found loaning money to individual Negroes, feeding them and their families from his kitchen, or defending "his Negroes" in court or elsewhere. All of the more prominent white citizens of Atlanta, during the riot, protected and fed many colored families who ran to them in their terror. Even Hoke Smith, Governor-elect of Georgia, who is more distrusted by the Negroes as a race probably than any other white man in Georgia, protected many Negroes in his house during the disturbance. In many cases white friends armed Negroes and told them to protect themselves. One widow I know of who had a single black servant, placed a shot-gun in his hands and told him to fire on any mob that tried to get him. She trusted him absolutely. Southern people possess a real liking, wholly unknown in the North, for individual Negroes whom they know.[8]

W. E. B. Du Bois Confronts the Racial Crisis

John W. Gardner, then secretary of Health, Education and Welfare, predicted in the 1960s that if no solution were found in the mounting racial conflict, the United States would end up as two nations, "with an embittered and angry nation within a nation, with two peoples who don't know each other, don't mingle, and meet only to vent their hostility."[9] Presaging this attitude was William Edward Burghardt Du Bois, a militant black leader in the United States who edited the monthly *Crisis* for the NAACP for almost a quarter of a century (1910–1934). He sought racial reconciliation on equal terms, not what he perceived as the surrender of former black leaders such as Booker T. Washington. Du Bois's activism obscured, to a certain extent, his prolific journalistic contributions, with the exception of *The Crisis*, so highly regarded that its entire file for the first fifty years has been reproduced as *A Record of the Darker Races*. Du Bois got his start in journalism as a correspondent for the prestigious *Springfield*

(Massachusetts) *Republican,* which trained generations of young newspapermen in the days before journalism schools.

The distinguished black leader was one of the cofounders of the NAACP in 1909 and also founded and edited *The Crisis* until 1934, when Roy Wilkins took over. Du Bois then headed the sociology department at Atlanta University and late in life became a member of the Communist Party. Like opera singer Paul Robeson, he despaired of finding racial justice in his own country, and Du Bois left the United States to live in the new African nation of Ghana until his death there in 1963 at the age of ninety-five. The American embassy did not send a representative to his funeral. But his lasting monument lies in *The Crisis* series, which elevated black journalism to new heights. Du Bois himself best tells of his long and fruitful association with that publication.

EDITING *THE CRISIS*

In 1910, I came to New York as Director of Publications and Research in the NAACP. The idea was that I should continue the kind of research into the Negro problem that I had been carrying on in Atlanta and that eventually I should become Secretary of the NAACP. But I did not want to raise money, and there were no funds for research; so that from the first, I urged that we have a monthly organ.

This seemed necessary because the chief Negro weekly *The New York Age* was then owned by friends of Mr. [Booker T.] Washington, and the Tuskegee organization had tight hold of most of the rest of the Negro press. The result was that the NAACP got a pretty raw deal from the colored press and none at all from the white papers.

In addition to that, the Negro press was at the time mainly organs of opinions and not gatherers of news.

I had the idea that a small publication would be read which stressed the facts and minimized editorial opinion, but made it clear and strong; and also published the opinion of others.

There were many on the board of directors who did not agree with me. I remember Albert Pilsbury, former Attorney General of Massachusetts, wrote to me and said: "If you have not already determined to publish a magazine, for heaven's sake drop the idea. The number of publications now is as many as the 'plagues of Egypt'!" But I was firm, and back of me stood William English Walling, Paul Kennedy, Charles Edward Russell, and John E. Mulholland and other members of the board.

But there again the matter of money was difficult. It was hard enough to raise the salaries of our two executive officers, and certainly we had no capital for investment in a periodical. I was persistent and two persons helped me: Mary Maclean, an English woman who was a writer on the *New York Times* and a loyal and efficient friend; and Robert N. Wood, a printer who was head of the Negro Tammany organization at that time.

Wood knew about printing and I knew nothing. He advised me, helped me to plan the magazine, and took the risk of getting me credit for paper and printing. The Board agreed that it would be responsible for debts up to but not exceeding $50.00 a month. It has always been a matter of pride to me that I never asked for that $50.00.

Finally after what seemed to me interminable delays on various accounts, the first number of *The Crisis* appeared in November 1910. It had sixteen 5 x 8 pages, with a cover which carried one little woodcut of a Negro child; as one of my critics facetiously said: "It is a shame to take the ten cents which this issue costs."

First because of the news which it contained, in four pages of "Along the Color Line"; then because of some blazing editorials which continually got us into hot water with friends and foes; and because of the pictures of Negroes which we carried in increasing number and often in color, *The Crisis* succeeded.

We condensed more news about Negroes and their problems in a month than most colored papers before this had published in a year. Then we had four pages of editorials, which talked turkey. The articles were at first short and negligible but gradually increased in number, length, and importance; but we were never able to pay contributors. Pictures of colored people were an innovation; and at that time it was the rule of most white papers never to publish a picture of a colored person except as a criminal and the colored papers published mostly pictures of celebrities who sometimes paid for the honor. In general the Negro race was just a little afraid to see itself in plain ink.

The circulation growth of the *The Crisis* was extraordinary, even to us who believed in it. From a monthly net paid circulation of 9,000 copies in 1911, it jumped to 75,000 copies in 1918. . . . In January 1916, *The Crisis* became entirely self-supporting, paying all items of its cost including publicity, light, heat, rent, etc., and the salaries of an editor and business manager and nine clerks. It circulated in every state in the union, in all the insular possessions, and in most foreign countries including Africa. . . .

We reached a circulation of 100,000 in 1919, following my revelation of the attitude of American army officers toward the Negroes in France. I shall never forget the circumstances of that scoop. I was in the office of Blaise Diagne in the spring of 1919. Diagne was a tall, thin, black Senegalese, French Under-Secretary of State for Colonies, and during the war, French Commissioner in West Africa, outranking the Colonial Governor. Diagne saved France by the black shock troops which he brought from Africa and threw against German artillery. They held the Germans until the Allies could get ready for them.

Diagne was consequently a great man and it was his word which induced Prime Minister Clemenceau to let the First Pan-African Congress meet in Paris against the advice of the Americans. Diagne did not like white Americans.

"Did you see," he stormed, "what the American Mission told the French about the way Negroes should be treated?" Then he showed me the official document. I read it and sat very still. Then I said, as carelessly as possible, "Would it be possible to obtain a copy of this?" "Take that," said Diagne.

Having the precious document, the problem was what to do with it. I dare not carry it nor trust it to the mails. But a white friend who was sailing home offered to take anything I wished to send. I handed him the document sealed, neglecting to say what dynamite was in it. The Crisis office and NAACP officials read it and dropped it until I returned. I published it in May 1919. The Post Office promptly held The Crisis up in the mails. But it proved too hot for them; if the Government held it that would be acknowledging its authorship. They let it go. We sold 100,000 copies!

Our income in 1920 was $77,000; that was our high-water mark. Then began a slump which brought the circulation down to 35,000 copies in 1924 and a cash income of $46,000.

The causes of this were clear and strike every modern periodical: the reading public is not used to paying for the cost of the periodicals which they read; often they do not pay even for the cost of the paper used in the edition. Advertisers pay for most of the costs and advertisers buy space in periodicals which circulate widely among well-to-do persons able to buy the wares offered. The Crisis was known to circulate among Negro workers of low income. Moreover it antagonized many white powerful interests; it had been denounced in Congress and many respectable Negroes were afraid to be seen reading it. Mississippi passed laws against it and some of our agents were driven from home.

We got some advertising, especially from Negro businesses; some advertisers we refused because we did not like the wares they offered or suspected fraud. The "Big" advertisers remained aloof; some looked us over, but nearly all fell back on the rule not to patronize "propaganda" periodicals. Besides, they did not believe the Negro market worth entering.

Our only recourse was to raise our price of subscription. In December 1919 we raised our price to a dollar and a half for a year and fifteen cents a copy; also we increased our size to sixty-four pages and cover. This might have extricated us if the prices of everything else had not gone up, while wages went down. The depression which burst on the nation in 1929, started among Negro workers as early as 1926. It struck the workers of the Negro race long before the country in general dreamed of it. I remember bringing the matter to the attention of the president of the board of directors, but he said "the country is unusually prosperous!" Nevertheless, I reported, the Negro worker is losing old jobs and not getting new ones.

There was a wider underlying cause: How far was *The Crisis* an organ of opinion and propaganda; and of whose opinion and just what propaganda? Or how far was it an organ of an association catering to its immediate plans and needs? The two objects and methods were not incompatible with each other in the earlier days of beginnings. Indeed from 1920 to 1925 or later *The Crisis* was the predominant partner, with income and circulation larger than the income and membership of the NAACP. For just this reason the NAACP became known outside its membership [which] . . . increased and the question of the future relation of *The Crisis* and NAACP had to be settled. Their complete separation was proposed; or if the income of *The Crisis* continued to fall, the subsidy of *The Crisis* by the NAACP; or further attempts [would be needed] to prolong the present relations and increase *The Crisis* income and circulation.

From 1925 to 1934, the latter method was tried. Various efforts were made to increase *The Crisis* circulation, by change of form and content. Considerable success ensued, but the depression which now fell heavier on the nation, convinced me that *The Crisis* could not be made to pay again for a long period and that meantime the only way to keep it alive was by subsidy from the NAACP. For this reason in 1934, I gave up my position as editor and publisher of *The Crisis* and went back to teaching and writing at Atlanta University.

In the nature of the case, there is a clear distinction between an organ of an organization and a literary magazine. They have different objects and functions. The one is mainly a series of reports and records of organizational technicalities and news notes of methods and routine notices. All large organizations need such a publication: But it is never self-supporting nor widely read. So far as it tries to be literary and artistic, it misses its main function and is too narrow to achieve any other.

On the other hand, a literary and news journal must be free and uncontrolled; in no other way can it be virile, creative, and individual. While it must follow an idea, and one of which one or more organizations approve, yet its right to deviate in particulars must be granted, else it misses its function of provoking thought, stimulating argument, and attracting readers. For many years the NAACP gave me such freedom and the public repaid them and me by wide support. But when public support lagged and the NAACP must furnish a large part of the supporting funds, it would have called for more faith than any organization was likely to have in one man, to leave me still in untrammeled control. And as for me, I had no interest in a conventional organ; I must be free lance or nothing.

Against, therefore, the strong pleas to close friends like Joel Spingarn; and against the openly expressed wish of the whole board, which did not wholly agree with me, but were willing to yield much to retain me, I resigned. And I resigned completely and not in part, I was not only editor and head of a department which was separate from that of the Executive Secretary, with my own office staff and separate bank account; I was also one of the incorporators of the NAACP and member of the board of directors since its beginning. Its officials from the first had come to consideration and election on my recommendation. I was a member of the Spingarn Medal Committee, and chief speaker at every annual conference. It was fair to say that the policy of the NAACP from 1910 to 1934 was largely of my making.

I would not have been honest therefore with my successors to have resigned in part and hung on to remnants of my former power. I went out completely. I think some sighed in relief. But many were genuinely sorry. Among the latter was myself. For I was leaving my dream and brainchild; my garden of hope and highway to high emprise. But I was sixty-five; my life work was practically done. I looked forward to a few final years of thought, advice, and remembrance, beneath the trees and on the hills beside the graves and with the friends where first my real life work had begun in 1897.[10]

Langston Hughes and Fifty Years of the *Chicago Defender*

During the smear-and-run days of Senator Joseph McCarthy when Cold War hysteria clouded judgments, W. E. B. Du Bois was indicted in 1951 for being a Soviet sympathizer. Although he was acquitted, the stigma of "traitor" hung over him, prompting a black columnist for the *Chicago Defender* to come to his aid. Langston Hughes, who was to become one of America's most distinguished poets, cut his writing teeth on the black newspaper the *Defender*, just as Ernest Hemingway and other authors had done on other newspapers. Concerning the Du Bois incident, Langston Hughes responded with anger in a column in the *Defender* of October 6, 1951, which concluded: "Somebody in Washington wants to put Dr. Du Bois in jail. Somebody in France wanted to put Voltaire in jail. Somebody in Franco's Spain sent Lorca, their greatest poet, to death before a firing squad. Somebody in Germany under Hitler burned the books, drove Thomas Mann into exile, and led their leading Jewish scholars to the gas chamber. Somebody in Greece long ago gave Socrates the hemlock to drink. Somebody at Golgotha erected a cross and somebody drove the nails into the hands of Christ. Somebody spat upon His garments. No one remembers their names."[11]

Langston Hughes had published his first book of poetry, *The Weary Blues*, in 1925, followed by sixteen more of verse, short stories, and essays on the contemporary American scene. He was a deeply committed writer who became known as the Poet Laureate of Harlem, the most prolific writer of the Harlem Renaissance of the 1920s and 1930s. For our purposes, it is essential to note that Hughes never turned his back on journalism, describing the *Chicago Defender* as a "journalistic voice of a largely voiceless people." His writings for that journal have been assiduously collected by Christopher C. De Santis in *Langston Hughes and the Chicago Defender* (1995). Like Latin American intellectuals, Hughes considered it not only an obligation but also an honor to write for the public prints long before the appearance of op-ed pages in U.S. newspapers. Moreover, early critics sneered at the "journalistic" writing of such towering figures as John Steinbeck and John Dos Passos. In 1955, on the occasion of the fiftieth anniversary of the *Chicago Defender*, Langston Hughes, who rose from boyhood in Kansas to international fame, recounted the long and often stormy career of the newspaper he loved.

During the year in which "The Chicago Defender" was founded in 1905 there were 57 Negroes lynched in the United States, an average of more than one a week. The following year, 1906, was the year of the great Atlanta race riot in which many in that city were killed. That same year in the United States 62 Negroes were lynched. In 1907 Alain Locke received a Rhodes Scholarship to Oxford University in England and 58 Negroes were lynched.

In 1906 when 89 Negroes were killed by mobs, Cole and Johnson produced the "Red Moon" in which Abbie Mitchell starred. In 1909, the year the National Association for the Advancement of Colored People was initiated, 69 Negroes were lynched. In 1910 there were 67 black lynchings. In 1911, when the National Urban League was organized, 60 Negroes were hanged or burned without trial. In 1912 the number was 61.

In 1913, however, when Harriet Tubman [of Underground Railroad fame] died, only 51 were lynched. And the same number in 1914 when [W. C.] Handy wrote "The Saint Louis Blues" and Mamie Smith made the first blues record. In 1915, the year that Booker T. Washington died, 56 of his fellow countrymen were put to death by white mobs.

So, in its early years, "The Chicago Defender" had a lot of lynching news to report, while at the same time it reported the upward progress of the Negro—the news of our leaders, show people, and prize fighters, and the more sensational of our crimes. The "Defender" kept its readers posted on happenings throughout the Negro world. In the Deep South, Middle West, and Far West it had many avid readers.

As a child in Kansas I grew up on "The Chicago Defender" and it awakened me in my youth to the problems which I and my race had to face in America. Its flaming headlines and indignant editorials did a great deal to make me the "race man" which I later became, as expressed in my own attitudes and in my writing. Thousands and thousands of other young Negroes were, I am sure, also affected the same way by this militant and stirringly edited Chicago weekly.

Then when World War I began and many new job opportunities for Negroes were created in the North, the "Defender's" Come-North campaign became a great social force that helped change the history of our race in this country. In 1916 there had been 50 lynchings in the sunny Southland. Though it might be cloudy and cold, in the North, the "Defender" said, "To die from the bite of frost is far more glorious than at the hand of a mob." Its founder and owner, Robert S. Abbott, urged his readers to come North, come North, come North.

Although the South mistreated its Negro citizens, it did not want to lose its basic supply of cheap labor. There were cities in the South where it was forbidden to sell or circulate "The Chicago Defender" and the Longview, Texas, race riot began when a mob of white men went into the Negro section looking for a colored teacher accused of sending news to the "Defender."

That was the year, 1919, when there were 76 lynchings in America, more than there have ever been in any single year since. That year, too, was the time of bloody race riots in an ever increasing number of U.S. cities. In Omaha, Nebraska, a white mob wrecked the Court House to drag a Negro from it through the streets, shooting him more than a thousand times. And in the great Chicago riot of 1919 which grew out of housing problems, 38 persons were killed and more than 500 injured. In 1921, a year of 59 lynchings of Negroes, there was a race war in Tulsa, Oklahoma. In Chicago then Dixieland jazz was beginning to catch on and, on the stages of the South Side, some of the best colored talent in the country was appearing.

In Harlem in the early twenties the now famous "Negro Renaissance" in the arts was underway. Negro themes and Negro performers were reaping applause on Broadway. In 1925 Alain Locke edited his anthology of the arts of that period, his widely read "The New Negro." That year there were only 17 lynchings. The "Defender" of this post-war period reported all these events of both sorrow and gladness, struggle and achievement—but with the accent always on the struggle and the goals of freedom still to be obtained. In its second decade, the "Defender" continued to be a great militant pro-democratic paper and a thorn in the side of bigoted, American racists.

From 1905 to 1925 the "Defender" said for the anonymous millions of Negroes all of the things pent up in their hearts concerning segregation, and fear of riots and lynchings and police brutality and joblessness, and their loathing of second-class citizenship. From New Orleans to Detroit, Chicago to the West Coast, this paper was the popular mouthpiece of the Negro masses.

In those days before our many regional Negro newspapers had grown to the positions they now occupy in various cities and sections of the country, and before some of the eastern Negro weeklies had become national in scope, it was the *Defender* that said best most of the things millions of Negroes wanted said about their needs, their dreams, and their demands in this America of ours. The "Defender" said them loudly and simply and clearly in big headlines, strongly worded editorials, and in pictures of mob fires and black bodies on Southern trees that cried "Shame!" from the printed page. The journalistic voice of a largely voiceless people, that was "The Chicago Defender."

Now, fifty years after the founding of this newspaper, conditions have changed greatly, racially speaking, in our country. But not so greatly that the Negro masses do not still need a great strong voice to speak up—and to speak out—for them. Integration is not here yet, not by a long shot.

America's highly publicized Supreme Count decisions of very recent years have been read of and heard of in many parts of our country, but have had as yet no practical effect whatsoever on Negro life in a great many localities. Outside of some of our larger cities, decent housing for Negroes is as hard to find as ever. Entrance to public places in thousands of American towns—movies, restaurants, hotels, and motels—is still either impossible to secure, or is available only on the old ugly insulting Jim Crow basis. Lynchings and race riots have died down, but the threat of lynchings, and of riots, too, is still in the air of more communities than it is pleasant to contemplate.

Police brutality is still present. Jim Crow cars still run on the rails of the South. The number of newly integrated public schools opening their doors this fall to all children will still be small compared to the number of segregated schools in operation. For all the noble work of the Negro press, the NAACP, the Urban League, the churches, fraternities and sororities and our race leaders, behind the average man or woman who buys a weekly copy of a Negro newspaper at a news stand, Jim Crow follows the reader as closely as his shadow.

The majority of the people who buy the Negro papers are not those lucky few in our race who have managed to escape the dark shadows of prejudice in America, or are fortunate enough to live in integrated communities where they can almost forget about race, or enough to buy their way to forgetfulness with vacations in New York or Europe.

The readers of the Negro papers are mainly those who still need a voice to say what they still want and have not yet gotten—namely full citizenship, full equality, full civil rights, job rights, and an absence from fear, want, and contempt. So long as millions of Negroes who shove out their small change every week for Negro papers, do not have these basic rights—and are hardly likely to have them tomorrow or the next day—just so long will the Negro press be of great value to its basic readers—providing the Negro press does not forget about them, and the publishers and editors of Negro papers do not grow too far away from the Negro masses to understand their needs.

My hope is that the "Defender" will remain a Negro paper as long as we Negroes need it. Personally, I think there is probably another fifty years of great racial and democratic service ahead for "The Chicago Defender." However, by the time its 100th anniversary rolls around, the "Defender" might well be an integrated newspaper—or maybe even a white paper—without loss to anybody.

Perhaps "integration" and "segregation" will be forgotten words by then, and maybe there will not have been a lynching since 1955 in Mississippi. When this desirable state of affairs comes about, the "Defender" will have played a great part in bringing into being such a wonderful day. Blessings on the "Defender" at fifty![12]

Carl T. Rowan Finds a Middle Way

As lynching declined in the first years of the twentieth century, and the black papers were at their peak of circulation and influence in the 1940s, another form of harassment of African-Americans took its place—the slur, the hurtful word, the despising glance. Even in World War II, 700,000 segregated black soldiers—ironically fighting for the freedom denied them at home—faced a wall of prejudice. John D. Stevens has documented this with his monograph *From the Back of the Foxhole: Black Correspondents in World War II*. The Navy called back, with embarrassment, a poster that depicted a Ubangi woman over the slogan "A Slip of the Lip May Sink a Ship." And the Treasury Department sent out mats of papers of a fat black woman with this slogan:

> A cheerful old mammy named Hannah
> Who'd lived 80 years in Savannah
> Said Sho 'nuff, I'll buy bonds cause ah
> Am in love with the Star Spangled Bannah.

Officially, an English-French pocket dictionary published by the military included the word "nigger."[13] Four black weeklies sent twenty-seven correspondents to cover the fighting, and in 1948 by executive order President Harry S. Truman ended segregation in the armed forces for all time.

Although it is debatable, the advent of television perhaps lessened tensions between the races. Norman Lear's series *All in the Family* poked fun both at the amiable bigot Archie Bunker and the doctrinaire liberalism of his son-in-law "Meathead." A few critics said it entrenched stereotypes, but others found in the series a safety valve of laughter.

Before all this, a serious young black man, Carl T. Rowan, had carved out a solid journalistic reputation for himself on the white *Minneapolis Tribune*. The best known African-American journalist of his time, Rowan sought reconciliation—not retribution. Some blacks might have called him a "white Negro," but he preferred to work for the betterment of his race within the existing system. In 1956, at the age of thirty, he became the only journalist ever to win three consecutive awards from Sigma Delta Chi (now the Society of Professional Journalists), and President Lyndon Baines

Johnson appointed him director of the U.S. Information Agency in 1964, along with other diplomatic assignments.

Rowan's early journalistic career coincided with the desegregation of public schools by the famous 1954 Supreme Court decision, with which this selection from *Go South to Sorrow* (1957) deals. Perhaps it was not a panacea, as school busing aroused protests and inner-city schools continued to deteriorate as parents clamored for government subsidies (vouchers) to send their children to private schools. While this undoubtedly would result in de facto segregation once again, some blacks by the 1990s themselves wanted separatism. But the 1954 Supreme Court decision integrating schools was greeted by Rowan and others as a giant leap forward for American blacks. Here is what he had to say.

"We conclude that in the field of public education the doctrine of 'separate but equal' has no place. Separate educational facilities are inherently unequal."

This was the unanimous opinion of the court, and it was an opinion that electrified the nation. I sat at my desk at the *Minneapolis Tribune*, reading the thousands of words that poured in from the South, from Negroes, from newspaper editors, and from foreigners.

"In the lives of nations there are moments when the ideal blazes forth with shattering intensity," declared the *New York Herald Tribune*. "Men see the truth they have known all along and yet have somehow managed to deny. Such a moment came with a clear, final decision of the court."

The *New York Times* envisioned problems as a result of the court's decision, because "the Constitution and the Bill of Rights are at times hard masters." The *Times* saw no chance that the ruling alone would solve this great social problem immediately, but it saw hope in the fact that a constitutional principle inherent in the Declaration of Independence had been restated. "The highest court in the land, the guardian of our national conscience, has reaffirmed its faith—and the undying American faith—in the equality of all men and all children before the law."

A day later, on May 18, 1954, United Press reported that the decision was front-page news in Europe and Asia. The *Manchester Guardian* expressed "immense relief" at America's "having put behind it what has long been its worst reproach."

In Zurich, Switzerland, *Neue Zeitung* called the ruling "an impressive example of the vitality of American democracy."

In color-conscious India, the ruling was praised, but Indians adopted an attitude of "wait and see."

Izvestia, the mouthpiece of Communist Russia, called the decision a sham perpetrated "for purely propaganda purposes." The Soviet newspaper called the ruling "a demagogic gesture designed for export as well as for lulling American public opinion." The Russians, who had often used the issue of school segregation to label Americans "imperialistic racists," obviously were referring to the fact that immediately upon receiving the decision, the United States government launched a full-scale campaign to get the words and import of the court ruling to the vast millions of Asia and Africa who are so vitally concerned about color problems in the United States. Within an hour after the ruling, the Voice of America beamed an English-language short-wave program to Communist-dominated eastern Europe. The full text of the decision and a 600-word dispatch on the ruling were sent to United States Information Services throughout the world. If the race problem was the "Achilles heel" of American democracy, we wanted to tell the world that the high court had found a cure. . . .

This campaign was expected, since both the Truman and Eisenhower administrations had urged the court to outlaw segregation because, they said, Jim Crow "furnishes grist for the Communist propaganda mills and it raises doubt even among friendly nations as to the intensity of our devotion to the democratic faith."

Thurgood Marshall, the brilliant lawyer for the National Association for the Advancement of Colored People who had argued for and won this monumental decision, spoke with a restrained sense of jubilation: "This decision gives the lie to Communist propaganda. This shows what can be done here; for once, our country can hold its head up, and for that I am eternally grateful. I am grateful, not just as a Negro, but as an American."[14]

Notes

1. Quoted in Roland E. Wolseley, *The Black Press, U.S.A.*, 2d ed. (Ames: Iowa State University Press, 1990), frontispiece.

2. Ibid., 405.

3. Gunnar Myrdal, *American Dilemma: The Negro Problem and Modern Democracy* (New York: Harper and Row, 1962).

4. I. Garland Penn, *The Afro-American Press, and Its Editors* (Springfield, MA: Willey and Company, 1891), 69.

5. Ibid., 448–50.

6. Alfreda M. Duster, ed., *Crusade for Justice: The Autobiography of Ida B. Wells* (Chicago: University of Chicago Press, 1970), 63–67.

7. Ray Stannard Baker, *Following the Colour Line: American Negro Citizenship in the Progressive Era* (New York: Harper and Row, 1906), editorial comment, 25, 196.

8. Ibid., 9–11.

9. Wolseley, *Black Press*, 402.

10. John Henrik Clarke, Esther Jackson, Ernest Kaiser, and J. H. O'Dell, eds., *Black Titan: W. E. B. Du Bois, An Anthology by the Editors of Freedomways* (Boston: Beacon Press, 1970), 268–73.

11. Christopher C. De Santis, ed., *Langston Hughes and the Chicago Defender: Essays on Race, Politics, and Culture, 1942-62* (Urbana: University of Illinois Press, 1995), 188.

12. "Langston Hughes Recalls Triumphs and Tragedies of a Race as Told by the Defender," *Chicago Defender*, August 6, 1955.

13. John D. Stevens, *From the Back of the Foxhole: Black Correspondents in World War II* (Lexington, KY: Association for Education in Journalism), Journalism Monographs no. 27, February 1973.

14. Carl T. Rowan, *Go South to Sorrow* (New York: Random House, 1957), 10–13.

9

Radio and Television

———————⟨◆⟩———————

In 1961, not long after the Golden Age of radio and television, Newton Minow, chairman of the Federal Communications Commission (FCC), described television fare as a "vast wasteland" of mediocrity or worse. In 1990, after Ken Burns aired his acclaimed documentary series on the Civil War on the Public Broadcasting System (PBS)—told in both images and the simple, beautiful language of the people themselves— he told the National Press Club in Washington, DC, that commercial television was "nearly the same thing everywhere . . . on dozens of clonelike channels." As for newscasting, "a kind of cultural peerage" has been conferred on a small group of TV commentators, he asserted, adding, "Issues and ideas are merely pushed around the plate, never digested, by the same people." Burns concluded, "In the worst of our television, we are addicted to personality, to the breathless embrace of celebrity, ensuring as we go a tyranny of the televised over the great mass of the untelevised."[1] In 1991, Philo T. Farnsworth, credited with developing television, on his deathbed lamented the use to which his invention had been put.

Yet as with any institution, there have been peaks of excellence as well as plains of banality in the electronic media. Only the highlights of the technical history of radio and television will be touched upon here, as specialists are still debating who did what first. But it boggles the mind to contemplate that within the span of one generation we went from primitive radio crystal sets to satellite transmission that covers the globe. This all rested on nineteenth-century advances in science, such as the invention of the telephone by Alexander Graham Bell in 1876 and the wireless transmission by telegraph achieved by Guglielmo Marconi in the 1890s. But voice broadcasting would not have been possible without the improvement by Lee De Forest in 1906 of the vacuum tube.

Through these pioneering efforts came radio and television as means of mass communication. In 1998 an estimated one billion people in the world watched the Academy Awards by satellite. The "global village" predicted by Marshall McLuhan is here, but will such technical mastery bring us more than "the breathless embrace of celebrity"? Mahatma Gandhi once described radio as the "talking book," and educational satellites in some Third World countries are teaching millions of illiterate persons.

After radio made its first tentative commercial debut in the 1920s, promoters wondered how to make money out of the popularity that greeted this new invention. At first, it was thought that sales of the radio sets themselves in retail stores would finance the new medium and yield a handsome profit. That idea was soon shoved aside, however, by the more lucrative advertising, and therein began a battle for the advertising dollar between the electronic and print media that persists to this day. Apparently no serious thought was given at the time toward independent government subsidy like that of the British Broadcasting Corporation, an autonomous unit partly financed by the government and partly by users. (The BBC now does have one commercial channel that accepts advertising.) In the United States, it was not until 1967 that Congress established the Public Broadcasting System, partly supported by viewers and partly by government, an arrangement dependent—often for political reasons—on those who hold congressional purse strings.

The early days of radio were like the Oklahoma land rush, with everyone furiously hurrying to stake out his or her claim. With a limited number of frequencies on the broadcast band, there was much overlapping. The result was chaos until the Radio Act of 1927—at which time there were 733 stations—created a five-person Federal Radio Commission to regulate all forms of radio communication. Licenses were granted for three years "in the public interest, convenience or necessity." Later, the Communications Act of 1934 set up the seven-person FCC to perform the above duties. Presumably, renewal of licenses every seven years for radio and five years for television would ensure continued high standards, but in fact the FCC has seldom denied a license renewal.

A case in point is that of the Rev. Charles Coughlin, the Catholic priest who built up his own radio network after being dropped by CBS for his controversial views—anti-Jewish and pro-Nazi; he acquired an audience of 40 million in the late 1930s. It was not the FCC that forced him off the air in 1940, however, but the National Association of Broadcasters. Relying then on the print medium, Father Coughlin blamed World War II on a British-Jewish-Roosevelt conspiracy. The postmaster general banned his publications from the mails, and his superiors ordered him to desist or be defrocked. The "Radio Priest" obeyed and died in obscurity.

The abuse of radio by demagogues such as Father Coughlin and Huey Long in Louisiana, not to mention Adolf Hitler and Benito Mussolini, poses the difficult problem of when freedom of expression becomes a threat to free society. As Francis R. McBride has written, "Whether or not Father Coughlin ever constituted a threat to democracy, he undoubtedly was one of the most powerful figures outside of the government during the Depression era." Despite talk shows today conducted by convicted perjurers and ex-convicts, radio, and later television, have also done much good historically. During the Great Depression, for example, Franklin Delano Roosevelt used radio masterly in his famous weekly "Fireside Chats" to reassure a country fearing economic collapse, and Winston Churchill in the Battle of Britain buoyed the spirits of a beleaguered people through his radio talks.

Actually, until recently the rules for social responsibility were quite different for radio/television and the print medium. The First Amendment offers greater latitude toward the latter because presumably anyone can start up a newspaper or magazine, whereas the electronic media channels were limited in number (until the advent of cable television), thrusting greater responsibility on the shoulders of those granted the right to use those channels.

The FCC has vacillated in control over the electronic media, depending on the political bent of those appointed to this important body. In 1941 the commission in a case concerning the Mayflower Broadcasting Corporation of Boston ruled against editorializing on radio, declaring that "the broad-caster cannot be an advocate." Eight years later, however, the FCC reversed itself and decided that broadcasters could—and should—"editorialize with fairness," including the right of reply. But the Fairness Doctrine has since been rescinded. No longer do broadcasters express their views in clearly labeled editorial comments at the end of a news program, but almost every segment on national television news today ends with a thinly veiled editorial assessment by the correspondent of the news just presented.

The "equal-time" rule—granting political opponents the same air space to reply—has proved more durable. In 1959 the FCC exempted legitimate newscasts and news programs from the "equal-time" requirement, and a decade later the Supreme Court upheld the "equal-time" rule. It took an act of Congress to allow the Kennedy-Nixon presidential cam-paign debate of 1960 to exclude the numerous other contend-ers. Yet since the administration of Ronald Reagan (1981–1989) deregulation has been the trend, with a noticeable deteriora-tion in program quality. The Telecommunications Act of 1996, the first since 1934, "gave away" $80 billion in free digital channels, in the view of Robert Dole, former senator and 1996 Republican presidential candidate.

Edward R. Murrow once said that the trouble with televi-sion news was that it could not decide whether to impart in-formation or entertainment. Unfortunately, the line has become blurred, as several of the following selections will show. And we have the phenomenon of the proliferating talk shows. What will some future historian or anthropologist think of a culture in which people sit around and passively watch other people talk—without any possibility of interac-tion? Opinions may be formed by listening to what comedi-ans, actors, singers, "analysts," "consultants" (and others who are plugging usually ghost-written books) think of national and world events.

The influence of these shows probably should not be un-derestimated. Larry King says that he is not a journalist but rather an "infotainer" whose prime-time show on CNN (the news channel) is beamed to 170 million households in 210 countries. As Fred Tasker has written, "King may perfectly embody the late '90s melding of TV entertainment and traditional journalism."² On the other hand, the NBC show *Meet the Press*, which reaches the opinion-makers and introduces the public to informed journalists discussing the issues, celebrated its fiftieth anniversary in 1997, the longest-running network program.

H. V. Kaltenborn: The Voice of Reason

Radio—and later television—networks created a mammoth audience with programs driven by ratings that even nationally printed newspapers such as the *New York Times*, the *Wall Street Journal*, the *Christian Science Monitor*, and *USA Today* cannot begin to match. The networks also brought celebrity status to persons ranging from the hate-mongering talk-show hosts to Walter Cronkite and other distinguished journalists. Newspaper columnists acquired followings, but not to the extent of the radio and television commentators. With radio we learned to respond to the authenticity of the voice, whether it be that of H. V. Kaltenborn, Edward R. Murrow, Lowell Thomas, Howard K. Smith, or other commentators.

The first of the networks to create these luminaries was the National Broadcasting Company, which was formed in 1927 under David Sarnoff as a subsidiary of the Radio Corporation of America; it was followed by the Columbia Broadcasting System led by William S. Paley. In 1934 four independent stations formed the now defunct Mutual Broadcasting System, and in 1943 pressure from the FCC brought the sale of NBC's Blue Network to Edward J. Noble, who renamed it the American Broadcasting Company.

Thus live radio newscasting was hitting its stride as World War II approached, and H. V. Kaltenborn performed a prodigious feat of live reporting during the Munich crisis of 1938 when Great Britain and France allowed Hitler to keep the Sudetenland of Czechoslovakia for "peace in our time." For twenty tense days when the world sought to avoid war, H. V. Kaltenborn made 102 broadcasts, ranging from two minutes to two hours each, grabbing a nap on a cot in the New York

CBS studio whenever possible. Bulletins from correspondents scattered across Europe were fed to him, and roundtable hook-ups with them also brought the crisis home.

As budgets for foreign coverage by all news media are being slashed today, it is well to remember that at the time of the Munich conference, NBC and CBS were willing to spend a total of $200,000 in uninflated currency to cover the crisis. And ultimately it taught the country a lesson against appeasement. Kaltenborn recalled the impact of his broadcasts:

> The intensity with which America listened to the radio reports of the Munich crisis was without parallel in radio history. Portable radio sets which had just been developed had a tremendous sale. People carried them to wherever they went, to restaurants, offices, and on the streets. That was the day of taxicab radios and every standing cab was surrounded by crowds as on World Series days. Here was a world series with a vengeance! Never before had so many listened so long to so much. Millions of Americans concentrated intently as they heard the words: "America calling Prague. . . . London. . . . Come in, Paris. . . . Berlin. . . . Munich."[3]

Yet, as Eric Sevareid points out below, television—which broke on the commercial scene in the late 1940s—is not radio with pictures. It is an entirely different medium, although there were bridges between the two. Newsreels such as Fox Movie-Tone News, although laden with propaganda and publicity gimmicks for Hollywood starlets, were shown in every theater before the feature film. Of higher caliber was Henry Luce's *March of Time* (1931–1951), which was a half-hour documentary aired on radio and later shown in theaters and on television.

Television also learned from Luce's *Life* photographers after that magazine was founded in 1936 and later became a victim of the new medium. In the concept of photojournalism, pictures do not illustrate the text but rather advance the story, or perhaps tell it entirely. Again, television was not illustrated radio (or should not be "talking heads"), although one bridge again was crossed by H. V. Kaltenborn. During World War II people were so avid for information that the commentator answered before a newsreel crew questions submitted by common Americans. His filmed responses were shown periodically in Newsreel Theatre in San Francisco, Embassy Newsreel Theatres in New York, and in the Telenews Theatres of Chicago and many other cities. The voice and demeanor of Kaltenborn, plus his great learning—except on election eve of 1948, when he early predicted victory for Thomas E. Dewey over Harry S. Truman—carried authority. Some of these questions and answers are presented in *Kaltenborn Edits the War News* by H. V. Kaltenborn (1941). From there it was just a hop, skip, and jump to television commentary.

Eric Sevareid Defends Television

While some whacked away at television's faults, others within the young industry defended its good points. Among these was commentator and journalist Eric Sevareid, who, like Walter Cronkite, had firm grounding in the print medium before going on the airwaves. In 1939, Sevareid joined Edward R. Murrow's staff in Europe, an illustrious group that continued to perform with distinction after going their separate ways after the war. In his thirty-eight years with CBS, Sevareid was news analyst at fifteen national political conventions and roving correspondent in Europe, offering nightly commentary from 1959 to 1961. Here are excerpts from his speech before the Washington Journalism Center in 1976: "What's Right with Sight-and-Sound Journalism," an important document adapted for publication in the *Saturday Review*.

A kind of adversary relationship between print journalism and electronic journalism exists and has existed for many years. As someone who has toiled in both vineyards, I am troubled by much of the criticism I read. Innumerable newspaper critics seem to insist that broadcast journalism be like *their* journalism and measured by their standards. It cannot be. The two are more complementary than competitive, but they *are* different.

The journalism of sight and sound is the only truly new form of journalism to come along. It is a *mass* medium, a universal medium; as the American public-education system is the world's first effort to teach everyone, so far as that is possible. It has serious built-on limitations as well as advantages, compared with print. Broadcast news operates in linear time, newspapers in lateral space. This means that a newspaper or magazine reader can be his own editor in a vital sense. He can glance over it and decide what to read, what to pass by. The TV viewer is a restless prisoner, obliged to sit through what does not interest him to get to what may interest him. While it is being shown, a bus accident at Fourth and Main has as much impact, seems as important, as an outbreak of a big war. We can do little about this, little about the viewer's unconscious resentments.

Everybody watches television to some degree, including most of those who pretend they don't. Felix Frankfurter was right, he said there is no highbrow in any lowbrow, but there is a fair amount of lowbrow in every highbrow. Television is a combination mostly of lowbrow and middlebrow, but there is more highbrow offered than highbrows will admit or even seek to know about. They will make plans, go to trouble and expense, when they buy a book or reserve a seat in the theater. They will not study the week's offerings of music or drama or serious documentation in the radio- and TV-program pages of their newspaper and then schedule themselves to be present. They want to come home, eat dinner, twist the dial, and find something agreeable ready, accommodating to *their* schedule.

For TV, the demand-supply equation is monstrously distorted. After a few years' experience with it in Louisville, Mark Ethridge said that television is a voracious monster that consumes Shakespeare, talent, and money at a voracious rate. As a station manager once said to a critic, "Hell, there isn't even enough mediocrity to go around."

TV programming consumes eighteen to twenty-four hours a day, 365 days of the year. No other medium of information or entertainment ever tried anything like that. How many good new plays appear in the theaters of this country each year? How many fine new motion pictures? Add it all together and perhaps you could fill twenty evenings out of the 365. As for music, including the finest music, it is there for a twist of the dial on any radio set in any big city of the land. It was radio, in fact, that created the audiences for music, good and bad, as nothing ever had before it. . . .

Now, at this point the reader must be thinking, what's this fellow beefing about? He's had an unusually long ride on the crest of the wave; he's highly paid. He's generally accepted as an honest practitioner of his trade. All true. I have indeed been far more blessed than cursed in my own lifework.

But I am saying what I am saying here—I am finally violating Ed Murrow's old precept that one never, but never, replies to critics—because it has seemed to me that someone must. Because the criticism exchange between print and broadcasting is a one-way street. Because a mythology is being slowly, steadily, set in concrete.

Why this intense preoccupation of the print press with the broadcast press and its personae? Three reasons at least: broadcasting, inescapably, is the most personal form of journalism ever, so there is a premium on personalities. The networks are the only true national news organs we have. And, third, competition between them and between local stations is intense, as real as it used to be between newspapers.

So the searchlight of scrutiny penetrates to our innards. Today we can scarcely make a normal organizational move without considering the press reaction. Networks, and even some stations, cannot reassign a reporter or anchorman, suspend anyone, discharge anyone, without a severe monitoring in the newspapers. Papers, magazines, wire services, don't have to live with that and would very much resent it if they did.

We live with myths, some going far back but now revived. The myth that William L. Shirer was fired by Ed Murrow and fired because he was politically too liberal. He wasn't fired at all; but even so good a historian as Barbara Tuchman fell for that one. The myth that Ed Murrow was forced out of CBS. At that point in his great career, President Kennedy's offer to Ed to join the government, at cabinet level, was probably the best thing that could have happened to him. The myth that Fred Friendly resigned over an issue of high principle involving some public-service air time. There are other such myths, and a new generation of writers are perpetuating them in their books, which are read and believed by a new generation of students and practitioners of journalism.

We have had the experience of people leaving, freely or under pressure, then playing their case in the papers to a fare-thee-well; they are believed because of that preconceived image of the networks in the minds of the writers. What does a big corporation do? Slug it out with the complainant, point by point, in the papers? Can it speak out at all when the real issue is the personal character and behavior of the complainant, which has been the truth in a few other cases? It can't. So it takes another beating in the press.

There is the myth that the CBS News Division—I am talking about CBS, of course, because it is the place I know and because it is the network most written about these days—has been somehow shoved out to the periphery of the parent corporation, becoming more and more isolated. What has happened is that it has achieved, and been allowed, more and more autonomy because it is fundamentally different from any other corporate branch. Therefore it is more and more independent.

There is the myth that the corporation is gradually de-emphasizing news and public affairs. In the last sixteen years since CBS News became a separate division, its budget has increased 600 percent, its personnel more than 100 percent. It does *not* make money for the company; it is a loss leader, year after year. I would guess it spends more money to cover the news than any other news organization in the world today. This is done because network news servicing has become a public trust and need.

There is the myth that since the pioneering, groundbreaking TV programs of Murrow and Friendly, CBS News has been less daring, done fewer programs of a hard-hitting kind. The Murrow programs are immortal in this business because they were the *first*. Since then we have dealt, forthrightly, with every conceivable controversial issue one can think of—drugs, homosexuality, government corruption, business corruption, TV commercials, gun control, pesticides, tax frauds, military waste, abortion, the secrets of the Vietnam War—everything. What shortage has occurred, has been on the side of the materials, not on the side of our willingness to tackle them.

In case I had missed something myself, I have recently inquired of other CBS News veterans if they can recall a single case of a proposed news story or a documentary that was killed by executives of the parent organization. Not one comes to anyone's mind. Some programs have been anathema to the top executive level, but they were not stopped. Some have caused severe heartburn at that level when they went on the air. Never has there been a case of people at that level saying to the News Division, "Don't ever do anything like that again."

For thirteen years I have done commentary—personal opinion inescapably involved—most nights of the week on the evening news. In that time exactly three scripts of mine were killed because of their substance by CBS News executives. Each one by a different executive, and none of them ever did it again. Three—out of more than 2,000 scripts. How many newspaper editorialists or columnists, how many magazine writers, have had their copy so respected by their editors?

There is the perennial myth that sponsors influence, positively or negatively, what we put on the air. They play no role whatever. No public-affairs program has ever been canceled because of sponsor objection. Years ago, they played indirect roles. When I started doing a six P.M. radio program, nearly thirty years ago, Ed Murrow, then a vice-president, felt it necessary to take me to lunch with executives of the Metropolitan Insurance Company, the sponsors. About fourteen years ago, when I was doing the Sunday-night TV news, a representative of the advertising agency handling the commercials would appear in the studio, though he never tried to change anything. Today one never sees a sponsor or an agency man, on the premises or off.

There is the myth, which seems to be one of the flawed premises of so successful a reporter as David Halberstam, that increased corporate profitability has meant a diminished emphasis on news and public affairs. The reverse, of course, is the truth. . . .

We are not the worst people in the land, we who work as journalists. Our product in print or on the air is a lot better, more educated, and more responsible than it was when I began, some forty-five years ago, as a cub reporter. This has been the best generation of all in which to have lived as a journalist in this country. We are no longer starvelings, and we sit above the salt. We have affected our times.

It has been a particular stroke of fortune to have been a journalist in Washington these years. There has not been a center of world news to compare with this capital city since ancient Rome. We have done the job better, I think, than our predecessors, and our successors will do it better than we. I see remarkable young talents all around.

That's the way it should be. I will watch them come on, maybe with a little envy, but with few regrets for the past. For myself, I wouldn't have spent my working life much differently had I been able to.[4]

Edward R. Murrow: A Tribute by Theodore White

In this country's first university course in radio broadcasting at Washington State College at Pullman in the late 1920s, one of the students was Edward R. Murrow, whose name conjures up the finest in American television news. Although a speech major, Murrow went on in 1937 to become head of CBS European news, where he fought to select such men for his staff as William L. Shirer and others for their reportorial skills, not the quality of their voices—in an age when radio was flourishing. Shirer later wrote *The Rise and Fall of the Third Reich* (1960), a classic of modern journalism and history. But Americans became most familiar with Murrow's deep, dramatic voice during the Battle for Britain in 1940 when he opened his live newscast every night, as air raid sirens and bursting bombs sounded in the background, "This . . . is London."

Constantly at odds with producers who regarded the electronic media as simply a business enterprise and not an educational force of living history, Murrow and Fred W. Friendly after the war produced *Hear It Now* on radio, which became *See It Now* on television in 1951. Murrow used the visual impact of the new medium to great effect, as in documentaries such as *Harvest of Shame*, portraying the plight of migrant farm workers. But he is perhaps best remembered for crossing swords with Senator Joseph R. McCarthy of Wisconsin, taking risks the print medium seemed unwilling to do. McCarthy, who bullied his way to national prominence by exploiting fear of communism at the depth of the Cold War, ruined unjustly many reputations with half-truths, innuendo, guilt by association, or outright lies. It all began in 1950 at a speech in West Virginia, when he waved a sheet of paper, declaring, "I have in my hand . . ." the names of 205 members of the State Department with Communist ties. Incredibly, not one of several reporters present asked to see the paper, which McCarthy later joked was his laundry list. The witchhunt was on, with probes that involved prominent persons in government, education, entertainment—even the military. Murrow unmasked McCarthy's demagoguery in a historic telecast of March 9, 1954, mainly using the senator's own recorded statements to indict him. But as Murrow pointed out, it was not communism that was on trial, but rather objectivity. Some reporters argued that McCarthy was a U.S. senator and what he said was news, but others asserted that putting quotation marks around a lie did not make it true. The televised Army-McCarthy hearings of 1954 further eroded McCarthy's credibility, and the Senate later censured him.

The following article from *TV Guide* in 1986 captures the human qualities of Murrow as remembered by a fellow journalist—of the print medium—Theodore White, who informed and amused America with his four timely book-length series on every presidential election between 1960 and 1972, *The Making of the President*. White, also the author of *In Search of History* and other books, pays tribute to his friend of twenty years.

It is so difficult to recapture the real Ed Murrow from the haze that now shrouds the mythical Ed Murrow of history. Where other men may baffle friends with the infinite complexity of their natures, Ed was baffling otherwise. He was so straightforward, he would completely baffle the writers who now unravel the neuroses of today's demigods of television. When Ed was angry, he bristled; when he gave friendship, it came without withholding.

He could walk with prime ministers and movie stars, GIs and generals, as natural in rumpled GI suntans as in his diplomatic homburg. But jaunty or somber, to those of us who knew him he was just plain old Ed. In his shabby office at CBS, cluttered with awards, you could loosen your necktie, put your feet up and yarn away. The dark, overhanging eyebrows would arch as he punctured pretension with a jab, the mouth would twist quizically as he questioned. And then there were his poker games, as Ed sat master of the table, a cigarette dangling always from his lips—he smoked 60 or 70 a day—and called the bets.

Then—I can hear him now—there was the voice. Ed's deep and rhythmic voice was compelling, not only for its range, halfway between bass and baritone, but for the words that rolled from it. He wrote for the ear—with a cadence of pauses and clipped, full sentences. His was an aural art but, in Ed, the art was natural—his inner ear composed a picture and, long before TV, the imagination of his listeners caught the sound and made with it their own picture.

We remember the voice. But there was so much more to Ed. He had not only a sense of the news but a sense of how the news fit into history. And this sense of the relation of news to history is what, in retrospect, made him the great pioneer of television journalism. His exploration of television's new range was so powerful in its impact on our dreams and lives that in American journalism only Horace Greeley and Walter Lippmann matched him in shaping our history.

He had begun very young, as assistant director of the Institute of International Education; gone to Europe; arranged broadcasts; then made them himself. And, as the Nazis attacked England, Ed gave his heart to the British. His sign off—"This . . . is London"—was the sound of resistance. To the heart Ed added his mastery of the microphone. He caught the thudding of the bombs over London, the patter of feet hurrying to shelter in the stinking subways. Ed flew with the bombers. A modern investigative reporter would have told us that the British bombers were hideous contraptions, deathtraps when hit. But, for Ed, the straight story was more important—the valor of the men who flew such planes into Nazi flak.

He stayed with radio after the war. He and Fred Friendly, his producer, created the radio show *Hear It Now* from their recording, "I Can Hear It Now." And then they moved on to television with *See It Now*.

Television was a giant step in the power of the electronic media—and its magic tantalized Ed. In the fall of 1951, the engineers of AT&T had just completed their hookup of microwave towers and coaxial cables that linked the country coast to coast. Ed tested it. On Sunday afternoon, Nov. 18, 1951, on *See It Now*'s first broadcast, he sat in a CBS studio in New York's Grand Central Terminal building and invited America to look at itself. He swiveled his chair and showed two monitors—on the one was the Brooklyn Bridge in New York, on the other the Golden Gate in San Francisco: both live and simultaneous. The country was now one continental arena. You could see it now—a moment equivalent to Leland Stanford driving the Golden Spike to link the Nation's railways at Promontory Point, Utah, in 1869. In 1948, only 18 states had been able to see the national conventions in Philadelphia on the East Coast hookup. By 1952, the whole country could watch the proceedings at the Republican convention in Chicago—and television's power became instant clout. Television destroyed [Robert] Taft and nominated Ike [Dwight D. Eisenhower].

Ed was never reluctant to use the power of the tube—and, when he used it, he could rouse thunder. By 1954, he had had enough of Joe McCarthy, that alcoholic and reckless political terrorist who perverted American loathing of communism into a witch hunt of innocents. Murrow took to the air. On the night of March 9, in an immaculate broadcast devoid of any denunciation, Murrow displayed the senator from Wisconsin at his wheezing, halting, tormenting best—which, of course, was his worst. When Ed had finished, McCarthy's career was finished, too.

CBS tried to make Ed into an executive—as vice-president of public affairs. Murrow was, of course, a superb executive, with exquisite taste in men and policy. During the war, he had put together from unknowns the world's finest corps of correspondents. He had chosen two young Rhodes scholars—Charles Collingwood, 23, and Howard K. Smith, 27. He chose Eric Sevareid, then 26. He had found and chosen, or was to choose, William Shirer, Fred Friendly, David Schoenbrun, Larry LeSueur, Winston Burdett, Richard Hottelet, Ed Morgan, all of whom went on to fame.

But Ed did not want to be an executive and he went back to broadcasting. He loved probing events and connecting them to history. Ed's boys, as they called themselves, were fundamentally newsmen who could report, talk—and also connect. He cherished them all, but liked to tease now and then by calling them "Buster." For those who fell behind in the race, Ed always had a job or knew an opening they could fill. Some he would put in place as drafters of his "think pieces." For others he would be the first who called in a time of misfortune, as he called me after *Collier's* magazine collapsed in 1956 and I was jobless. "I saw what happened," he said, "How would you like to go to Washington as our correspondent?" To another, burnishing his new celebrity with mock modesty, Ed said, "Listen, Buster, you aren't important enough to be that modest."

By the late 1950s, Ed was suffering from burnout—a psychological afflic-tion of television's personalities akin to silicosis among miners. He was no longer content to observe and report; he wanted to be part of the action itself—history was his calling, news only his trade. So he joined the adminis-tration of John F. Kennedy and, as director of the U.S. Information Agency, insisted on a voice in policy. He was wiser than either Kennedy's Secretary of Defense or Secretary of State. But he had not long to go. The ever-dangling cigarette had ravaged his health. One lung was removed on Oct. 6, 1963, and so he was in his bed the day Kennedy was shot. But he was alert to the tube, and when I called him that weekend, he was savoring the tech-nical wizardry of the funeral ceremonies.

Ed was not to last long after that. The cancer spread to a tumor near the brain and, when I last saw him, his head was swathed in white bandages. I thought this would be a solemn and mournful visit to a friend I cherished, but Ed opened the conversation by saying, "Say, Buster, how do you like my new haircut?" And we went on to happy reminiscence.

He died shortly after that—at 57, so young that it now seems that fate itself had decided to cut short his honors.

He is very large now, for it was he who set the news system of television on its tracks, holding it, and his descendants, to the sense of history that gives it still, in the schlock-storm of today, its sense of honor. Of Ed Murrow it may be said that he made all of us who clung to him, and cling to his memory still, feel larger than we really were.[5]

David Brinkley: A Nation Goes to a Funeral

More than a decade before David Brinkley finally retired from newscasting in 1998, leaving his Sunday-morning ABC show, *This Week with David Brinkley*, he had, in his words, "done the news longer than anyone on earth." Network television news began with the fifteen-minute evening broadcasts for NBC of John Cameron Swayze, supplanted in 1956 by the team of Brinkley in Washington, DC, and Chet Huntley in New York. On other occasions, both men did individual shows. But un-til Huntley retired in 1970 (he died four years later) and Brinkley moved from NBC to ABC in 1981, for fourteen years the *Huntley-Brinkley Report* was often the top-ranked news program in television. It was a felicitous combination—the straightforward Huntley from Montana and the wry Brinkley from North Carolina. The latter once described Washington as "ten square miles surrounded on all sides by reality." To critics who said he editorialized by his mere facial expressions he responded, "The smirks and sneers are entirely in the eye of the beholder."[6] Actually, there was no tomfoolery such as in local television shows today, where performers—whom Walter Cronkite has called "pretty faces"—seem compelled to make little comments and laugh at their own inane "happy talk" as they read the news. In this regard, Chet Huntley's resolutions for 1955 on objectivity in the news bear repeating: "Resolved: To stop and think at least thirty minutes before offering one of my own opinions in a broadcast; that if my own opinion must be used, to label it as just opinion with the biggest verbal sign or billboard; . . . and to remember that some citizens don't deserve silencing—just answering . . . to face the East each morning and thank Mr. Sulzberger for the New York *Times*."[7]

The potential power of television over the printed word was made most vivid by the televised coverage of the events in Dallas on November 22, 1963, when John F. Kennedy was assassinated. The killing was followed by seventy-two hours of funeral coverage in Washington that tied together a nation mourning the loss of its youngest president. In his *Memoir*, David Brinkley recounts what it was like for a veteran reporter on that Friday afternoon in 1963 that no one will ever forget.

On Friday, November 22, 1963, I was in my office at NBC on Nebraska Avenue in Washington thinking about that night's *Huntley-Brinkley Report* and what news to put on it. There wasn't much. Some NATO business in Europe with Charles de Gaulle objecting as he usually did. President John Kennedy, a day or two before, when asked about some recent scandals in Washington, said he thought the ethical climate there was about the same as in other places. And now, on this Friday, he had gone to Texas at the invitation and urging of Vice President Lyndon Johnson. Since Kennedy's first term would end in about a year and since he had barely carried Texas in the 1960 election, it seemed a little politicking down there would not hurt. We decided to lead that night's news program with Kennedy's trip to Texas. Not because it was such a big story. It wasn't. But because that day there was nothing else.

It was a quiet Friday, and we were all looking forward to two days off, and my wife and I were planning to spend two days with friends in a pretty little country town in Virginia.

Robert MacNeil, then an NBC correspondent, went to Texas for NBC and rode along in an open-top car in a motorcade behind the president. He heard shots fired up ahead. He was young enough and fleet of foot enough to get to a telephone ahead of some dozen other newspeople desperately grasping for the few telephones available around Dealey Plaza in Dallas. MacNeil dialed the news desk at NBC in New York, somebody answered, he screamed, "This is MacNeil in Dallas!" Before he could get the terrible news out, the voice in New York said, "Just a minute," put the phone down and *never came back* leaving MacNeil with the agony of having the biggest news story of his life and unable to get it out. These were the most agonizing moments he ever knew. Merriman Smith of United Press International was riding in a Secret Service car with a built-in phone. He grabbed it and dictated to UPI one of the two shortest news stories ever written: "JFK shot." The only other news flash this short was moved on the INS wire in 1945 when Franklin Roosevelt died: "FDR dead."

At NBC, whoever answered the phone and then left MacNeil hanging was tracked down and fired the next morning, his crime so hideous the network would never say who he was. In the meantime, Huntley and I were told to get into our New York and Washington studios and keep the news going. Before we could reach the studios, an NBC staff announcer gave the news, his voice trembling so severely he could hardly get the words out: "President Kennedy was shot in Dallas today. Blood was seen on the President's head as they rushed him to a hospital. Mrs. Kennedy was heard to exclaim, 'Oh, no!' "

At that hour, 1:45 in the afternoon, the network normally is not busy and the affiliate stations are running local programs, but in less than two minutes it was all pulled together and stayed together for seventy hours and twenty-seven minutes, all day and all night, giving the American people the horrible news and showing them everything as fast as we could bring it in. From that Friday afternoon we went, as all the networks did, without a halt until 1:16 A.M. the following Tuesday morning with no entertainment programs and no commercials. Such wretchedly terrible news was frightening to people who already were afraid the country was coming apart, and in times of such stress we all knew as everyone knew that ugly rumors begin and spread rapidly. We stayed on the air to show the new president being sworn in, showing that our constitutional processes were continuing as usual and giving President Johnson the microphone to speak some reassuring words to a people who desperately needed them. All of us in television believed or hoped that in these three days we had helped the American people get through one of the most difficult and frightening times in their history.

Even so, there were rumors that this was a part of a plot emanating from Communist Cuba or the Soviet Union or some other dangerous place. In the first hours we did not know for sure which of the rumors, if any, were true, and so we all decided we could do nothing but report the news as we got it and deliver it without histrionics or emotional displays.

In the years after, speculation and guesswork about the Kennedy murder became somewhere close to a heavy industry. More than two hundred books and one very bad movie tried, or pretended to try, to prove who shot Kennedy, why, who else was involved and what the motive was. Many of them were nonsensical. For example, a very silly book by Edward Jay Epstein argued tediously that Earl Warren and the other famous members of his commission did very little of its work, leaving most of it to the staff. Of course they did. That was how it was, and is, always done. The chief justice and the other respected public figures were appointed to give the commission a weight and seriousness and to encourage public acceptance of its report when it came. They could not be expected to spend months studying reports from the FBI, the CIA, the Dallas police, the Zapruder film, ballistics experts, the surgeons, the pathologists and hundreds of eyewitnesses. They were not equipped for this kind of work anyway, so the controversy was unending. In late summer 1993, there was one more book, *Case Closed*, by Gerald Posner, that seemed to me and to some others to finally settle it all. I think Posner's book proved that Lee Harvey Oswald alone killed Kennedy and that no other country nor any other person or group was involved, and the motive, if it can be called that, was a product of madness. Which is what I had always believed. Others still argue there was some evil conspiracy. I doubt all the questions will ever be answered.

The networks stayed on the air throughout, down to the funeral, Kennedy's young son saluting his father's coffin, and the American flag being folded into a triangle. I believe it was television's finest hour.[8]

"Why Television News Is on the Decline"

The above was the headline on the Commentary page of the *Philadelphia Inquirer* on March 30, 1993, reacting to the revelation that *Dateline-NBC* producers had rigged explosives under a GM pickup truck being tested, producing a bigger bang for the television buck when the vehicle hit a solid wall.

The outcome is detailed below by Arthur A. Lord, a senior producer for NBC News and one of three NBC News veterans assigned to look into the matter.

Unfortunately, faking the news crops up every so often in the history of American journalism, from the Moon Hoax of the nineteenth century to Janet Cooke's fictitious account of an eight-year-old heroin addict for the *Washington Post* that won her a Pulitzer Prize—recalled when the hoax was discovered—and ended her job. More recently, it was revealed that artists accentuated the Negroid facial features of O. J. Simpson for a *Time* cover during his murder trial, and straightened the teeth of the mother of the septuplets. All of this comes straight out of the "Jazz Journalism" of the 1920s, when photographs were cut and pasted to form misleading composite pictures.

The visual media are much more vulnerable to this kind of manipulation. Great photographs become icons, but some were posed. It was reported afterward, for example, that AP photographer Joseph Rosenthal had the Marines who were hoisting the flag on Mt. Suribachi on Iwo Jima in 1945 repeat it several times before he got what he wanted. General MacArthur waded ashore several times when he returned to the Philippines so the newsreel cameras would get a good shot. The badly burned baby at the fall of Shanghai was grabbed from its mother's arms and placed on a train platform against a backdrop of burning buildings by an overly eager photographer. Finally, the most famous fake of all was the newsreel showing Hitler doing a little victory jig while walking away from the camera after learning of the fall of Paris. Actually, the film was advanced and reversed and advanced again by the British propaganda office to simulate the cocky little victory dance while the lights went out in Paris.

No one denies that all of the media are in business to make money, but some creative persons are led astray to dramatize and exaggerate at any cost whatever will increase circulation or boost television ratings. Faking the news, in whatever medium, destroys credibility and ultimately may impair markets themselves. When one criticizes the current wave of sensationalism in tabloid television, which blurs fact and fiction while posing as news shows, the answer is usually, "But that's what people want!" Perhaps, but a balance must be struck between responsibility and revenue. As William Allen White said long ago, "The purpose of the press is not to follow public opinion, but to lead it." Here's what Arthur A. Lord has to say on the subject.

On the desk beside me as I write this is a document titled "Report of Inquiry Into Crash Demonstrations Broadcast on Dateline NBC Nov. 17, 1992." The report, containing more than 70 pages, is the end result of six weeks of investigation by a team of highly paid and capable lawyers, examining how a national news network of high repute managed to put 57 seconds of video on the air—57 seconds that put in jeopardy 67 years of broadcasting achievement.

On the plus side, NBC News has been exceedingly candid by revealing the lawyers' findings to the employees of the company, to the public and to the rest of the media. Those who were responsible for the rigged GM pickup truck crash test were named and held accountable. Three Dateline producers have resigned. The correspondent who voiced the broadcast, Michelle Gillen, has been transferred to the NBC station in Miami.

The biggest personnel casualty was Michael Gartner, president of NBC News, who resigned after unsuccessfully trying to justify what turned out to be one of the biggest gaffes in the history of broadcast journalism. Detailed explanations of sloppy journalistic practice, errors in judgment and a serious lack of a sense of fairness are hanging out there between those pages for everyone to see, warts and all.

On the minus side, for someone like me, who has invested 25 years of personal and professional life at NBC News, I view the report as having the size, weight and gaiety of a tombstone. For anyone who cares about the news profession, the GM/Dateline-NBC affair is painful and embarrassing.

Even after reading the report, there's a tendency to ask a self-delusional question, "How did this happen?" In truth we know how it happened.

The entire news business, broadcast and print, has experienced a gradual but steady downward spiral in the last 15 years. Most metropolitan areas in the United States have only one daily newspaper. Many local TV stations put on newscasts that are a joke and most local radio stations don't even bother to cover news in the communities they're supposed to serve.

More media have fallen into fewer hands. Absentee owners or huge corporations may run the news in a town where the only time they appear there is for a board meeting, for window dressing, or to figure out new ways to squeeze more money out of the property. At the networks, we thought we were immune to this kind of thing. We were wrong.

At ABC News, when State Department employee Felix Bloch was accused a few years ago of passing secrets to the Soviets, they hired a pair of actors to simulate the crime.

At CBS News last January, the *Evening News with Dan Rather* did a story on Katie Beers, a 10-year-old girl from Long Island who had been held prisoner in a dungeon under the family garage. They had no access to Katie because she was under the protection of juvenile authorities, so they put together a video tone poem where the viewer saw a youngster in scruffy clothes representing Katie, wandering the streets, photographed from the waist down.

In both cases many in the viewing audience did not realize that they were watching a re-enactment. The fine line between real video shot as it happens and some contrived event staged for the camera became fuzzy.

Pile onto that the plethora of tabloid TV shows like *Current Affair* and *Inside Edition*, and there is little wonder why the public is confused about the veracity of what it is seeing. Even some of our colleagues who labor in the vineyards have seemingly forgotten what they learned in journalism school.

Since the General Electric Company bought NBC, the news division has been under relentless pressure to cut costs and make profits, just as GE's light bulb factories do. Experienced correspondents, producers and technicians were let go, to be replaced by freelancers, daily hires and the inexperienced.

NBC News bureaus in Houston, San Francisco, Miami, Paris, Rome and Frankfurt were closed to save money. So now we cover stories in Central America from Washington, the war in Bosnia from London and so on.

Satellite communication makes it easy. If there's a massacre in Sarajevo, some cameraman we don't even know will make it to the transmission point and feed pictures of the incident to the network. Maybe the cameraman is a propagandist, maybe the video is faked. Our people receiving the transmission try to check it out by remote control, but there's no substitute for having your own person on the ground.

Given the climate, it is fair to say the GM/Dateline-NBC fiasco did not happen in a vacuum. It may, in fact, be the result of a general decline in standards. Too much emphasis has been placed on ratings and profits and not nearly enough on sound journalism. Tabloid values have found their way into some of our news programs. Quality has been sacrificed in an effort to attract ever larger audiences at ever lower costs. Such pressure creates situations where inexperienced, insecure or overly ambitious people cut corners to achieve what they perceive to be management's goals.

After the report was released on March 22, NBC President Robert Wright cleared up any doubts about management's goals. "These journalistic and administrative failures are indefensible," he said. "They should not have happened. They should never again be allowed to happen, and they must not happen again at NBC News."

A blaring wake-up call for all of us.[9]

Walter Cronkite: *A Reporter's Life*

In 1973 an Oliver Quayle public opinion survey revealed that 73 percent of those polled regarded Walter Cronkite, the CBS newscaster, as the most trusted public figure in the United States, outranking the president himself, who came in with 57 percent. The results, with the usual margin of error but reasonably accurate, were a tribute to the evenhandedness of Cronkite as a television journalist and as a person, but it raised some disturbing questions about the cult of personality in television; some readers still preferred to get their news by the printed word, eliminating the middleman in the form of the broadcaster. Walter Cronkite is the first to criticize sharply the electronic media to which he has devoted most of his life, as indicated in his autobiography *A Reporter's Life* (1996). How does one account for Cronkite's continuing popularity from the time he joined CBS News in 1950—after solid print experience with the United Press—until his "retirement" in 1981? Perhaps David Halberstam of the *New York Times* put it best when he referred to Cronkite's appeal as that of "the definite centrist American who reflects the essential decency of American society as much as anyone can."[10]

Cronkite was anchorman of the *CBS Evening News with Walter Cronkite* from 1962 to 1981. He had become a United Press correspondent in 1939, covered many of the decisive battles of World War II, and then served as UP bureau chief in Moscow until 1948. A veteran reporter, he urged early on that the evening news on television be allotted an hour rather than half an hour, to do justice to the complexities of the present world (PBS later did this with the *MacNeil-Lehrer Report*, then the *Lehrer Report*). Cronkite also has fought tenaciously to keep opinion out of television news segments, maintaining in an interview for the *Christian Science Monitor* (December 26, 1973): "I am a news presenter, a news broadcaster, an anchorman, a managing editor—not a commentator or analyst. I feel no compulsion to be a pundit." His autobiography is another matter, however, and in it Cronkite speaks his mind. A portion of his concluding chapter is given below.

A career can be called a success if one can look back and say: "I made a difference." I don't feel I can do that. All of us in those early days of television felt, I'm sure, that we were establishing a set of standards that would be observed by, or at least have an influence on, generations of news professionals to come. How easily these were dismissed by the Van Gordon Sauters and those who felt they had to imitate to compete.

The infotainment trend has been exacerbated in recent years by the network fight to hang on to a viable share of a shrinking pie. Cable, the increasingly important independent stations and video recordings have reduced the total network audience to barely half of what it once was. The news departments have moved from the loss leaders of my years to profit centers, and management now considers ratings more important than prestige.

I don't envy those many serious broadcast journalists on both sides of the microphone who must live in this environment. The lack of respect in which they are held by their network managers is rubbed in their noses every day when the network-owned stations put the trashy syndicated tabloid "news" shows on in the preferred evening hours once occupied by the genuine news programs. That is a discouraging message from the executive suites to the newsrooms of the tastes, preferences and sense of responsibility of network brass.

Newspapers, under similar pressure of falling circulation, are also guilty today of trivializing the news. Much of the news is featurized, and a lot of it is condensed into "What Happened Today" columns. This led in the mid-nineties to a spate of criticism of the press, but most of it was misdireced, aimed as it was at the journalists. Basically, the problem is, again, the bottom line.

The shame is that most of our newspapers, for a variety of understandable reasons (not the least of which is confiscatory inheritance taxes), have passed from the hands of individual publishers to large chains. These corporate behemoths are forced by their stockholders and the "get mine" mores of the nineties to seek constantly expanding profits. Adequate profits are obviously necessary to the survival of any institution, but stockholder greed now demands super profits, their "maximization."

Newspapers and broadcasting, insofar as journalism goes, are public services essential to the successful working of our democracy. It is a travesty that they should be required to pay off like any other stock-market investment.

To play the downsizing game, the boards and their executives deny to their news managers enough funding to pay for the minimum coverage necessary to serve their consumers well. They reduce the amount of expensive newsprint available until editors do not have enough space for the news they need to cover. Good reporters, writers and editors are spread so thin that they cannot spend the necessary time developing the stories that the public needs and deserves. A more responsible press depends not upon individual journalists but upon more responsible owners. That is the real bottom line.

The future is cloudy in this area. The profits for the networks and the other big players may be further fragmented in the new communications era. How willing will they be then to finance the news and public affairs programming which the public expects, to which it is entitled, and which is fundamental to the nation's welfare?

As for the hundreds of special interests that in the future will supply programming for the multitude of satellite or cable channels or news sites on the Internet, it is unlikely that they will have the resources or the will to provide highly expensive, well-rounded, comprehensive news services. The big question is whether the major players in the new alignment—the entertainment and industrial giants—with no background in news and their focus primarily on profits from other sources, will be willing to underwrite the budget-bending business of serious news reporting. Will they continue even the level of reduced news and public affairs programming that their networks are providing today?

Will the journalism center hold in the changed economic environment of the future? In the last decade the networks have cut back news budgets while supporting in syndication the emergence of tabloid news shows, travesties of genuine news presentations. They bear the same relationship to the network news broadcasts as the *Enquirer* does to *The New York Times*.

Unfortunately, by targeting the lowest common denominator among the potential viewership, these schlock broadcasts lure audiences and make money. Financially hard-pressed network and local station executives, with their substantial budgets for legitimate news gathering, must look at the size of the audience for the tabloids with a gleam of jealousy and wonder if this might be the way to go. The danger, of course, is that the profitable bad has a way of driving out the unprofitable or marginally profitable good.

The major problem is simply that television news is an inadequate substitute for a good newspaper. It is not too far a stretch to say that the public's dependence on television for the bulk of its news endangers our democratic system. While television puts all other media in the shade in its ability to present in moving pictures the people and the places that make our news, it simultaneously fails in outlining and explaining the more complicated issues of our day.

For those who either cannot or will not read—equally shameful in a modern society—television lifts the floor of knowledge and understanding of the world around them. But for the others, through its limited exploration of the difficult issues, it lowers the ceiling of knowledge. Thus, television news provides a very narrow intellectual crawl space between its floor and ceiling.

The sheer volume of television news is ridiculously small. The number of words spoken in a half-hour broadcast barely equals the number of words on two thirds of a standard newspaper page. That is not enough to cover the day's major events at home and overseas. Hypercompression of facts, foreshortened arguments, the elimination of extenuating explanation—all are dictated by television's restrictive time frame and all distort to some degree the news available on television.

The TV correspondent as well as his subjects is a victim of this time compression, something that has come to be known as "soundbite journalism." With inadequate time to present a coherent report, the correspondent seeks to craft a final summary sentence that might make some sense of the preceding gibberish. This is hard to do without coming to a single point of view— and a one-line editorial is born. Similarly, a story of alleged misdeeds frequently ends with one sentence: "A spokesman denied the charges." No further explanation.

Television frequently repeats a newspaper story that is based on "informed sources." The newspaper may have carefully hedged the story with numerous qualifiers, but the time-shy newscast does not. More distortion.

The greatest victim in all this is our political process, and in my view this is one of the greatest blots on the recent record of television news. Soundbite journalism simply isn't good enough to serve the people in our national elections. Studies have shown that in 1988 the average block of uninterrupted speech by a presidential candidate on the network newscasts was 9.8 seconds. Nine point eight seconds! The networks faithfully promised to do better in 1992. The average sound bite that year was just 8.2 seconds. The networks promised to do better in 1996.[11]

Notes

1. *Philadelphia Inquirer*, October 30, 1990.

2. *Philadelphia Inquirer TV Week*, May 25, 1997.

3. H. V. Kaltenborn, *Fifty Fabulous Years, 1900-1950: A Personal Review* (New York: G. P. Putnam's Sons, 1950), 208.

4. Eric Sevareid, "What's Right with Sight-and-Sound Journalism," *Saturday Review* (October 2, 1976): 18–21.

5. Theodore H. White, "When He Used the Power of TV, He Could Rouse Thunder," *TV Guide* (January 18, 1986): 13–14.

6. Quoted in *Current Biography Yearbook 1987* (New York: H. W. Wilson, 1987), 70.

7. Reprinted in the *Reporter*, January 27, 1955, quoted in *Current Biography Yearbook 1956* (New York: H. W. Wilson, 1956), 291.

8. David Brinkley, *David Brinkley, A Memoir* (New York: Alfred A. Knopf, 1995), 155–58.

9. Arthur A. Lord, "Why Television News Is on the Decline," *Philadelphia Inquirer*, March 30, 1993.

10. Quoted in *Current Biography Yearbook 1975* (New York: H. W. Wilson, 1975), 95.

11. Walter Cronkite, *A Reporter's Life* (New York: Alfred A. Knopf, 1996), 373–76.

10

The Press and World Revolution

———⟨◆⟩———

Americans traditionally have been insular, with little or no interest in international affairs. Even today, a survey by the Associated Press of U.S. editors and broadcast news directors, as reported in *World Press Review* (March 1998), revealed that they included only three stories that remotely could be considered international in their selection of the top ten news stories for 1997. These were the death of Princess Diana (ranking first), the death of Mother Teresa (third), and turmoil in the financial markets (fourth). In his trip to Africa in 1998, President Clinton stated in Rwanda that he had not known the true dimensions of the genocidal slaughter that claimed 800,000 lives in the civil war there. The American news media had failed to cover one of the most tragic stories of the twentieth century, leaving both the public and policymakers uninformed.

Herbert L. Matthews, the celebrated and controversial reporter for the *New York Times* who covered the Republican, or anti-Fascist, side of the Spanish Civil War (1936–1939) and interviewed Fidel Castro in the Sierra Maestra of Cuba in 1957, entitled his memoir *A World in Revolution*.[1] Indeed it has been—and continues to be—despite the false sense of security that may have lulled many Americans into the comfortable belief that we "won" the Cold War and all is right with the world. Tragedies, such as that which some of the African and Asian and Latin American countries experience while struggling toward nationhood, are seen not only in Bosnia and the Middle East but also occur from Northern Ireland to North Korea. There are only a few areas in the world that have not been targeted by terrorists—and therefore also journalists, who are on the cutting edge of world revolution.

With some exceptions, three of which are presented below, American reporters have generally been insensitive or badly informed about the history unfolding before their eyes. Matthews in 1976, toward the end of his life, explained why there was so little reporting of Latin America in the United States and so much misunderstanding about the region: "The problem is one of *sustained* interest. When there is a revolution or assassination, of course, some news is printed. I decided that it was a vicious circle: readers are generally interested in what is familiar to them; since they are *not* interested in Latin America, editors will not provide money, personnel or space to educate them."[2]

The veteran correspondent went further: "The American mass media . . . tend to create a fantastic world. The picture they draw is a response to a pre-disposed public opinion which is both satisfied and molded by it."[3] Matthews, to stress his point, added: "Readers or radio and television listeners believed (in fact, wanted to believe) the worst about Cuba long before it became as bad as they thought. The result of this type of approach was to bring about, or to hasten, this 'worst' and that is what can happen whenever a leftist revolutionary situation develops or threatens in Latin America or anywhere else in the world."[4]

In fact, we in the United States today have so little concept of the meaning of the word "revolution" that we must be redundant and say "social revolution" to distinguish profound social change, usually but not always initiated with an armed phase, from a simple coup d'état, whether palace or barracks revolt. Social revolutions, such as those that unfolded in France after 1789, Mexico after 1910, Russia after 1917, China after 1949, and Cuba after 1959, have been relatively rare in world history. The Chinese, for example, had no word for "revolution" and had to describe the experience of their country after 1949 as "Change of Mandate from Heaven."

In the former British colonies that now comprise the United States, the dilemma was similar. In the judgment of Carl Becker and other historians, the events of 1776–1783 meant little more than a change of rulers—not home rule but who should rule at home. J. Franklin Jameson concurs, in his seminal work, *The American Revolution Considered as a Social Movement,* for there were no significant social changes in American life after victory at Yorktown. Political freedom is another matter altogether, although it too seems to have run its course. As historian Richard Maxwell Brown has written, "The long-range era of the American Revolution has at last come to an end, for it seems that the Revolution now has little impact as an inspiration for dissent and reform whether peaceable or violent."[5]

In his book *Listen, Yankee* the late sociologist C. Wright Mills expressed the thought that it is impossible for U.S. reporters to cover a social revolution adequately because the phenomenon is completely alien to their experience. He wrote: "Many North American journalists simply do not know how to understand and to report a revolution. If it is a real revolution—and Cuba's is certainly that—to report it involves more than the ordinary journalist's routine. It requires that the journalist abandon many of the clichés and habits which now make up his very craft. It certainly requires that he know something in detail about the great variety of left-wing thought and action in the world of today."[6]

Mills also blamed newspaper editors for their "demand for violent headlines [that] restrict and shape the copy journalists produce. Editors and journalists tend to feel that the American public would rather read about executions than about new lands put into cultivation. They print what they think is the salable commodity."[7] Mills implied that U.S. journalists, with their traditional up-the-ladder training, tend to cover the world as if it were a giant police court—with good guys and bad guys and themselves in the judge's seat. Matthews, who had firsthand experience in Cuba, concurred: "The academic world has been waking up to the true significance of the Cuban revolution before our mass communications media. This was perhaps to be expected because there is a goodly number of Latin Americanists in our universities and very few in journalism."[8] With the exception of Matthews and Ernest Hemingway, the reporters who wrote the selections that follow did not comment on their own work. Nor for the most part did their reportage appear in the mainstream

American press, so we must examine by indirection how they regarded coverage of the major social revolutions of their time.

Upheaval in Mexico

Signs of impending revolution frequently go completely unnoticed. The most salient example is the famous interview in 1908 by American journalist James Creelman with Porfirio Díaz, who ruled Mexico with an iron fist to create one of the lengthiest dictatorships in Latin American history (1876–1911). Creelman, who joined the staff of the *New York Herald* in 1878, worked there for two decades before becoming associate editor of *Pearson's Magazine*; the *Pearson's* interview with Díaz unwittingly touched off a social revolution. This adulatory interview of 1908 was entitled "President Díaz, Hero of the Americas," and it triggered political opposition that had largely lain dormant for decades. A presidential election was coming up in 1910, and the nearly octogenarian Díaz startled Mexicans with his declaration in the interview that "no matter what my friends and supporters say, I retire when my present term of office ends, and I shall not serve again. I shall be eighty years old then."[9] Apparently intending his remarks only for foreign consumption, Díaz went on to say, "I welcome an opposition party in the Mexican Republic. If it appears, I will regard it as a blessing, not as an evil. And if it can develop power, not to exploit but to govern, I will stand by it, support it, advise it and forget myself in the successful inauguration of complete democratic government in the country." Translated into Spanish, the interview appeared in the capital newspaper *El Imparcial* on March 3, 1908—probably because of Creelman's glowing comments on the Díaz regime. By promising honest elections, later thwarted, the Creelman interview set the political pot bubbling in Mexico that boiled over into revolution. (The Mexican government considered this interview so decisive in the revolutionary process that it published a facsimile edition, with translation, in 1963.) Creelman himself went on to write a book on *Díaz, Master of Mexico* (1911) that revealed his blindness to reality, as the dictator fell in that year.

The main challenger to Díaz in the rigged election of 1910 was the son of a wealthy landowner from the north of Mexico, Francisco Madero, who drew ever larger crowds during the campaign but incredibly won only 196 votes in the official tally, compared with millions for Díaz. Mexico was soon plunged into revolution. In answer to written questions submitted to him by William Randolph Hearst, Madero later wrote: "I knew that General Díaz could only be defeated by means of arms, but the democratic [electoral] campaign [of 1910] was indispensable in order to make a revolution because this would prepare public opinion and justify the armed uprising."[10]

John Reed Witnesses Revolution

When in 1910 the Mexican Revolution broke out—it was to cost a million lives before revolutionary goals were codified in the Constitution of 1917—American intellectuals flocked to the scene. Among them were writers Katharine Anne Porter, whose *Flowering Judas and Other Stories*, based on her Mexican experiences, added to her literary fame, and later the poet Hart Crane, who committed suicide on his way back to the United States. The filmmaker Sergei Eisenstein came from Russia to make a documentary, *¡Que Viva Mexico!* which was never finished, and American reporters attached themselves to various revolutionary factions in the prolonged fighting. Lincoln Steffens decided to hitch his star to the fortunes of Venustiano Carranza, first chief of the Constitutionalist Army, which from the north opposed the counterrevolutionary Victoriano Huerta in Mexico City. The twenty-six-year-old John Reed, son of a wealthy lumber family in Oregon, rode with Doroteo Arango (Pancho Villa) in the northwest. Reed actually waded across the Rio Grande to hitch up with Villa, regarded by many simply as a bandit but who became a social reformer similar to Emiliano Zapata in the south. Concerning his surreptitious entry into Mexico, Reed later wrote in *Almost Thirty*, an unfinished autobiography: "When I first crossed the border deadliest fear gripped me. I was afraid of death, of mutilation, of a strange land and strange people whose speech and thought I did not know. But a terrible curiosity urged me on."[11]

These journalists developed an almost proprietary interest in their subjects, as critics claimed that Herbert L. Matthews did later with Fidel Castro. The revolutionary leaders became their "babies," and the fortunes of the reporters rose and fell with the ascendancy or defeat of the chieftains, an attachment that may have clouded the journalists' judgment. Also, the experience of Reed, who reported for *Metropolitan Magazine* and the *New York World*, illustrates that "checkbook journalism"—paying for interviews or information—is unfortunately nothing new. In a hitherto unpublished letter to Carl Hovey (courtesy of his daughter Tamara Hovey, author of *John Reed: Witness to Revolution*), then editor of *Metropolitan Magazine*, Reed wrote his boss: "The story of Villa's life by himself will commence as soon as we can get on a train going South. He says 'I will conceal nothing.' The two-fifty [$250] I have spent already on presents etc., so we won't have to pay him anything. I bought Villa a saddle and a rifle with a gold name plate on it and a Maxim silencer. He is hugely delighted and will do anything for me now."

After four months in revolutionary Mexico observing firsthand the campaigns of Pancho Villa, Reed returned to New York, where he collected his writings in 1914 under the title *Insurgent Mexico*. The book lends credence to the claim that Reed was the first of the so-called "New Journalists" of the 1970s and 1980s because of its vivid descriptions and penetration of character—a more literary and immediate journalism than formula writing. But more was yet to come. With the outbreak of World War I he covered both the western and eastern fronts before moving on to Russia, where he witnessed the Bolshevik revolution of 1917, including the storming of the Winter Palace, and wrote the classic of modern journalism *Ten Days that Shook the World*.

In the selection that follows, we have John Reed's first encounter with Pancho Villa, as the journalist reported it in *Insurgent Mexico*. Reed—young, impetuous, idealistic—served as a minor official in the Soviet regime but became somewhat disillusioned with the Russian revolution before contracting typhus and dying at the age of thirty-three. He is buried, along with three other Americans, beside the Kremlin wall—the highest honor the former Soviet Union could bestow on foreigners. It was a long way from Portland, Oregon.

PANCHO VILLA GETS A MEDAL

The roar began at the back of the crowd and swept like fire in heavy growing crescendo until it seemed to toss thousands of hats above their heads. The band in the courtyard struck up the Mexican national air, and Villa came walking down the street.

He was dressed in an old plain khaki uniform, with several buttons lacking. He hadn't recently shaved, wore no hat, and his hair had not been brushed. He walked a little pigeon-toed, humped over, with his hands in his trouser pockets. As he entered the aisle between the rigid lines of soldiers he seemed slightly embarrassed, and grinned and nodded to a *compadre* here and there in the ranks. At the foot of the grand staircase, Governor Chao and Secretary of State Terrazas joined him in full dress uniform. The band threw off all restraint, and, as Villa entered the audience chamber, at a signal from someone in the balcony of the palace, the great throng in the Plaza de Armas uncovered, and all the brilliant crowd of officers in the room saluted stiffly.

It was Napoleonic!

Villa hesitated for a minute, pulling his mustache and looking very uncomfortable, finally gravitated toward the throne, which he tested by shaking the arms, and then sat down, with the Governor on his right and the Secretary of State on his left.

Señor Bauche Alcalde stepped forward, raised his right hand to the exact position which Cicero took when denouncing Catiline, and pronounced a short discourse, indicting Villa for personal bravery on the field on six counts, which he mentioned in florid detail. He was followed by the Chief of Artillery, who said: "The army adores you. We will follow you wherever you lead. You can be what you desire in Mexico." Then three other officers spoke in the high-flung, extravagant periods necessary to Mexican oratory. They called him "The Friend of the Poor," "The Invincible General," "The Inspirer of Courage and Patriotism," "The Hope of the Indian Republic." And through it all Villa slouched on the throne, his mouth hanging open, his little shrewd eyes playing around the room. Once or twice he yawned, but for the most part he seemed to be speculating, with some intense interior amusement, like a small boy in church, what it was all about. He knew, of course, that it was the proper thing, and perhaps felt a slight vanity that all this conventional ceremonial was addressed to him. But it bored him just the same.

Finally, with an impressive gesture, Colonel Servín stepped forward with the small pasteboard box which held the medal. General Chao nudged Villa, who stood up. The officers applauded violently; the crowd outside cheered; the band in the court burst into a triumphant march.

Villa put out both hands eagerly, like a child for a new toy. He could hardly wait to open the box and see what was inside. An expectant hush fell upon everyone, even the crowd in the square. Villa looked at the medal, scratching his head, and, in a reverent silence, said clearly: "This is a hell of a little thing to give a man for all that heroism you are talking about!" And the bubble of Empire was pricked then and there with a great shout of laughter.

They waited for him to speak—to make a conventional address of acceptance. But as he looked around the room at those brilliant, educated men, who said that they would die for Villa, the peon, and meant it, and as he caught sight through the door of the ragged soldiers, who had forgotten their rigidity and were crowding eagerly into the corridor with eyes fixed eagerly on the *compañero* that they loved, he realized something of what the Revolution signified.

Puckering up his face, as he did always when he concentrated intensely, he leaned across the table in front of him and poured out, in a voice so low that people could hardly hear: "There is no word to speak. All I can say is my heart is all to you." Then he nudged Chao and sat down, spitting violently on the floor; and Chao pronounced the classic discourse.[12]

Ernest Hemingway and the Spanish Civil War

Like many before and after him, Ernest Hemingway cut his writing teeth as a reporter on a newspaper—for him it was the *Kansas City Star* and later the *Toronto Star*, between 1920 and 1924—and some critics believe that that experience honed his terse, staccato style. But it was not until the Spanish Civil War (1936–1939) and the publication of his novel depicting that bitter conflict, *For Whom the Bell Tolls*, that Hemingway burst into international fame. Sympathetic to the legitimate government of Spain, the Republicans, and vehemently opposed to the fascism of the usurper Gen. Francisco Franco and his Nationalists, Hemingway shuttled between besieged Madrid and the United States raising money for the cause. But neither the Americans, British, nor French would enter the struggle—which might have prevented World War II. On the opposite side, Franco was supported with arms, aircraft, and troops by the Germany of Adolf Hitler and the Italy of Benito Mussolini. Only the Soviet Union aided the Republican cause, and the Soviets were more interested in containing fascism than furthering social revolution.

Hemingway was acutely aware of the value of propaganda in combating the verbal blitz of the Fascists, who resurrected the slogans of World War I: "War is to a man what maternity is to a woman," "War is the salt of civilization," and "War is beautiful." Most famous of all was Gen. Millan Astray's epithet hurled at the Spanish philosopher Unamuno, "Down with intelligence! Long live death!"[13] In the face of this irrationality, Hemingway, along with his literary endeavors, directed a documentary film, *The Spanish Earth*, with John Dos Passos and Archibald MacLeish. Hemingway was holed up in Madrid in the Victoria Hotel, which according to British historian Hugh Thomas, who wrote the definitive *Spanish Civil War*, was bombed more than thirty times. There Hemingway wrote a play—his only one—entitled *The Fifth Column*. It described a city besieged by Franco's four columns but whose fatal enemy was within Madrid itself, the fifth column of sympathizers and enemy agents. The slogan of Madrid's defenders was "They shall not pass!" but after the fall of Barcelona in early 1939, resistance in the capital crumbled and the war was over, clamping Franco's dictatorial rule on Spain until his death in 1975. The selection below by Hemingway was published in *Esquire* in 1934, shortly before the Spanish Civil War. It sets forth more clearly than any of his other writings what he thought of the mission of journalism.

HEMINGWAY: "OLD NEWSMAN WRITES A LETTER FROM CUBA"

I don't know what was on the mind of the good grey baggy-pants of the [columnist] when he used to write those I, me, pieces but I am sure he had his troubles even before he took over the world's troubles and, anyway, it has been interesting to watch his progress from an herbivorous (out-doors, the spring, baseball, an occasional half-read book) columnist to a carnivorous (riots, violence, disaster, and revolution) columnist. But personal columnists, and this is getting to read a little like a column, are jackals and no jackal has been known to live on grass once he had learned about meat—no matter who killed the meat for him. [Walter] Winchell kills his own meat and so do a few others. But they have news in their columns and are the most working of working newspaper men. So let us return to the ex-favorite who projects his personality rather than goes for the facts.

Things were in just as bad shape, and worse, as far as vileness, injustice and rottenness are concerned, in 1921, '22 and '23 as they are now but our then favorite columnist did not get around as much in those days or else he didn't read the papers. Or else we had to go broke at home before anybody would take the rest of the world seriously.

The trouble with our former favorite is that he started his education too late. There is no time for him, now, to learn what a man should know before he will die. It is not enough to have a big heart, a pretty good head, a charm of personality, baggy pants, and a facility with a typewriter to know how the world is run and who is making the assists, the put-outs and the errors and who are merely the players and who are the owners. Our favorite will never know because he started too late and because he cannot think coldly with his head.

For instance the world was much closer to revolution in the years after the war than it is now. In those days we who believed in it, looked for it at any time, expected it, hoped for it—for it was the logical thing. But: everywhere it came it was aborted. For a long time I could not understand it but finally figured it out. If you study history you will see that there can never be a Communist revolution without, first, a complete military debacle. You have to see what happens in a military debacle to understand this. It is some-thing so utterly complete in its disillusion about the system that has put them into this in its destruction and purging away of all the existing stan-dards, faiths and loyalties, when the war is being fought by a conscript army, that it is the necessary catharsis before revolution. . . .

Now a writer can make himself a nice career while he is alive by espous-ing a political cause, working for it, making a profession of believing it and if it wins he will be very well placed. All politics is a matter of working hard without reward, or with a living wage for a time, in the hope of booty later. A man can be a Fascist or a Communist and if his outfit gets in he can get to be an ambassador or have a million copies of his books printed by the Gov-ernment or any of the other rewards the boys dream about. Because the literary revolution boys are all ambitious. I have been living for some time where revolutions have gotten past the parlor or publishers' tea and light picketing stage and I know. A lot of my friends have gotten excellent jobs and some others are in jail. But none of this will help the writer as a writer unless he finds something new to add to human knowledge while he is writ-ing. Otherwise he will stink like any other writer when they bury him; except, since he has had political affiliations, they will send more flowers at the time and later he will stink a little more.

The hardest thing in the world to do is to write straight honest prose on human beings. First you have to know the subject; then you have to know how to write. Both take a lifetime to learn and anybody is cheating who takes politics as a way out. It is too easy. All the outs are too easy and the thing itself is too hard to do. But you have to do it and every time you do it well, those human beings and that subject are done and your field is that much more limited. Of course the boys are all wishing you luck and that helps a lot. (Watch how they wish you luck after the first one.) But don't let them suck you in to start writing about the proletariat, if you don't come from the proletariat, just to please the recently politically enlightened critics. In a little while these critics will be something else. I've seen them be a lot of things and none of them was pretty. Write about what you know and write truly and, tell them all where they can place it. They are all really very newly converted and very frightened, really, and when Moscow tells them what I am telling you, then they will believe it. Books should be about the people you know, that you love and hate, not about the people you study up about. If you write them truly they will have all the economic implications a book can hold.

In the meantime, since it is Christmas, if you want to read a book by a man who knows exactly what he is writing about and has written it marvelously well, read *Appointment in Samarra* by John O'Hara.

Then when you have more time read another book called *War and Peace* by Tolstoi and see how you will have to skip the big Political Thought passages, that he undoubtedly thought were the best things in the book when he wrote it, because they are no longer either true or important, if they ever were more than topical, and see how true and lasting and important the people and the action are. Do not let them deceive you about what a book should be because of what is in the fashion now. All good books are alike in that they are truer than if they had really happened and after you are finished reading one you will feel that all that happened to you and afterwards it all belongs to you: the good and the bad, the ecstasy, the remorse and sorrow, the people and the places and how the weather was. If you can get so that you can give that to people, then you are a writer. Because that is the hardest thing of all to do. If, after that, you want to abandon your trade and get into politics, go ahead, but it is a sign that you are afraid to go on and do the other, because it is getting too hard and you have to do it alone and so you want to do something where you can have friends and well wishers, and be part of a company engaged in doing something worth doing instead of working all your life at something that will only be worth doing if you do it better than it has ever been done.

You must be prepared to work always without applause. When you are excited about something is when the first draft is done. But no one can see it until you have gone over it again and again until you have communicated the emotion, the sights and the sounds to the reader, and by the time you have completed this the words, sometimes, will not make sense to you as you read them, so many times have you re-read them. By the time the book comes out you will have started something else and it is all behind you and you do not want to hear about it. But you do, you read it in covers and you see all the places that now you can do nothing about. All the critics who could not make their reputations by discovering you are hoping to make them by predicting hopefully your approaching impotence, failure and general drying up of natural juices. Not a one will wish you luck or hope that you will keep on writing unless you have political affiliations in which case these will rally around and speak of you and Homer, Balzac, Zola and Link Steffens. You are just as well off without these reviews. Finally, in some other place, some other time, when you can't work and feel like hell you will pick up the book and look in it and start to read and go on and in a little while say to your wife, "Why, this stuff is bloody marvelous."

And she will say, "Darling, I always told you it was." Or maybe she doesn't hear you and says, "What did you say?" and you do not repeat the remark.

But if the book is good, is about something that you know, and is truly written and reading it over you see that this is so you can let the boys yip and the noise will have that pleasant sound coyotes make on a very cold night when they are out in the snow and you are in your own cabin that you have built or paid for with your work.[14]

Herbert L. Matthews and the Cuban Story

The question of objectivity in news stories is a thorny one. Some say it is impossible, given the socioeconomic backgrounds of the journalists and editors and owners, who see the world from their particular points of view. Others view efforts toward objectivity, while imperfect, as the culmination of centuries of press development that should be defended at all costs. Herbert L. Matthews, who in 1957 made the arduous journey into the Sierra Maestra of eastern Cuba to prove to the world that rebel leader Fidel Castro was still alive after the disastrous *Granma* landing one year earlier, came down on the side of the committed writer. As the *New York Times* reporter noted in 1946, "True journalism, like true historiography, is not mere chronology, not (to cite Von Ranke's famous definition of the purpose of history) 'simply to describe the event exactly as it happened,' but placing the event in its proper category *as a moral act and judging it as such*."[15]

Again, in *The Yoke and the Arrows*, an account of Franco's Spain published in 1961, Matthews stated quite candidly:

> I would never dream of hiding my own bias or denying it. I did not do so during the Spanish Civil War and I do not do so now. In my credo, as I said before, the journalist is not one who must be free of bias or opinions or feelings. Such a newspaperman would be a pitiful specimen, to be despised rather than admired. There is only one quality that the reader has a right to demand—the truth as the man sees it and all the truth. He must never change or suppress that truth; he must never present as the truth anything that he does not honestly believe to be true.[16]

As far as Cuba was concerned, Matthews faced bitter opposition after his favorable interview with Castro helped the latter gain power on January 1, 1959. Eight months before Castro made his famous speech in which he said, "I am a Marxist-Leninist and will be until the day I die," on December 3, 1961, Matthews wrote in a memorandum to *New York Times* editors: "My now famous criticism of the American press to the effect that in my nearly 40 years in journalism, I have never seen a big story [the Cuban Revolution] so badly handled, is based on the fact that the American press has been very biased. This goes just as much for the pro-Fidel elements like Professor C. Wright Mills and the Fair Play for Cuba Committee as it does for the vast body of the American press which has been intensely hostile and emotional."[17]

Matthews was right in forecasting stormy times ahead. Cuban-exile picket lines repeatedly denounced him in front of the *Times* building. An alleged plot by exiles to kill him brought FBI protection. After receiving a massive amount of hate mail, and a bomb scare prevented him from concluding a speech at the University of New Mexico, Matthews was dropped from the board of directors of the Inter American Press Association, almost censured by that organization, and shunned at the Overseas Press Club. How did the newsman himself stand on Cuba? Here are excerpts of his informed opinion from a speech he gave at the City College of New York on March 15, 1961:

No mind could grasp all the forces at play in a given situation even if you could get hold of *all* the facts—which you cannot. Clausewitz wrote of the fog of war; there is also a fog of history through which we journalists grope our way as best we can. At least we are in the midst of what is happening. . . . Cuba has been drowned in emotions and ignorance in the United States during the last few years. There has been a woeful lack of understanding.

This is a Cuban phenomenon to be interpreted in Cuban, and therefore in Latin American, terms. Not merely in terms of communism, and still less in terms of our democratic, free enterprise, capitalistic, stable, mature, Anglo-Saxon way of life.

Cuba was ripe for revolution. The roots of this event go so deeply into Cuban and American history and spread so wide that it would require a whole lecture to do justice to them. Boiled down, what you saw in Cuba was a revolt against a small, corrupt, wealthy ruling class whom the United States had put in power and helped to keep in power. . . .

We live in a world where nationalism is the most important of all political emotions. It takes a destructive, xenophobic and often revolutionary form. Therefore, of course, the Communists profit by nationalism and we suffer. In Latin America, nationalism inevitably becomes anti-Yankeeism. . . . It was this combination of nationalism with genuine pressures for social, political and economic reforms that gave us the Cuban revolution. Communism had nothing to do with it.

A social revolution was narrowly averted in Cuba in 1933, when another brutal and predatory dictator, Gerardo Machado, was gently eased out by our diplomacy. We then prevented a social revolution from taking place, and Cuba had 27 more years of corruption, inefficiency and profitable business, this time under the domination of Fulgencio Batista. The General ended with seven years of straightforward military dictatorship that were in the worst Latin American tradition, during which time he had the friendship or the benevolence of the United States. . . .

I doubt that historians will ever be able to agree on whether the Castro regime embraced communism willingly or was forced into a shotgun wedding. My own belief is that Fidel Castro did not want to become tied up with the Communists and dependent on them. . . . After an event happens it takes on an inevitability and one feels that it had to happen. Historians—and journalists—build a neat pattern to explain just how a course of events progressed naturally and inescapably to its conclusion. Those who live close to the events, who are a part of them, who know that the forces and pressures involved at any given time on any particular circumstance are enormously complex, that those who are making the history are driven by emotions, consumed with doubts and fears, unable to understand how their opponents feel, unable to grasp all the complicated factors at work—those who understand and see this know that there is no inevitability. . . .

What you are seeing in Cuba, as I said before, is a social revolution. You read little about it in the American press and see and hear little on the radio and television, but this is the supremely important thing about Cuba. This is why it is making such an impact throughout Latin America. . . . This means that if we succeed in destroying, or helping to destroy, the Castro regime, we and Cuba would be facing the same pressures, the same ideals and aspirations and demands for social justice. . . . Because of the appalling and unbroken record of corruption and immorality of Cuban governments and Cuban ruling classes, a revolution, to be effective, had to be honest, and this regime for the first time in Cuban history, is an honest regime in that sense of the word. . . .

No one knows the Cuban revolution who does not know Fidel Castro. Yet his is a character of such complexity, such contradictions, such emotionalism, such irrationality, such unpredictability, that no one can really know him. The men who make history have to be extraordinary men. The man in the street, the journalist, the opponent is tempted to dismiss such men in their lives by applying comforting labels such as paranoia, megalomania, manic depression or—in our day, depending on the political complexion—Communist or Fascist.

This is a waste of time with Fidel Castro. He is not certifiably insane; he is certainly not a Fascist and it is most unlikely that he was, or is today, a Communist. He is himself, and he fits no category although one can get some vague help from the knowledge that he is a Galician Spaniard by blood, a Cuban by birth and upbringing, and a creature—a very wild creature—of our times. He will be written about as long as historians write about hemispheric affairs. No single person has made such a mark on Latin American history since the wars of independence 150 years ago. . . .

One of the baffling facts about the Cuban revolution is this fact that it is Fidel Castro's revolution, and he is an emotional, incalculable force. You may be sure they are as puzzled about him in Moscow and Peiping as they are in Washington. One hears a great deal nowadays about the charismatic leader, a term invented by the sociologist, Max Weber. No doubt the term is abused and used too loosely, but I have always felt that Fidel Castro is a perfect example of the charismatic leader, one whose authority rests upon a popular belief in qualities like heroism, sanctity, self-sacrifice, even in superhuman, miraculous powers. He is the object of hero worship and, in turn, he demands blind obedience of all.[18]

Edgar Snow Opens the Door to China

Few Americans of this generation have even heard of Edgar Snow, but at the University of Beijing one crosses a little arched bridge framed by willows in the Chinese mist and unexpectedly comes across the grave of Snow—the American journalist who did more than anyone other than Pearl Buck to bring the realities of China to an American audience. Snow was an advertising major at the University of Missouri School of Journalism and was on his way around the world when he arrived in Shanghai in 1928—and remained in Asia until 1941. It was a fateful and mutual attraction: Snow went to Yenan province to interview the Communist leader Mao Tse-tung (who later came to power in 1949), during the Long March, covered the Sino-Japanese War, and lived to see the beginnings of rapprochement between the United States and the People's Republic of China in 1972.

Edgar Snow was a committed journalist. Some may have questioned his detachment when he encouraged friendly student demonstrations in 1935 or later stood on the reviewing stand in Tiananmen Square with Mao Tse-tung. During the McCarthy era, Snow was charged with sympathy for the Chinese Communist movement, but in 1960 *Look* magazine hired him to be the first American journalist to return to the Chinese mainland after the successful revolution. As early as the 1940s, he predicted the results of the French withdrawal from Vietnam and the fate awaiting the United States there. His *Red Star over China* (1937) is a classic of modern journalism and underlines the necessity of having informed journalists in the field.

Georgie Anne Geyer, formerly of the *Chicago Daily News* and now a syndicated columnist, illustrates the other side of the coin. Her editors had her hopscotch from Latin America to China to the Middle East, without plumbing the cultures of any of those places in any depth. Edgar Snow stayed thirteen years in China, in addition to his later visits, and thus acquired an expertise that no other American journalist could match. In an increasingly complex world, the need for specialization cannot be emphasized too strongly. When Sino-American relations began to thaw, the *New York Times*, for example, sent a reporter to the Royal Institute of International Studies in London for a year to learn something of the Chinese language, history, and culture before assigning him to their newly opened bureau in Beijing.

Snow died of cancer in his home in Switzerland on February 15, 1972, only three days before Richard Nixon visited Beijing on his historic mission to reestablish diplomatic relations between the two countries. Perhaps Edgar Snow summed up his own career best when he said, "In working overseas you were bound to notice that fifteen of every sixteen people on earth were not Americans. Those fifteen were likely to behave as if their interests were more important than any of ours which conflicted with them."

Many are the answers and speculations [Snow wrote in 1971] offered to explain why President Nixon sought and accepted an invitation to Peking, but why were the Chinese responsive? Is it forgotten in Peking that Nixon built his early career on witch-hunting and climbed to the Senate and vice-presidency on the backs of "appeasers in the State Department" who sold China to Russia? Why should Mao Tse-tung, with a fierce domestic purge safely behind him, seeing America's Vietnam venture a shambles and believing its political and economic position to be in serious trouble abroad and at home, accept a belated olive branch? And, if Nixon is not going to China just to eat shark fins, what may his hosts serve as side dishes—and what may they expect in return? . . .

My *Life* article was translated and widely circulated in China among political and army leaders. They could not, therefore, have been much astonished by the recent Peking-Washington joint announcement. Though China's press may carry only a few lines, the whole subject today is undoubtedly being cautiously discussed and explained down to the commune level. Only one thing may have surprised the Chinese: Mr. Kissinger's success in keeping his visit secret. Experience with American diplomats during World War II had convinced Chinese leaders that Americans could not keep secrets.

The Chinese are, of course, well aware not only of the international impact of Mr. Nixon's plans, but also of the domestic effects and side benefits to his present and future political career. Discussing Nixon's possible visit to China, the chairman [Mao] casually remarked that the presidential election would be in 1972, would it not? Therefore, he added, Mr. Nixon might send an envoy first, but was not himself likely to come to Peking before early 1972.

By 1970 China had passed through the ordeal of the great purge, much time had been lost in domestic construction, and many fences had to be mended or newly built to end China's international isolation. The period of internal tension was largely over. Now, if there was a chance to recover Taiwan—Mao's last national goal of unification—and for China to be accepted as an equal in recognition of her great size, achievements and potential, why not look at it? Nothing in Mao's thought or teaching ever called for a war against the U.S. or for a war of foreign conquest, and nothing in Mao's ideology places any faith in nuclear bombs. The burden of building bombs and counterattack silos is very heavy indeed and likely to become more so. China has more than once called for their total abolition. . . .

Whatever the Chinese may think of Nixon's motives, he has earned their appreciation by the courtesy of coming to see them, thereby according prestige of Mao Tse-tung and amour-propre to the whole people. Vassal kings of the past brought tributes to Peking, but never before the head of the world's most powerful nation. The gesture in itself may go far to assuage the rancor and resentment accumulated during the past two decades. There is some risk that the gesture could be misinterpreted to the Americans' disadvantage, but more likely it will be accepted with full grace and improve chances of mutual accommodation.

The millennium seems distant and the immediate prospect is for the toughest kind of adjustment and struggle. China must satisfy Korea and Vietnam, and the U.S. cannot jettison Japan. The danger is that Americans may imagine that the Chinese are giving up Communism—and Mao's world view—to become nice agrarian democrats. A more realistic world is indeed in sight. But popular illusions that it will consist of a sweet mix of ideologies, or an end to China's faith in revolutionary means, could only serve to deepen the abyss again when disillusionment occurs. A world without change by revolutions—a world in which China's closest friends would not be revolutionary states—is inconceivable to Peking. But a world of relative peace between states is as necessary to China as to America. To hope for more is to court disenchantment.[19]

Notes

1. Herbert L. Matthews, *A World in Revolution: A Newspaperman's Memoir* (New York: Charles Scribner's Sons, 1971).

2. Matthews to the author, January 2, 1976. Emphasis in original.

3. Herbert L. Matthews, "Dissent over Cuba," *Encounter* (July 1964): 84.

4. Ibid.

5. Richard Maxwell Brown, "Violence and the American Revolution," in *Essays on the American Revolution*, ed. Stephen G. Kurtz and James H. Hutson (Chapel Hill: University of North Carolina Press, 1973), 116.

6. C. Wright Mills, *Listen, Yankee: The Revolution in Cuba* (New York: McGraw-Hill, 1960), 10.

7. Ibid., 9–10.

8. Jerry W. Knudson, *Herbert L. Matthews and the Cuban Story* (Lexington, KY: Association for Education in Journalism), Journalism Monographs, no. 54 (February 1978): 18.

9. Quoted in James Creelman, *Pearson's Magazine* (March 1908): 242.

10. Jerry W. Knudson, "Document: When Did Francisco I. Madero Decide on Revolution?" *Americas* (April 1974): 529.

11. Tamara Hovey, *John Reed: Witness to Revolution* (New York: Crown Publishers, 1975), 93.

12. John Reed, "Villa Accepts a Medal," *Insurgent Mexico* (New York: Simon and Schuster, 1969), 113–15.

13. Jerry W. Knudson, "The Ultimate Weapon: Propaganda and the Spanish Civil War," *Journalism History* (Winter 1988): 103.

14. Ernest Hemingway, "Old Man Writes a Letter from Cuba," *Esquire* (December 1934): 25–26.

15. Herbert L. Matthews, *The Education of a Correspondent* (New York: Harcourt, Brace and Company, 1946), 11. Emphasis added.

16. Herbert L. Matthews, *The Yoke and the Arrows: A Report on Spain* (New York: George Braziller, 1961), 225.

17. Herbert L. Matthews to Dryfoos, Markel and Catledge, March 31, 1961, in Herbert L. Matthews Papers, Butler Library, Columbia University, New York.

18. Matthews Papers, Butler Library, Columbia University, Cuban Revolution, Box 2.

19. Edgar Snow, "China Will Talk from a Position of Strength," *Life* (July 30, 1971): 22–26.

11

The Contemporary Press and Criticism

———⟨◆⟩———

Whenever something bad happens in the United States or the world, it eventually is blamed by someone or other on "the media." If there is anything the American public knows, it's how to raise children and how to run a newspaper. Much of the criticism is merited, and journalists themselves are their own harshest critics—when the mood strikes them to speak out. And they are the critics who should be heard, because they know the realities of their profession and the problems. Under the pressures of time, limited access to information, and available space, journalists may present a truncated view of society. But all are agreed that there are more sins of omission than commission. Significant stories should be covered that reporters and editors seem largely unaware of. Thus it is not necessarily a conspiracy of publishers that these stories go unreported, but lack of knowledge all the way down the line. Turn on your local television news and you will usually get little more than murders and fires, and the networks have gone in for "tabloid TV" or news magazines that seem designed mainly for entertainment rather than information. And many of the panelists on some shows have dubious credentials. What used to be called "gossip columnists," for example, are now "celebrity journalists." And it seems that anyone can set up shop as an "analyst" or "commentator," while those who used to be called "lobbyists" are now "legislative consultants."

Despite the slough of sensationalism we are wallowing in as the twentieth century comes to an end, sensationalism that equals or surpasses that of the "Jazz Journalism" of the 1920s (when jazz was at first considered discordant and disreputable), the American press has improved greatly in the three centuries since Benjamin Harris first offered his little *Publick Occurrences Both Forreign and Domestick* to his readers. No one wants to go back to the mud-slinging of the overtly politically partisan press (although we have some of that in television political commercials today) or the jingoism of the War with Spain. But we can look with pride at the courage of the abolitionists and the muckrakers' efforts to improve society and expose corruption, a tradition not dead, as Watergate clearly showed, and hundreds of other papers have demonstrated in their own communities.

Yet we are in a period of acute sensationalism, accentuated by the overkill coverage of the O. J. Simpson murder trial while more important issues go begging. The greater metropolitan area of Philadelphia has a population of 4,922,257, according to the 1990 census, and yet it is essentially a one-newspaper town: Both the *Philadelphia Daily News* and *Philadelphia Inquirer* are owned by the Knight-Ridder chain, and the former has become hardly a step above the supermarket tabloids. Consider the lurid color and the full front-page headlines such as "Too Nuts to Die?" (April 12, 1997) and "Don't Kill My Daddy" (April 21, 1997). And the *Inquirer*, which has garnered its share of Pulitzer prizes, gave a banner front-page headline to a local murder on the same day (October 31, 1997) that Jiang Zemin, president of the People's Republic of China, spoke in Philadelphia (he got a box below the headline).

In such a situation, where does one turn for balanced information? There are other printed sources, of course. The *New York Times* and the *Washington Post* are available, among others, but they ususally do not cover Philadelphia events. And there are other alternatives. According to the *Statistical Abstract of the United States* for 1997, although there is some overlap, among those over eighteen years of age, 82.25 percent read newspapers, 82.75 listen to the radio, and 77.63 view prime-time television. Significantly, the percentage of those who accessed the Internet was 15.06 and rapidly growing, perhaps to become the news conveyor of the future. In a landmark ruling on June 26, 1997, the U.S. Supreme Court ruled 7–2 that the Federal Communications Decency Act unconstitutionally restricted free speech, thus clearing the way for the Internet to become a full-fledged member of the family of communications. Video cassettes, compact disks, and cable television also have widened the horizons of millions of people who are willing to pay for what they want to see without commercial interruptions.

Yet we still come back to the question of who pays the piper. Many will say, when the press is criticized, that the public gets what it wants, that journalism is a business like any other, and that it is bound to sell the product most salable. One can reply to those comfortable with this status quo, however, that the First Amendment does not protect shoe manufacturers. In other words, the Founding Fathers gave special status to the press because they viewed it as beneficial to society and a democratic government. Freedom of the press, speech, religion, assembly, and right to petition for redress of grievances were all included in the very first amendment to our Constitution, part and parcel of the whole, because they were considered to be our most valuable civil liberties. With freedom, however, comes responsibility, and some of the journalists whose excerpts are printed below believe that many of their colleagues have never come to grips with that concept.

Refreshingly, there is now increased criticism of the performance of the press. Journalists have contributed to *Quill* since it was first published in 1912 by Sigma Delta Chi (now the Society of Professional Journalists), eight years before Upton Sinclair privately published *The Brass Check* urging reform in American journalism. Exaggerated as some of Sinclair's criticisms were, they may have stimulated the American Society of Newspaper Editors to adopt "The Canons of Journalism" in 1923. These ethical guidelines coincided with the beginnings and growth of professional education itself, whereby today the Association for Education in Journalism and Mass Communication accredits university journalism programs. The press has come under professional scrutiny as never before. The fifth edition of *The Iowa Guide*, for example, lists 124 scholarly journals in mass communication and related fields. Most influential in criticism is the *Columbia Journalism Review* (1961), which preceded municipal journalism reviews—some short-lived after the turmoil of the 1960s had passed, such as the *Washington Journalism Review* (1977), which became the *American Journalism Review* (1993).

Television self-criticism has been rare by comparison and less stringent. ABC's *Nightline* occasionally takes a look, however defensively, at news media performance, as also do the Fred Friendly Seminars on public television. It is noteworthy that television roundtables on public affairs still rely mainly on print journalists as panelists, with some exceptions. Bernard Kalb moderates CNN's weekly *Reliable Sources*, and others include such venerable programs as *Meet the Press*, *Face the Nation*, and *Washington Week in Review*. Hodding Carter III is frequently chief correspondent for the PBS *Frontline*, but with notable exceptions one is inclined to think that the electronic news media still have not developed a sturdy infrastructure of their own reporters. But let's hear what the journalists have to say about their own work, beginning on a lighter note with Finley Peter Dunne, who ranks somewhere between Mark Twain and Will Rogers as one of the most celebrated humorists of the early twentieth century.

Mr. Dooley Sizes Up Newspapers

Finley Peter Dunne, creator of Mr. Dooley—America's most famous Irish bartender—began his career as a young reporter on the *Chicago Daily News*, did his stint as a muckraker, and rose to become editor of the *Chicago Journal* in 1898. In syndicated columns, Mr. Dooley held court on issues of the day at his Chicago saloon on Archy Road with his faithful audience—and interlocutors—Hennessy and Hogan. The simulation of Mr. Dooley's Irish brogue in print seemed to delight rather than perplex Dunne's followers. Mr. Dooley, who seemed almost a real person to his readers, did not always cast a jaundiced eye on journalism, however, as "Newspaper Publicity," a column in its entirety that follows, might indicate. On the contrary, he had this to say on another occasion: "Th' newspa-apers are-re a gr-reat blessing. I don't know what I'd do without thim. If it wasn't f'r thim I'd have no society fit to assocyate with—on'y people like ye'ersilf an' Hogan. But th' pa-apers opens up life to me an' gives me a speakin' acquaintance with th' whole wurruld. . . . I know more about th' Impror iv Chiny [Emperor of China] thin me father knew about th' people in th' next parish."[1]

FINLEY PETER DUNNE: "NEWSPAPER PUBLICITY"

"Was ye iver in th' pa-apers?" asked Mr. Dooley.

"Wanst," said Mr. Hennessy. "But it wasn't me. It was another Hinnissy. Was you?"

"Manny times," said Mr. Dooley. "Whin I was prom'nent socyallly, ye cud hardly pick up a pa-aper without seein' me name in it an' th' amount iv th' fine. Ye must lade a very simple life. Th' newspaper is watchin' most iv us fr'm th' cradle to th' grave, an' before an' afther. Whin I was a la-ad thrippin' continted over th' bogs iv Roscommon, ne'er an iditor knew iv me existence, nor I iv his. Whin annything was wrote about a man 'twas put this way: 'We undhershtand on good authority that M—l—chi H——y, Esquire, is on thrile before Judge G——n on an accusation iv l—c—ny. But we don't trhink it's true.' Nowadays th' larceny is discovered be a newspa-aper. Th' lead pipe is dug up in ye'er back yard be a rayporther who knew it was there because he helped ye bury it. A man knocks at ye'er dure arly wan mornin' an' ye answer in ye'er nighty. 'In th' name iv th' law, I arrist ye,' says th' man seizin' ye be th' throat. 'Who ar-re ye?' ye cry. 'I'm a rayporther f'r th' Daily Slooth,' says he. 'Phottygrafter, do ye'er jooty!' Ye're hauled off in th' circylation wagon to th' newspaper office, where a con-fission is ready f'r ye to sign; ye're thried be a jury iv th' staff, sintinced be th' iditor-in-chief an' at tin o'clock Friday th' fatal thrap is sprung be th' fatal thrapper iv th' fam'ly journal.

"Th' newspaper does ivrything f'r us. It runs th' polis foorce an' th' banks, commands th' milishy, conthrols th' ligislachure, baptizes th' young, marries th' foolish, comforts th' afflicted, afflicts th' comfortable, buries th' dead an' roasts thim aftherward. They ain't annything it don't turn its hand to fr'm explainin th' docthrine iv thransubstantiation to composin' saleratus biskit. Ye can get anny kind iv information ye want to in ye'er fav'rite newspaper about ye'ersilf or annywan else. What th' Czar whispered to th' Imp'ror Willum whin they were alone, how to make a silk hat out iv a wire mattress, how to settle th' coal sthrike, who to marry, how to get on with ye'er wife whin y're married, what to feed th' babies, what doctor to call whin ye've fed thim as directed,—all iv that ye'll find in th' pa-apers.

"They used to say a man's life was a closed book. So it is but it's an open newspaper. Th' eye iv th' press is on ye befure ye begin to take notice. Th' iditor obsarves th' stork hoverin' over th' roof iv 2978 1/2 B Ar-rchey Road an' th' article he writes about it has a wink in it. 'Son an' heir arrives f'r th' Hon'rable Malachi Hinnissy,' says th' pa-aper befure ye've finished th' dhrink with th' doctor. An' afther that th' histhry iv th' offspring's life is found in th' press:

" 'It is undhershtud that there is much excitement in th' Hinnissy fam'ly over namin' th' lates' sign. Misther Hinnissy wishes it call Pathrick McGlue afther an uncle iv his, an' Mrs. Hinnissy is in favor iv namin' it Alfonsonita afther a Pullman car she seen wan day. Th' Avenin Fluff offers a prize iv thirty dollars f'r th' best name f'r this projeny. Maiden ladies will limit their letters to three hundherd wurruds.'

" 'Above is a snapshot iv young Alfonsonita McGlue Hinnissy, taken on his sicond birthday with his nurse, Miss Angybel Blim, th' well-known specyal nurse iv th' Avenin Fluff. At th' time th' phottygraft was taken, th' infant was about to bite Miss Blim which accounts f'r th' agynized exprission on that gifted writer's face. Th' Avenin Fluff offers a prize iv four dollars to th' best answer to th' question: "What does th' baby think iv Miss Blim?" '

" 'Young Alf Hinnissy was siven years ol' yisterdah. A raporther iv th' Fluff sought him out to intherview him on th' Nicaragooan Canal, th' Roomanyan Jews, th' tahriff an' th' thrusts. Th' comin' statesman rayfused to be dhrawn on these questions, his answer bein' a ready, "Go chase ye'ersilf, ye big stiff!" After a daylightful convarsation th' rayporther left, bein' followed to th'gate be his janial young host who hit him smartly in th' back with a brick. He is a chip iv th' ol' block.'

" 'Groton, Conn., April 8. Ye'er rayporther was privileged to see th' oldest son iv the Hon'rable Malachji Hinnissy started at this siminary f'r th' idjacation iv young Englishmen bor-rn in America. Th' heir iv the Hinnissys was enthered at th' exclusive school thirty years before he was bor-rn. Owin' to th' uncertainty iv his ancesthors he was also enthered at Vassar. Th' young fellow took a lively intherest in th' school. Th' above phottygraft riprisints him mathriculatin'. The figures at th' foot ar-re Misther an' Mrs. Hinnissy. Those at th' head ar-re Professor Peabody Plantagenet, prisident iv th' instichoochion an' Officer Michael H. Rafferty. Yooung Hinnissy will remain here till he has a good cukkin' idjacation.'

" 'Exthry Red Speshul Midnight Edition. Mumps! Mumps! Mumps! Th' heir iv th' Hinnissy's sthricken with th' turr'ble scoorge. Panic on th' stock exchange. Bereaved father starts f'r th' plague spot to see his afflicted son. Phottygrafts iv Young Hinnissy at wan, two, three, eight an' tin. Phottographts iv th' house where his father was born, his mother, his aunt, his uncle, Professor Plantagenet, Groton School, th' gov'nor iv Connecticut, Chansy Depoo, statue iv Liberty, Thomas Jefferson, Niagara Falls be moonlight. Diagram iv jaw an' head showin' th' prob'ble coorse iv the Mumpococcus. Intherviews with J. Pierpont Morgan, Terry McGovern, Mary McLain, Jawn Mitchell, Lyman J. Gage, th' Prince iv Wales, Sinitor Bivridge, th' Earl iv Roslyn, an' Chief Divery on Mumps. We offer a prize iv thirty million dollars in advertisin' space f'r a cure f'r th' mumps that will save th' nation's pride.—Later, it's croup.'

"An' so it goes. We march through life an' behind us marches th' phottygrafter an' th' rayporther. There are no such things as private citizens. No matter how private a man may be, no matter how secretly he steals, some day his pitcher will be in th' pa-aper along with Mark Hanna, Stamboul 2:01 1/2, Fitzsimmons' fightin' face, an' Douglas, Douglas, Tin dollar shoe. He can't get away from it. An' I'll says this f'r him, he don't want to. He wants to see what bad th' nighbors are doin' an' he wants thim to see what good he's doin'. He gets fifty per cint iv his wish; niver more. A man keeps his front window shade up so the pa-apers can come along an' make a pitcher iv him settin' in his iligant furnished parlor readin' th' life iv Dwight L. Moody to his fam'ly. An' th' lad with th' phottygraft happens along at th' moment whin he is batin' his wife. If we wasn't so anxious to see our names among those prisint at th' ball, we wudden't get into th' pa'aper so often as among those that ought to be prisint in th' dock. A man takes his phottygraft to the iditor an' says he: 'Me attintion has been called to th' fact that ye'd like to print this mug iv a prom'nent philanthropist;' an' th' iditor don't use it till he's robbed a bank. Ivrybody is inthrested in what ivrybody else is doin' that's wrong. That's what makes th' newspapers. An' as this is a dimmycratic counthry where ivrybody was bor-rn akel to ivrybody else, even if they soon outgrow it, an' where wan man's as good as another an' as bad, all iv us has a good chanst to have his name get in at laste wanst a year. Some goes in at Mrs. Rasther's dinner an' some as victims iv a throlley car, but ivrybody lands at last. They'll get ye afther awhile, Hinnissy. They'll print ye'er pitcher. But on'y wanst. A newspaper is to intertain, not to teach a moral lesson."

"D'ye think people likes th' newspapers iv the prisint time?" asked Mr. Hennessy.

"D'ye think they're printed f'r fun?" said Mr. Dooley.[2]

The Press under Scrutiny

The humor of Mr. Dooley around 1900 turned to anger after the middle of the century as the United States became mired in the Vietnam War amidst mounting racial and social tensions at home. Chicago journalists felt that the established media of their city did not adequately or fairly cover the student and police riots during the Democratic Party convention there in 1968 and founded the *Chicago Journalism Review* for purposes of evaluating the local press.

Ironically, it was also in Chicago that the first sweeping assessment of American press performance had been carried out, in 1947. Funded by Henry Luce of Time-Life, Inc., and headed by Robert M. Hutchins, chancellor of the University of Chicago, the Commission on Freedom of the Press was composed of journalists, scholars, and members of the public. It held seventeen two-day sessions, interviewed 225 journalists, publishers, and government officials, and studied 176 documents prepared by its staff. The upshot of its findings, published as *A Free and Responsible Press* (1947), was that if the press did not conduct itself more responsibly, it would risk government intervention.

A second major examination of press performance came in 1973, *A Free and Responsive Press*, conducted by the Twentieth Century Fund, founded in 1919 and endowed by Edward A. Filene. Note the shift in emphasis within a quarter of a century between these two comprehensive studies, from a *responsible* to a *responsive* press. Most people do not have access to newspaper columns except through the limited space for letters to the editor, and the Twentieth Century Fund may be credited with opening up the press with op-ed pages. Most important, the fund established a national press council to hear complaints and mediate their resolution. Great Britain had had such a council since 1963, as did Sweden and New Zealand later, along with local councils such as those of Minnesota and Honolulu. The only means of enforcing the council's decisions was through publicity about grievances, and its proceedings were published in the *Columbia Journalism Review*. Major newspapers such as the *New York Times* refused to take part, however, claiming a threat to editorial independence. Another reason for the demise of the council is that there is no truly national press in the United States. One might cite *USA Today*, whose skeletal news has caused it to be dubbed *McPaper*—the fast food of journalism— along with complaints that *USA Today* is to journalism what the *Reader's Digest* is to literature.

At another level, in the search for a better press, old voices sounded as vigorously and persistently as always. Among these critics were A. J. Liebling, who wrote some eighty-seven articles on "The Wayward Press" for *The New Yorker* over the years, and *I. F. Stone's Weekly*, which manned the parapets to make sure no one poached on the Constitution.

The precursor of these press critics was H. L. Mencken, who, with a solid background on the *Baltimore Sun*, launched the *American Mercury* in 1924. When he began as a reporter, Mencken wrote (in *Newspaper Days*) that he was "young, goatish and full of an innocent delight in the world." He added that his work was "the maddest, gladdest, damndest existence ever enjoyed by mortal youth." At the same time, however, he wrote, "The illusion that swathes and bedizens journalism, bringing in its endless squads of recruits, was still full upon me, and I had yet to taste the sharp teeth of responsibility."[3] Many people, however, got their idea of reporters as being cynical if not callous creatures with a half-pint of bourbon in their back pocket, slouched hat, and no morality other than getting the story—as depicted in Ben Hecht's and Charles MacArthur's play *The Front Page*, which spawned numerous film versions and imitators.

At a quite different level, the New Journalism of the 1960s and 1970s spread its wings in the face of traditional ways of doing journalism. In competition with television news, newspaper writing became more literary. It made use of fictional techniques such as foreshadowing, realistic dialogue, a point (or points) of view, symbolic or revealing detail, and scenic rather than historical narrative. The best of this genre did not twist the facts but marshaled them in a new way to convey a greater reality. It was investigative reporting with soul. The gurus of this new form included among others Tom Wolfe, Norman Mailer, Gay Talese, and Jimmy Breslin. Truman Capote called his epic of a Kansas murder, *In Cold Blood* (which was based on two years of relentless research on the scene), "the nonfiction novel," while others derided the new form as "journalit"—neither journalism nor literature. Yet the New Journalists left their mark, with more engaging and perceptive writing in today's newspapers.

The underground press also put its indelible stamp on the 1960s and 1970s, before "hippies" became "yuppies." The father of the movement was Norman Mailer, who with four others founded *Village Voice* in 1955; but it was so successful, taking the middle ground, that it, too, soon became Establishment. Probably the first underground newspaper as such was the *Los Angeles Free Press*, which opened up shop in 1964, followed by the *Berkeley Barb* in 1970, which soon had a circulation of 85,000—six times that of its established rival, the Berkeley commercial newspaper.

These newspapers opened the floodgates for many more alternative publications, including those published by university and high-school students, militant blacks and Chicanos, American Indians and Asians, soldiers and prisoners, abortion advocates and death-penalty foes—the list seems endless. John Wilcock, who left the established press to found his own underground paper, *Other Scenes*, had this to say about the phenomenon, headlining his 1968 article "Foolosophy of Flower Children": "There is a credibility gap between the press and the people, because the newspaper owners are plain and simple liars. They have fostered wars and want the people to believe that the Viet Nam war is a holy war. As a result, the Hippies just don't read the national papers."[4]

Technology again was partly responsible for this proliferation of viewpoints, as the photo-printing or "cold type" offset process brought the cost of a small edition within the job-printing reach of countless groups. And for those who could not afford that, there was always the mimeograph machine. It was a heady time, coupled with the student revolt that began in Paris in 1968 and spread to American campuses. One remembers seeing young persons offering free copies of their mimeographed underground sheets to motorists stopped for a red light at busy intersections.

The driving force behind the underground press was not only vitality but also anger. This was best expressed by Marty Glass, who, in the *Dock of the Bay*'s third issue in August 1969, in powerful terms offered a new definition of news. Coverage by the mainstream press of some of Glass's complaints since that time attests to the impact of the underground press. Like third political parties, who have no hope of winning a race, the alternative or advocacy newspapers goaded the established press into taking stock of itself and dealing with some of these matters. Third political parties had advocated women's suffrage, direct election of U.S. senators, graduated income tax, referendum, recall and primaries—all considered radical measures in their time. But this forum belongs to Mr. Glass:

There's been a lot of murder and rape in the Bay Area during the past few weeks. . . .

The Bay Area newspapers blazed out the news in giant headlines. "Savage Slaying Mystery," "Shocking Murder," "A Story of Savagery," "Big Search for Knife Killer of Two San Jose Girls," "Big Hunt for Picnic Killer," and so on.

There's a big lie behind all this. The stories are more or less true; the accounts bear some police-filtered relation to the truth, but there's still a big lie behind the grisly intimate details of bloody mayhem and brutal sexual assault.

The lie is linked to the idea of 'news' in the daily papers. What does 'news' mean? 'News' is what stands out on the vast, flat and presumably irrelevant plain of mundane events, 'news' is what deviates from the ordinary and the normal, 'news' is what someone else decides is important.

Supposedly, everything which isn't worth knowing about isn't of public concern. The daily papers convey a very strong and very indirect message; there's a normal, everyday life which is OK and unexceptional—not worth talking about. And then there's 'news': anything which stands out, anything that doesn't happen all the time and is, therefore, of interest.

Life is good. That's the realm where things are taken care of. 'News' is when something goes wrong.

This is pure bullshit. The real news isn't in distinct, bizarre events. The real news is what happens 24 hours a day all day long everywhere. This is the news we don't read about in the daily papers because the people who control those papers don't want us to know about it and do everything they can to distract our attention from it.

Fortunately, they can't succeed. We don't need their papers to tell us about the real news. All we have to do is open our eyes.

The real news is the expression on the faces of children sitting in tenement doorways with nothing to do. The real news is the tenement itself.

The real news is the despair and humiliation on the faces of people waiting for hours for a lousy check in the welfare or unemployment offices. And it's also on the emptied faces of people who have jobs they hate, jobs where their creative potential is stifled and crushed under the weight of meaningless labor performed to make enough money to survive.

The real news is jobs created solely to provide profits for those who don't work at all, or for a corporation which is nothing but a bankbook.

The precious unredeemable time of our lives is sacrificed for numbers in bankbooks.

The real news is elderly people rotting away in dilapidated Old Folks' Homes or in spare rooms in their children's houses, unwanted, resented, feeling they might as well as be dead. The real news is in the millions of people who don't get enough to eat, who receive inadequate medical care, who suffer and die from diseases which could be cured and should never have been contracted in the first place.

The real news is when there's a giant traffic jam on the Bay Bridge because the market economy and capitalism require profit and there's no profit in safe, comfortable, efficient, rapid public transportation. The real news is that there are hardly enough parks and playgrounds for a fraction of our children, that schools are falling apart, overcrowded, repressive, irrelevant and hated by the children imprisoned there.

The real news is that guys are getting beaten by sadistic psychopaths in prisons and army stockades all over the country, kids watch hours of obscene commecials on TV, women are forced to waste their lives in shopping and cooking because private consumption is the syphilitic deity of our society.

The real news is that people who can't take it any more—and they're mostly black or poor whites—are called mentally ill and given shock treatment or mind-killing drugs.

The real news is that ten thousand women die every year in the United States from slipshod expensive abortions, because this system doesn't permit half the population to decide what goes on in their own bodies, doesn't provide for any way outside of the decayed institution of marriage for children to be cared for.

The real news is that cops who murder black men are given medals and a guy found with two joints gets ten years.

The real news is that guys are being forced to kill their brothers in Vietnam. . . .

The real news is that Huey Newton is in jail and Richard Nixon isn't.[5]

The Pentagon Papers

In the strife of the Vietnam War, a New York court on June 15, 1971, issued an injunction ordering the *New York Times* to stop printing installments taken from the Pentagon Papers, commissioned by Secretary of Defense Robert S. McNamara in 1967 for the use of future historians. It was the first time in the nation's history that prior restraint had been invoked, a drastic action not even contained in the Alien and Sedition Acts of 1798–1801. The *New York Times* had published three installments of the Papers after months of editorial labor on copies of the original documents supplied by Daniel Ellsberg, earlier an employee of the Rand Corporation, commissioned to do the study. Once a hawk, he had become disillusioned with our involvement in Vietnam and, after trying unsuccessfully for two years to get the Papers before the public legally, he surreptitiously photocopied the forty-seven volumes consisting of seven thousand pages and handed them over to the *New York Times*, which decided to publish excerpts and summaries—against legal advice from its own counsel.

What was so revealing in the series that the government wanted to suppress? At the risk of oversimplifying complex issues, one can offer a précis of the Rand study. It concluded that as early as the administration of Harry S. Truman (1945–1953) the United States had become directly involved in Indochina by aiding France in its colonial war there. Dwight D. Eisenhower (1953–1961) undermined the Geneva settlement of 1954, and John F. Kennedy (1961–1963) expanded American involvement from a few advisors to a "broad commitment." Finally, Lyndon Baines Johnson (1963–1969) waged a covert war and planned an overt one long before revealing that fact either to Congress or the American public. It took courage to publish the series, not only because of possible governmental reprisal but also because the Pentagon Papers clearly showed that the *New York Times* had failed to report the full inside story of the war as it had unfolded.

Two days after the *Times* was enjoined from publishing any more installments, the *Washington Post* took up the gauntlet, published some of the Papers, and suffered the same fate.

But on June 30, fifteen days after the third installment had been published by the *New York Times*, the Supreme Court ruled in favor of the two newspapers in a landmark 6–3 decision. At issue was not so much freedom of the press under the First Amendment as national security, particularly the possible violation of the Espionage Act of 1917. The defense pointed out that forty-two books containing much of the same information had been written on Vietnam before the Papers began to appear in print. What the Papers stressed was the insensitivity of American policymakers to the forces of nationalism and self-determination in Vietnam.

Eighteen other newspapers printed portions of the Pentagon Papers while the litigation was in process, but only two besides the *Times* and *Post* were prosecuted—the *Boston Globe* and the *St. Louis Post-Dispatch*. All four papers had opposed the administration of Richard M. Nixon. The significance of the entire confrontation was summed up best by Professor Don Pember: "For 15 days the government of the United States successfully stopped the presses of two of the nation's most influential newspapers. For 15 days the freedom of the press was held in abeyance. For 15 days the people were denied the right to read a report prepared by their government about a war in which they have fought and died."

Watergate and Beyond

After Richard M. Nixon was elected president in 1968, an all-out offensive against the press was launched by Vice President Spiro T. Agnew. In speech after speech he attacked the "effete, eastern establishment" of the news media and its reporters, those "nattering nabobs of negativism." A "law and order" proponent, Agnew later pleaded "no contest" to income-tax evasion and resigned from the vice presidency in disgrace.

The greatest disgrace was yet to come, however, after police arrested five men trying to break into the Democratic National Committee headquarters in the Watergate apartment-office complex on the night of June 17, 1972. Ronald Ziegler, Nixon's press secretary, dismissed Watergate as a "third-rate burglarly attempt." But due largely to the perseverance of two reporters for the *Washington Post*, Bob Woodward and Carl Bernstein, the burglary and subsequent cover-up mushroomed into the biggest scandal in American political history—greater even than the Teapot Dome swindle of the administration of Warren G. Harding or the widespread corruption under that of Ulysses S. Grant. Before Watergate prosecutions had run their course, the House of Representatives voted 410–4 to begin impeachment hearings. Nixon resigned (he was later pardoned by his successor, Gerald Ford), and eighteen members of Nixon's staff, including Attorney General John Mitchell, pleaded guilty or were convicted.

The *Washington Post* won a Pulitzer prize for community service, but it should be borne in mind that of the hundreds of reporters in Washington, DC, only two—Woodward and Bernstein—uncovered the Watergate story. It was not an election issue in 1972, even though details of the story were then unfolding. One press critic calculated that of the 433 Washington-based journalists who might have been assigned to the Watergate scandal, only fifteen actually were at that time. Nevertheless, Woodward and Bernstein and their boss, Ben Bradlee, at the *Washington Post* restored prestige to journalism still reeling under the attacks by Agnew. The two newsmen became folk heroes, especially after the later appearance of the movie *All the President's Men*.

The credibility of the American press soared to new heights, although it has diminished since then. Some felt the press became too aggressive in its watchdog role after Watergate (Benjamin Franklin had called newspapers "the highest court of judicature" in America), but others thought the press had become too timid, not risking criticism. Polls show that many people regard the press as hostile and arrogant, which is perhaps why some journalists, not wanting to appear vindictive, did not push the Iran-Contra scandal far enough. Certainly there was no closure on that issue, which marred the presidency of Ronald Reagan (1985–1993) whereby secret funds from arms sales to Iran were illegally diverted to the anti-Sandinista counterrevolutionaries in Nicaragua. Or perhaps the public was tired of exposés. The U.S. government had been practically paralyzed for twenty-six months as the Watergate story was threshed out in the courts and Congress and newspapers. As Gerald Ford, who became president after Nixon resigned, put it, "Our long national nightmare is over. Our Constitution works."

Ben Bradlee, who below sets forth the impact on reporting of Watergate, was named vice president and executive editor of the *Washington Post* in 1968; he had also worked on *Newsweek*, which the *Post* company under publisher Katharine Graham had acquired in 1961. Interviewed by Theodore White about the flak the *Post* received as the Watergate story unfolded, Bradlee said, "I kept asking from June of 1972 on how could their [the government's] contempt be so great as to think that Ben Bradlee would publicly destroy himself and the paper he loved by printing something not true. The only answer was that they *had* to attack us for their own survival . . . which led me to the conviction that we were right."[6] The following is an excerpt from Bradlee's autobiography, *A Good Life: Newspapering and Other Adventures* (1995).

Woodward and Bernstein were still creating their legacy, but already new reporters coming on stream were plainly looking for the same kind of stardom, using what they thought was the same kind of brash persistence they'd seen in the movie. We joked about bright-eyed, bushy-tailed young Woodsteins coming back from covering a fire in Prince Georges County, reporting that the fire chief was anti-Semitic, there was gasoline in the hoses, and a guy who looked like Howard Hunt had been seen fleeing into the woods. Some of my colleagues in the business started making speeches about the need to rein in the young hotheads before they got newspapers into trouble. I think now we worried too much about the trouble and not enough about the newspapering. After all, good editors and good copy editors can prevent the excesses of exuberance; it is not that hard to take the elbows out of a lead like: "Despite overwhelming evidence to the contrary, the mayor today refused to admit that he had accepted sexual favors from the wife of an associate trying to sell the city a new health plan."

But there is no question that the Watergate legacy did include a major infusion of bright, young, motivated and talented men and women, who might have drifted off into other professions. Scotty Reston, the dean of Washington journalists, gave a speech about this time, urging the press not to relax their investigative pressure just because the public was leery of going through another Watergate, and just because some editors were listening to vague complaints that the press had accumulated too much power. Just the opposite, he said. Now was the time to pour it on, turn up the volume. Take a look at everything government was doing. Watergate had proved they weren't playing by the rules. He was right, but for the most part his peers were not listening.

However, it was neither the influx of hungry young journalists eager for notoriety nor the notoriety itself that made journalism forever different after Watergate. But journalism was forever changed by the assumption—by most journalists—that after Watergate government officials generally and instinctively lied when confronted by embarrassing events. "Look for the lies" replaced "Look for the woman" or "Follow the money" as the new shibboleth of journalism.

Most journalists working their way slowly up the ladder from cub reporter on small newspapers quickly learned that some public officials lie when cornered. I think back now to Jimmy O'Neil, the police chief of Manchester, New Hampshire (and later national commander of the American Legion), who lied to me rather than admit that a trap which had been set for a rapist misfired and resulted in another rape. But that involved only a small-town chief of police and, of course, the victim.

I think back now to the lies of Senator Joe McCarthy, but these were the lies of a mind gone manic.

I remember President Eisenhower authorizing lying about the U-2 incident in 1960, when the Russians shot down our supersecret spy plane, piloted by Francis Gary Powers. I didn't have any trouble rationalizing that lie, even as I wished for a world where such subterfuges were unnecessary.

And in that same category I remember Kennedy suddenly returning to Washington in October 1962, "with a bad cold," when in fact he had returned to cope with the Cuban Missile Crisis. Almost forgivable, I felt when I learned the truth, two weeks later.

But in Watergate, President Richard Milhous Nixon lied over and over again with intent to deceive the American public and thereby save his ass from the consequences of his crimes.

In Watergate, Attorney General John Mitchell, the chief law enforcement officer of the republic, lied with intent to obstruct the justice he was charged with imposing. He, too, lied to save his ass from the consequences of his crimes, and he went to jail for it. The only U.S. Attorney General in American history to go to jail.

All of these lies were on-the-record lies, before television cameras, before reporters, on the telephone, before large audiences, in front of grand juries, and in front of each other. These lies marked a generation of Washington reporters, generally considered by every generation of editors to be the finest reporters in the land.

The liars went to jail, and spent the rest of their lives trying to live down their disgrace. But the reporters went on to report tomorrow's news, with permanently jaundiced eyes.

Twenty years after Watergate, at some Twentieth Century Fund conference on journalism, I remember telling Republican Congressman Jim Leach of Iowa, a man full of common sense and compassion, that I found it easier to cope with Washington by assuming that no one ever told the complete truth in Washington. At least the first time. I was exaggerating to make my point about the new skepticism of journalists when I said that Vietnam, followed by Watergate, had changed the rules forever. Leach was appalled.

No matter how many spin doctors were provided by how many sides of how many arguments, from Watergate on, I started looking for the truth *after* hearing the official version of a truth. And it didn't make much difference whether it was George Bush telling the world that Clarence Thomas was the best-qualified Supreme Court candidate in the land, and that his color had nothing to do with his appointment. Or Ronald Reagan saying he knew nothing about Iran-Contra. Or Tonya Harding saying she knew nothing about the knee-capping of Nancy Kerrigan . . . to widen the circle beyond governmental lies.

Journalism after Watergate changed in another important way, more subtle and harder to define. And I realize I may be speaking about myself, here, although I believe I am speaking about my colleagues, too. I had already declined an invitation to join the newspaper establishment's Valhalla, the Gridiron Club. I felt that newspaper people and newsmakers should keep a civil distance from each other.

Watergate marked the final passage of journalists into the best seats of the establishment. This trip had begun long before when men such as Walter Lippmann and Arthur Krock separated themselves from the rough-and-tumble, hard-drinking journalists made famous in the 1920s in Hecht and MacArthur's *Front Page*, and emerged in the 1930s as leaders of a new tribe of intelligent, educated, eminently presentable newspaper people, mostly male. In their wake came the Scotty Restons, the Alsop brothers, Marquis Childs, Ed Lahey, Roscoe Drummond, and finally the pioneers of television like Murrow, Huntley, Brinkley, and Cronkite, who mixed easily with leaders of government and business. If they all weren't making Wall Street money yet, they were well on their way to respectability. Watergate was the last leg of this trip, bestowing the final accolade of establishmentarianism, or the semblance of it, on the daily press.

With membership in the establishment went a heightened sense of responsibility. At least I began to feel subconsciously that what the world did *not* need right away was another investigation that might again threaten the foundations of democracy. What the newspaper did *not* need right away was another fight to the finish with another president—especially a Republican president, and especially a successful fight. Without the suggestion of a formal decision, I think the fires of investigative zeal were allowed to bank. There wasn't all that much to investigate, nor that much time to investigate it, during the Ford administration. (In the story conference room on the news floor of *The Washington Post* hangs a large framed color photograph of a smiling President Ford, superimposed with the caption: "I got my job through *The Washington Post.*" It originally appeared in a skit on "Saturday Night Live," and it is cheerfully signed: "To Ben Bradlee and all my friends at *The Washington Post* . . . Jerry Ford." I can't think of another president who would have done the same thing.)

The Carter administration fascinated the Washington press corps for its regional stamp and religious quality. But except for the occasional excesses of a Bubba-like Bert Lance, the small-town Georgia banker and Carter friend who resigned in September 1977 as Budget Director in a controversy over his tangled financial affairs, there was still remarkably little smoke to suggest much of a fire to reporters.

It wasn't until the arrival of Reagan and Bush that the post-Watergate caution of editors was again visible. At last there was plenty to investigate: the scandals in public housing, the collapse of the savings and loan industry, and especially the Iran-Contra scandal. Lieutenant Colonel Ollie North's erratic zeal led the White House into some unconstitutional adventures that threatened democracy more than Watergate.

The press, to its discredit, never tumbled to the housing or the savings and loan stories, and editors have to take the blame. The press did investigate Iran-Contra to a fare-thee-well, however, and still never managed to engage the nation's attention or conscience. The public's throat was never seized by Iran-Contra as it had been seized by Watergate. Ronald Reagan was popular; there was no one to impeach him on the Hill. He was near the end of his term.[7]

"Molly Ivins Can't Say That, Can She?"

This was the title of the first collection of columns written by Molly Ivins, the Texas journalist, which remained on the *New York Times* bestseller list for more than twelve months, followed by *Nothin' But Good Times Ahead* (1993), from which the following selection is taken, and *You Got to Dance with Them What Brung You: Politics in the Clinton Years* (1998). Molly Ivins probably would not object to being called, like the late Senator Hubert Humphrey, "the happy warrior" of journalism. She has worked on the *New York Times* and various Texas and other Western newspapers, and has been a columnist for the *Fort Worth Star-Telegram* since 1992. She is not afraid to speak her mind. In the election of 1992 she characterized on his own turf the multi-billionaire presidential candidate Ross Perot as "a dangerous demagogue."

Newspaper columns probably evolved out of the sketches and travel articles written in the nineteenth century, according to Professor Sam Riley of Virginia Tech, who published *A Biographical Dictionary of American Newspaper Columnists* in 1995 and *The American Newspaper Columnist* in 1998, along with other work on the topic. Columns later also siphoned off the opinion that had proliferated in "news" columns of the Colonial and early national period, and later enlivened the editorial page itself. Certainly signed columns afforded the writer greater latitude, for better or worse; sometimes they were abusive. Westbrook Pegler, for example, once referred to Franklin Delano Roosevelt as "that cripple in the White House." Columnist Doris Fleeson would not go along with the herd when Josef Stalin died in 1953. Other columnists were lamenting the passing of "our great ally" of World War II, but Fleeson reminded her readers that Stalin had purged dissidents ruthlessly and deliberately starved to death millions of peasants in his collective farm program. The world was better off without him, she concluded.

Molly Ivins, while never minimizing serious news, believes in "the cleansing lash of laughter," in the phrase of Walt Kelly, creator of the comic strip "Pogo." Here is one of her columns, originally headlined "With U.S. Media, Malice is Absent—But So Is Attention."

Having recently been involved in media criticism in three different forums— including that ghastly soporific yawner of a *Nightline* special edition the other night—the topic is much on my mind.

Election season always brings out people who are mad because their candidate doesn't get written about or seen on TV the way they think he should. And the postelection season always brings a merry round of journalism conferences in which we slap our foreheads and beat our breasts and promise that next time we'll do it better.

The thing that surprises me most is that both journalists and our readers sit around criticizing what we do. The problem is not what we do. It's what we don't do. I think most journalists will go to professional hell (which is something like being edited by the *The New York Times* copy desk for eternity) for their sins of omission, not their sins of commission.

The 1980s was a particularly grim decade for journalistic dereliction of duty.

While we were busy keeping you informed about Bush's dislike of broccoli and about Donald [Trump] and Ivana's love life, the whole S&L crisis—estimated cost upward of $500 billion—occurred without a peep from your watchdogs in the press. Had it not been for a newspaper in Beirut, we would have missed the Iran-Contra scandal entirely.

Washington, D.C., which boasts more journalists per square inch than anywhere else on earth, hadn't even the wit to spot the open scandals at HUD, the EPA, and elsewhere in the federal bureaucracy.

And above all, despite the fact that David Stockman laid it all out for the press early in the Reagan administration, we never reported that the government was in the process of committing economic suicide with an untested and patently silly policy. Instead, we were bringing you "celebrity journalism," breathless accounts of what Calvin Trillin once listed as "glitzhounds, Eurotrash, dress designers and countesses from New Jersey."

It was the decade when *Vanity Fair* was the "hot book" among the magazines and political people liked to read *The New Republic* because it was so "unpredictable."

While reporters were missing major stories all around them, the pundit corps was increasingly peopled by those straight from the front lines of partisan political warfare. Kenneth Adelman, Richard Perle, Mona Charen, David Gergen, Caspar Weinberger, Edwin Meese, Patrick Buchanan, Jeane Kirkpatrick, and Henry Kissinger (briefly) were all Reagan-administration officials who became syndicated columnists.

Since columnists are supposed to have opinions—as opposed to reporters, who are supposed to have prefrontal lobotomies—you may see no great harm in this development. But I submit to you that training and experience as a reporter, while it doesn't always make a good columnist (look at Evans and Novak), does inspire some respect for the squiggly nature of truth.

To instill respect for the craft of journalism, there's nothing like going out to interview both drivers and all five eyewitnesses to an auto accident, and then coming back and trying to write an accurate story about what happened.

The great exception to this rule was Walter Lippmann, who never worked as a reporter but was the towering pundit of Washington.

OK, so Lippmann never covered a beat, but he brought to the trade a degree of learning unmatched since. There may be a few other exceptions. William Safire of the *Times*, a former ad man and Nixon speech writer, is not only a terrific writer but also a whale of a reporter. I can't imagine where he learned it.

The stories the press is most apt to miss are what Gene Roberts, former editor of *The Philadelphia Inquirer*, used to call "the stories that seep and creep." The ones no one ever calls a press conference to announce.

The classic example is the greatest internal migration in the history of this country: the mass migration of rural Southern blacks to Northern cities starting in the 1920s. The trend was never covered by the white press in this country.

Now that the eighties are over, we look up to find 37 million poor people among us; to find that the average American family hasn't been able to get by on one salary since 1973; that most of us are working longer hours and doing less well than we were a decade ago. How come you didn't learn that before 1992? Perhaps it is because no one called a press conference.

One of the stories the press doesn't cover well is the press. When Ben Bagdikian first published *Media Monopoly* in 1982, he found that fifty corporations controlled almost every major media outlet in this country: daily newspapers, magazines, radio stations, television stations, book publishers, and movie studios. By the time the revised edition came out in 1987, the number was twenty-nine corporations, and it is lower today.

At the end of World War II, 80 percent of American newspapers were independently owned. Today, almost without exception, they are owned by one of fifteen chains.

Hodding Carter, a sometime media critic, suggests that the Achilles' heel of most journalists is that we seek the approval of our peers. Having recently survived a small spate of approval myself (like getting invited on *Nightline*), I'm taking as my credo an observation once made by the great political organizer Saul Alinsky, who once got an award from some prestigious foundation.

He called his staff together and said, "Don't worry, boys, we'll weather this storm of approval and come out as hated as ever."[8]

Walter Lippmann: Columnist and Critic

World Press Review notes whether the publishers of each piece of material it culls from the global media is conservative, centrist, or liberal. None of those neat categories would apply to Walter Lippmann, however, as the independent and reasoned opinion in his column, syndicated to more than two hundred newspapers, defies classification. He was so widely read because he could separate the wheat from the chaff, ever since those student days when he was founding president of Harvard's Socialist Club. Then he wrote for *The New Republic* after it began publication in 1914 and later a regular column for *Vanity Fair*, before finally becoming assistant director of the *New York World*'s editorial page. His column, "Today and Tomorrow," began appearing in 1931, and Lippmann was well on his way to becoming the foremost American columnist of the twentieth century. After the demise of the *World*, Lippmann joined the staff of the *New York Herald Tribune* and later moved to the *Washington Post* before his death in 1974.

It is fitting to close this section on press criticism with excerpts from the following column by Walter Lippmann, who worried about freedom of the press and urged that professionalism and responsibility safeguard it. It should be borne in mind that this column was written before the Commission on Freedom of the Press and the Twentieth Century Fund (see above) held their deliberations, but the practical results of their findings on working journalists is debatable. Also, Lippmann urged the strengthening of journalism schools, which has been done, although some observers believe they have become too technical, turning out graduates who can operate video display terminals but who may find it difficult to craft a decent paragraph. If he lived today, Lippmann would have demanded a return to the basics of news reporting and writing, buttressed by solid education in the liberal arts and humanities. But let Walter Lippman, as relevant today as when he wrote half a century ago, have the last word.

This whole subject [liberty and the news] is immensely difficult, and full of traps. It would be well worth an intensive investigation by a group of publishers, lawyers, and students of public affairs. Because in some form or other the next generation will attempt to bring the publishing business under greater social control. There is everywhere an increasingly angry disillusionment about the press, a growing sense of being baffled and misled; and wise publishers will not pooh-pooh these omens. They might well note the history of prohibition, where a failure to work out a programme of temperance brought about an undiscriminating taboo. The regulation of the publishing business is a subtle and elusive matter, and only by an early and sympathetic effort to deal with great evils can the more sensible minds retain their control. If publishers and authors themselves do not face the facts and attempt to deal with them, some day Congress, in a fit of temper, egged on by an outraged public opinion, will operate on the press with an ax. For somehow the community must find a way of making the men who publish news accept responsibility for an honest effort not to misrepresent the facts.

But the phrase "honest effort" does not take us very far. The problem here is not different from that which we begin dimly to apprehend in the field of government and business administration. The untrained amateur may mean well, but he knows not how to do well. Why should he? What are the qualifications for being a surgeon? A certain minimum of special training. What are the qualifications for operating daily on the brain and heart of a nation? None. Go some time and listen to the average run of questions asked in interviews with Cabinet officers—or anywhere else.

I remember one reporter who was detailed to the Peace Conference by a leading news-agency. He came around every day for "news." It was a time when Central Europe seemed to be disintegrating, and great doubt existed as to whether governments would be found with which to sign a peace. But all that this "reporter" wanted to know was whether the German fleet, then safely interned at Scapa Flow, was going to be sunk in the North Sea. He insisted every day on knowing that. For him it was the German fleet or nothing. Finally, he could endure it no longer. So he anticipated Admiral Reuther and announced, in a dispatch to his home papers, that the fleet would be sunk. And when I say that a million American adults learned all that they ever learned about the Peace Conference through this reporter, I am stating a very moderate figure.

He suggests the delicate question raised by the schools of journalism: how far can we go in turning newspaper enterprise from a haphazard trade into a disciplined profession? Quite far, I imagine, for it is altogether unthinkable that a society like ours should remain forever dependent upon untrained accidental witnesses. It is no answer to say that there have been in the past, and that there are now, first-rate correspondents. . . . But they are eminences on a rather flat plateau. The run of the news is handled by men of much smaller caliber. It is handled by such men because reporting is not a dignified profession for which men will invest the time and cost of an education, but an underpaid, insecure, anonymous form of drudgery, conducted on catch-as-catch-can principles. Merely to talk about the reporter in terms of his real importance to civilization will make newspaper men laugh. Yet reporting is a post of peculiar honor. Observation must precede every other activity, and the public observer (that is, the reporter) is a man of critical value. No amount of money or effort spent in fitting the right men for this work could possibly be wasted, for the health of society depends upon the quality of the information it receives.[9]

Notes

1. Quoted in Finley Peter Dunne, *Mr. Dooley at His Best*, ed. Elmer Ellis (New York: Charles Scribner's Sons, 1938), 227.

2. Finley Peter Dunne, *Observations by Mr. Dooley* (New York: R. H. Russell, 1902), 239–44.

3. H. L. Mencken, *Newspaper Days, 1899–1906* (New York: Alfred A. Knopf, 1941), v, ix–x.

4. Quoted in Robert J. Glessing, *The Underground Press in America* (Bloomington: Indiana University Press, 1970), 53.

5. Ibid., 108–10.

6. Quoted from Theodore White, *Breach of Faith*, in entry for Ben Bradlee in *Current Biography Yearbook 1975*, 42.

7. Ben Bradlee, *A Good Life: Newspapering and Other Adventures* (New York: Simon and Schuster, 1995), 405–9.

8. Molly Ivins, *Nothin' But Good Times Ahead* (New York: Random House, 1993), 146–48.

9. Walter Lippmann, *Liberty and the News* (New Brunswick, NJ: Transaction Publishers, 1995), 68–72.

12

Objectivity at
the Barricades

––––––––––⟨◆⟩––––––––––

As the world lurches into a new millennium, the plethora of news coverage of two high-profile cases revealed the flaws of contemporary American journalism. With the advent of saturation reporting, many readers and viewers, still reeling from the year-long coverage of the O. J. Simpson trial, were then drenched with the most intimate details of President Bill Clinton's affair with White House intern Monica Lewinsky. Thoughtful Americans seemed to be asking themselves, Do we really need to know this? Two fleeting television images illustrate the range of opinion. One person said, "He [the President] has been humiliated enough," while a hysterical woman chased after the departing presidential limousine, screaming, "Shame on you! Shame on you!"

Specifically, some observers attacked the concept of objectivity itself in the news. There cannot be "objectivity," they say, when the entire news process is subjective—choice by the editor of what is to be covered, choice by the reporter as to which facts are salient and which should be left out, and choice by the copy editor and others in assigning display or headlines. On the other hand, scholars and some working journalists insist that although complete objectivity may be impossible, considering the socioeconomic backgrounds of the reporters, the ideal should be strived for. Unfortunately, most journalists carry with them long-entrenched and outmoded news values, such as prominence. And there is the "scoop" mentality that all too often ignores the dictum, "Get it first, but get it right." As for prominence, the courts themselves are partly guilty. The trial for the average American charged with murder lasts about two weeks, whereas O. J.

Simpson's took almost a year. It was a symbiotic relationship—the news media fueled the trial, and the trial fueled the news media. It required some three centuries of struggle to obtain what objectivity we have, so it should not be discarded lightly.

"Cash for Trash"—The O. J. Simpson Trial

Americans have always liked their murders on a grand scale, ranging from the butchery that did in Lizzie Borden's parents to the bizarre touches added by Jeffrey Dahmer. It really did not matter whether it was the prominence of the victim, such as Stanford White at the turn of the century, or that of the suspect, such as Dr. Sam Sheppard, prototype of *The Fugitive*, much later. The murders of Nicole Brown Simpson and her friend Ronald Goldman in June 1994 had all the ingredients of a best seller—O. J. Simpson, Nicole's husband charged with the crime, had been an enormously popular football star who could afford to hire some of the best legal talent in the country.

In the Simpson trial itself, racial tensions surfaced in a predominantly black jury. Los Angeles African-Americans had witnessed only two years before the brutal beating on the street of black Rodney King by white policemen as recorded on a bystander's videoscope. When white jurors cleared the policemen, Los Angeles erupted into rioting and looting that cost more than fifty lives. (In 1994, King was awarded 3.8 million in civil damages.) Perhaps television was partly to blame in the Los Angeles violence, as stations showed the videotape of the beating over and over again as the trial progressed, further inflaming the black community. Later, in the Simpson trial, the defense "played the race card" in favor of the African-American defendant. Prestigious lawyer F. Lee Bailey repeatedly used the word "nigger" in an inflammatory way to force Detective Mark Furman to admit that he had used the same term.

The question also arises about the presence of television cameras in the courtroom. This dilemma dates back to post-World War II when news executives urged judges to allow still cameras in their courtrooms. With faster lenses and film, they argued, gone forever were the days when photographers ignited magnesium in a hand-held trough that went off in a disruptive flash and puff. While television cameras may be less obtrusive, one wonders whether the Simpson trial would have lasted so long if the participants had not played to the cameras rather than to the jury. "It's educational," say proponents of cameras in the courtroom, "and it shows the public how our judicial system works." Or does not work, as the Simpson case demonstrated all too well. As it turned out, the "dream team" of defense lawyers won an acquittal after almost a year's testimony and only four hours of jury deliberation. (Later, however, in a civil suit Simpson had to pay $8.5 million to the Goldman family, $12.5 million to Nicole's estate, and $25 million in punitive damages.) Like Lizzie Borden, also acquitted by a sympathetic jury, Simpson seems destined to live out his life as a pariah.

Even though the Simpson jury was sequestered, questions arose as to "trial by newspaper" and racism before the panel reached its decision. *Time* magazine, for example, touched up a cover photograph of Simpson to emphasize his Negroid features, a move straight out of the "Jazz Journalism" of the 1920s when photos were cut and manipulated to create a false impression. (After the vote for acquittal in the Senate impeachment trial of Clinton, the *Philadelphia Daily News* doctored a front-page photograph of the president to make it appear that he was battered—Band-aid on forehead, black eye, and missing teeth—over the caption, "The Winner."[1]) This kind of creativity is hardly the stuff of which responsible newspapers are made.

Throughout the Simpson trial, the press ballyhooed its coverage of "the trial of the century." Had these reporters never heard of the Loeb-Leopold trial of 1924, the Scopes evolution trial in Tennessee in 1925, or the trial for the kidnapping and murder of the Lindbergh baby in 1934? Entertainers also voiced their opinions on late-night talk shows as if their views weighed more than those of the man or woman in the street.

Out of the rumors and innuendos sprang ghost-written books that tried to cash in on the topic of the day. The same was true in the aftermath of the Watergate scandal, when the sardonic motto was "Buy a book from a crook." In the following excerpt, Jeffrey Toobin of *The New Yorker* examines another aspect of this phenomenon—selling "information" to the tabloids—with its legal implications. The lead-in to the article, "Cash for Trash," states prophetically, "The tabloid stories surrounding O. J. Simpson are damning, but, following the latest trend in high-profile criminal cases, they may help set him free."

Robert Owens, an attorney from Los Angeles, had a cellular phone in one hand, a pen in the other, the sand of a Maui beach between his toes, and the riches of an O. J. Simpson-obsessed media on his mind. He represents Dale St. John, the owner of Town & Country Limousine, of Torrance, California, which is the company that sent a car to pick up the former football star and take him to the airport on what is now invariably referred to as "the fateful night" of June 12, 1994. "Obviously, Dale was one of the first people the police spoke to, and I know that what he said to them has not been published anywhere so far," Owens told me, over his phone in a tone of shared intimacy. "Remember, Dale drove O. J. personally for several years, and he also had a lot of contact with the driver on the night of the murders. He hasn't made a deal with anyone yet, and he hasn't spoken to anyone yet, but he's at the point now where he's ready to make a deal with someone. That's why he called me."

Owens symbolizes the state of the art in one of the newest specialties in the legal market—the brokering of interviews to the tabloid media. The cash-for-trash bar is not organized in any official sense—many of its practitioners dip in and out for just a single sale—but its influence is soaring in the prosecution of high-profile criminal cases. Because witnesses who take money from tabloids automatically raise questions about their credibility, and because defense attorneys can so successfully vilify those witnesses on cross-examination, the practice of buying and selling interviews seriously threatens prosecutors' abilities to try high-profile cases. Ironically, the print and television tabloids that fuel this industry have been widely denounced for their supposed rush to convict celebrity defendants before they have even been tried; as it happens, however, the tabloids can so taint the central witnesses in the government's case that tabloid infotainment may actually be the best friend a famous defendant can have. The torrent of press coverage of the Simpson case, tabloid and otherwise, has already cost the prosecution dearly. On June 24th, Judge Cecil J. Mills, of the California Superior Court, dismissed the grand jury investigating the case, because some jurors had been exposed to "potentially prejudicial matters not officially presented to them by the district attorney."

Certainly, it seems, the Los Angeles Police Department has come to recognize the costs of saturation coverage. This official acknowledgment came in a little-noticed coda to the first public announcement of the murder of Nicole Brown Simpson and her friend Ronald Goldman. After giving the basic facts about the case, such as the names of the victims and the place where the bodies were found, Commander David Gascon issued a plea to the news media. "Over the next few days, detectives will continue to interview possible witnesses, and gather and analyze evidence," Gascon said on June 13th. "Detectives are requesting that the media not attempt to contact potential witnesses in this case, as those contacts may delay and negatively impact the course of this investigation. I need to stress that. It's critically important."

Steve Dunleavy, who is the lead correspondent for Fox Television's "A Current Affair" and is also the Australian elder statesman of the tabloid industry, first heard about Gascon's request when I mentioned it to him, a few days later, in the course of a telephone call. "With all due respect to the L.A. police, they're a little Pollyanna when they ask reporters not to talk to witnesses," Dunleavy said. "We have an L.A. guy, and I'm just sort of tits on a reindeer out here, mate, but this is the story people are talking about, and we've got to be here." In fact, on the day that Dunleavy and I spoke, he had just interviewed Michael Mesko, a caddie at the Riviera Country Club, who had toted O. J. Simpson's bag around the course only hours before the murders took place. Mesko told Dunleavy that Simpson was alternatively angry and maudlin during his round, and that at one point Simpson "turns to me and says, 'Mitch, I'm a pathetic person.' " Mesko added, "I was shocked." Dunleavy now chuckled, and said, "Nice little scoop for us. But, if that's how the police feel, best of luck to them, eh?"

Dunleavy's view also seems to be that of his colleagues in the tabloid press. "It's not just going to be witnesses in the case itself," one reporter for a supermarket tabloid told me. "Every woman O. J. went out with, every secretary, everyone who worked with him—they're all going to be hitting the money." Indeed, the buying of witnesses has already begun. A week after the murders, Paramount's television tabloid "Hard Copy" agreed to pay a potentially crucial witness named Jill Shively five thousand dollars for her recollections of the night of June 12th. Holding up her grand-jury subpoena for the cameras, Shively said that she had seen a harried O. J. Simpson driving his Ford Bronco wildly near his home in Brentwood at about eleven o'clock. Adapting nicely to the overheated tabloid idiom, she declared that Simpson looked "like a madman gone mad, insane." At around the same time, the supermarket tabloid the *Star* paid Shively two thousand six hundred dollars for a print interview. And last week, at the preliminary hearing in the Simpson case, two of the prosecution's opening witnesses revealed that they, too, had been paid for interviews with a tabloid. Allen Wattenberg, a co-owner of Ross Cutlery, the store where O. J. Simpson bought a knife shortly before the murders, and José Camacho, a salesman at the store, testified that they would be splitting a twelve-thousand-five-hundred-dollar payment from the *National Enquirer* with Allen's brother and partner, Richard.

Shively and the knife dealers sold themselves cheap. The *Enquirer* offered at least a hundred thousand dollars for an interview with Kato Kaelin, a family friend who was staying in the guesthouse at Simpson's estate on the night of the murders. "The guy from the *Enquirer* made it clear that the hundred thousand was negotiable," Kaelin's lawyer, William Genego, told me shortly after the offer was received. "He was clearly willing to go higher." Indeed, the *Enquirer* raised its offer to two hundred and fifty thousand dollars last week. But, Genego said, his client turned the offer down, along with all other interview requests, because "he didn't want to get into that whole distasteful business." Yet the tabloids expect to find no shortage of takers as they continue to offer money to witnesses in the Simpson case. "The thing of it is that the really big guns have not come up for bid yet," a tabloid editor told me ten days after the murders. "No one even knows the name yet of the limo driver. He'd be worth plenty. And the biggest money of all is for Al Cowlings"—Simpson's best friend, who was the driver in his nationally televised chase along the Los Angeles freeways.

But as Dale St. John, for one, is discovering, this form of information entrepreneurship is treacherous, and calls for negotiating expertise. In the days immediately after the murders, St. John erred by peddling his story directly to tabloid reporters instead of leaving it up to his lawyer to drop tantalizing morsels. "Dale calls here every day, but we're done with him now," a "Hard Copy" employee told me. Indeed, this person said, St. John was the source for a "Hard Copy" scoop, on June 16th, reporting that Simpson was not at his estate when the limousine driver came to pick him up at ten-forty-five on the night of the murders; it was fifteen minutes later that a sweaty and agitated Simpson showed up for his ride. "Dale's got nothing more to sell us," the "Hard Copy" employee said.

Owens, St. John's lawyer, remained confident. "Dale's been approached by a number of different media outlets, a couple of TV shows, and two of the magazines," he said. "Our low offer at this point is fifteen thousand dollars and a trip to Hawaii for Dale, his wife, and their three kids. The top offer is fifty thousand dollars, from the *Enquirer*, but Dale doesn't want to deal with them. I'm still expecting more, and I figure Dale and I will be closing the deal any day now. That's why I interrupted my vacation to help him."

Credit (or blame) for the creation of the modern cash-for-trash industry belongs to the United States Supreme Court, according to John Terenzio, a former executive producer of "A Current Affair." "When they struck down the Son of Sam law, that's when everything started to change," he told me recently. The so-called Son of Sam law was passed by the New York State Legislature in 1977 to prevent David Berkowitz (who sent notes to the police signed "Son of Sam") from capitalizing on his notoriety as a serial killer. The measure made it illegal for criminals to earn income from selling stories about their misdeeds. In 1991, however, the Supreme Court ruled that the law violated the First Amendment. "Once that law was gone, we knew that the day would come when the Jeffrey Dahmers of the world would make a bundle," Terenzio said. "I wouldn't pay a convicted criminal, but it opened our eyes to what was out there—the deals to be made." The supermarket tabloids, led by the *Enquirer*, which has a weekly readership of nearly twenty million, have had no trouble keeping pace. I was told by David Perel, an editor at the *Enquirer*, "If someone has a great story to sell, and it can be exclusive for us, the price may be in the hundreds of thousands of dollars, and we're going to pay it."[2]

"What Went Wrong"—Clinton in the Dock

Americans, increasingly skeptical of the press, were further turned off by the overkill of journalistic coverage in the sensational treatment of the Clinton story. There was little else on CNN, for example, the all-news television channel, leading one to wonder if all-news really means no-news because nothing stands out—"a moving paper fantasy," in the words of the rock musical, *Hair*. And the avalanche of information (or disinformation) narcotized the audience. As Toni Morrison, Pulitzer Prize-winning author, wrote most succinctly in *The New Yorker* during the course of the president's difficulties: "This summer [1998], my plan was to do very selective radio listening, read no newspapers or news magazines, and leave my television screen profoundly, mercifully blank. There were books to read, others to finish, a few to read again. It was a lovely summer, and I was pleased with the decision to recuse myself from what had become since January The Only Story Worth Telling."[3]

Thus, when unilateral warfare was launched in the Balkans by the North Atlantic Treaty Organization (NATO) against the genocidal policies of Yugoslav President Slobodan Milosevic in the province of Kosovo, news-weary Americans seemed disengaged from the crisis. Along strictly party lines, Bill Clinton was impeached by a vote of 258 to 176 in the House of Representatives on December 19, 1998—the second president in our history to be so indicted—but acquitted in the Senate trial with several Republicans in the 50–50 vote crossing over to vote for acquittal, two-thirds needed for conviction. The outcome was that only partisans seemed to think that the president was guilty of "treason, bribery, or other high crimes and misdemeanors," as specified by the Constitution of the United States.

In the cases of the coverage of the Simpson and Clinton trials, however disparate, the foremost casualty was objectivity in the American press. Gossip—as illegally recorded on more than twenty hours of tapes by Linda Tripp—was reported, and the very fact that it was reported lent it credence. Gone were the days of meticulous Watergate reporting when *Washington Post* editor Ben Bradlee insisted on two substantiated sources for every allegation. On the contrary, for the first time the supermarket tabloids were taken seriously, and their stories were followed up by part of the mainstream press. Thus, these tabloids became the tail that wagged the dog of the established press.

Throughout the eight months of coverage of the Lewinksy affair, President Clinton's ratings in the polls remained high, indicating that the public had lost confidence in the press, which seemed to be telling another story. But, as it turned out, Clinton was exonerated, special prosecutor Kenneth Starr had his day in court and lost, and Monica Lewinsky appeared on the cover of *Time*, was interviewed by Barbara Walters, and made a book tour of England. Some 150 newspapers that had called for Clinton's resignation when the scandal first broke were left with the proverbial egg on their faces, and everyone went home to write a non-book. While there was some contemporary analysis of press coverage of the Clinton affair, we could have learned from the once-great Argentine newspaper, *La Prensa*, which stated as its motto in its first issue in 1868, "Independence, respect for the private individual, and reasoned criticism of public officials but not of their individual personalities will be our creed."

Beginning with the Simpson trial, however, self-appointed "analysts," "consultants," and "commentators" clogged the airwaves and viewed the fate of an individual as if it were a tennis match, with so many points scored by the prosecution and so many by the defense at the end of each day. The judicial process was trivialized, and these pundits continued on other shows purporting to explain the inner workings of justice long after the Simpson trial ended. Journalism was the loser.

As for the Clinton melodrama, let a working newsman evaluate the coverage. The following, "What Went Wrong," by Jules Witcover, is reprinted in its entirety from the *Columbia Journalism Review* (March/April 1998). Witcover, now of the *Baltimore Sun*, has covered Washington as a reporter and columnist for forty-three years and is the author of thirteen books on U.S. presidential politics and history.

In the sex scandal story that has cast a cloud over the president, Bill Clinton does not stand to be the only loser. No matter how it turns out, another will be the American news media, whose reputation as truth-teller to the country has been besmirched by perceptions, in and out of the news business, about how the story has been reported.

The indictment is too sweeping. Many news outlets have acted with considerable responsibility, especially after the first few frantic days, considering the initial public pressure for information, the burden of obtaining much of it from sealed documents in legal proceedings and criminal investigations, and the stonewalling of President Clinton and his White House aides.

But the explosive nature of the story, and the speed with which it burst on the consciousness of the nation, triggered in the early stages a piranha-like frenzy in pursuit of the relatively few tidbits tossed into the journalistic waters by—whom? That there were wholesale leaks from lawyers and investigators was evident, but either legal restraints or reportorial pledges of anonymity kept the public from knowing with any certainty the sources of key elements in the saga.

Into the vacuum created by a scarcity of clear and credible attribution raced all manner of rumor, gossip, and, especially, hollow sourcing, making the reports of some mainstream outlets scarcely distinguishable from supermarket tabloids. The rush to be first or to be more sensational created a picture of irresponsibility seldom seen in the reporting of presidential affairs. Not until the story settled in a bit did much of the reporting again begin to resemble what has been expected of mainstream news organizations.

The Clinton White House, in full damage-control mode, seized on the leaks and weakly attributed stories to cast the news media as either willing or unwilling collaborators of sorts with independent counsel Kenneth Starr's investigation of alleged wrongdoing by the president. Attacking the independent counsel and his office was a clear diversionary tactic, made more credible to many viewers and readers by suggesting that the overzealous news business, so suspect already in many quarters, was being used by Starr.

Unlike the Watergate scandal of twenty-five years ago, which trickled out over twenty-six months, this scandal broke like a thunderclap, with the direst predictions from the start. Whereas in the Watergate case the word impeachment was unthinkable and not uttered until much later in the game, the prospect of a premature end to the Clinton presidency was heard almost at once. "Is He Finished?" asked the cover line on *U.S. News & World Report*. Not to be outdone, *The Economist* of London commanded, "If It's True, Go."

ABC News's White House correspondent Sam Donaldson speculated on *This Week with Sam and Cokie* [Roberts] on January 25 that Clinton could resign before the next week was out. "If he's not telling the truth," Donaldson said, "I think his presidency is numbered in days. This isn't going to drag out. . . . Mr. Clinton, if he's not telling the truth and the evidence shows that, will resign, perhaps this week."

After Watergate, it was said that the president [Richard Nixon] had been brought down by two reporters, Bob Woodward and Carl Bernstein, and their newspaper, *The Washington Post*, and they were widely commended for it. This time, after initial reporting by Michael Isikoff of *Newsweek*, there was a major piling-on by much of American print and electronic journalism, for which they have been widely castigated. A *Washington Post* poll taken ten days after the story broke found 56 percent of those surveyed believed the news media were treating Clinton unfairly, and 74 percent said they were giving the story "too much attention."

The advent of twenty-four-hour, all-news cable channels and the Internet assured the story of non-stop reportage and rumor, augmented by repeated break-ins of normal network programming and late-night rehashes. Viewing and listening audiences swelled, as did newspaper and magazine circulation, accommodated by special press runs.

Not just the volume but the methodology of the reporting came in for sharp criticism—often more rumor-mongering than fact-getting and fact-checking, and unattributed appropriation of the work and speculation of others. The old yardstick said to have been applied by the *Post* in the Watergate story—that every revelation had to be confirmed by two sources before publication—was summarily abandoned by many news outlets.

As often as not, reports were published or broadcast without a single source named, or mentioned in an attribution so vague as to be worthless. Readers and listeners were told repeatedly that this or that information came from "sources," a word that at best conveyed only the notion that the information was not pure fiction or fantasy. As leaks flew wildly from these unspecified sources, the American public was left as seldom before in a major news event to guess where stories came from and why.

Readers and listeners were told what was reported to be included in affidavits and depositions in the Paula Jones sexual harassment case—information that supposedly was protected by a federal judge's gag order—or presented to independent counsel Starr. Leakers were violating the rules while the public was left to guess about their identity, and about the truth of what was passed on to them through the news media, often without the customary tests of validity.

In retrospect, it was sadly appropriate that the first hint of the story really broke into public view not in *Newsweek*, whose investigative reporter, Isikoff, had been doggedly pursuing for more than a year Paula Jones's allegations that Clinton had made inappropriate sexual advances to her when he was governor of Arkansas. Rather, it surfaced in the wildly irresponsible Internet site of Matt Drudge, a reckless trader in rumor and gossip who makes no pretense of checking on the accuracy of what he reports. ("Matt Drudge," says Jodie Allen, Washington editor for Bill Gates's online magazine *Slate*, "is the troll under the bridge of Internet journalism.")

Drudge learned that *Newsweek* on Saturday, January 17, with its deadline crowding in, had elected not to publish. According to a February 2 *Newsweek* report, prosecutors working for Starr had told the newsmagazine they needed a little more time to persuade former White House intern Monica Lewinsky to tell them about an alleged relationship she had with the president that had implications of criminal conduct.

Early Saturday morning, according to the same *Newsweek* report, the magazine "was given access to" a tape bearing conversations between

Lewinsky and her friend Linda Tripp. But the *Newsweek* editors held off. Opting for caution of the sort that in earlier days was applauded, they waited.

The magazine also reported that publication was withheld because the tapes in themselves "neither confirmed nor disproved" obstruction of justice, because the magazine had "no independent confirmation of the basis for Starr's inquiry," and because its reporters had never seen or talked with Lewinsky "or done enough independent reporting to assess the young woman's credibility." If anything, such behavior if accurately described resonated with responsibility, although holding back also left *Newsweek* open to speculation by journalists that its action might have been a quid pro quo for information received.

Drudge, meanwhile, characteristically feeling no restraints, on Monday morning, January 19, jumped in and scooped *Newsweek* on its own story with a report that the newsmagazine had "spiked" it after a "screaming fight in the editors' offices" on the previous Saturday night. Isikoff later said "there was a vigorous discussion about what was the journalistically proper thing to do. There were no screaming matches."

Drudge was not without his defenders. Michael Kinsley, the editor of *Slate*, argued later that "the Internet beat TV and print to this story, and ultimately forced it on them, for one simple reason: lower standards. . . . There is a case to be made, however, for lower standards. In this case, the lower standards were vindicated. Almost no one now denies there is a legitimate story here." Kinsley seemed to harbor the crazy belief that had Drudge not reported that *Newsweek* had the story, the newsmagazine never would have printed it the next week, and therefore the Internet could take credit for "forcing" the story on the mainstream news media.

Newsweek, not going to press again until the next Saturday, finally put the story on its American Online site on Wednesday, January 21, after *The Washington Post* had broken it on newsstands in its early Wednesday edition out Tuesday night, under the four-column banner atop page one: CLINTON ACCUSED OF URGING AIDE TO LIE. The story was attributed to "sources close to the investigation." ABC News broadcast the gist of it on radio shortly after midnight Wednesday.

The *Los Angeles Times* also had the story in its Wednesday editions, but *The New York Times*, beaten badly by the *Post* on the Watergate story a quarter of a century earlier, was left at the gate again. The lead on its first story on Thursday, January 22, however, was a model of fact: "As an independent counsel issued a fresh wave of White House subpoenas, President Clinton today denied accusations of having had a sexual affair with a twenty-one-year-old White House intern and promised to cooperate with prosecutors investigating whether the president obstructed justice and sought to have the reported liaison covered up."

The story spread like an arsonist's handiwork. *The Washington Post* of Thursday reported from "sources familiar with the investigation" that the FBI had secretly taped Lewinsky by placing a "body wire" on Tripp and had got information that "helped persuade" Attorney General Janet Reno to ask for and receive from the three-judge panel overseeing the independent counsel authorization to expand the investigation.

On that same Thursday, the *Times* identified Lucianne Goldberg, the literary agent who later said she had advised Tripp to tape her conversations with Lewinsky. But *The Washington Post* continued to lead the way with more information apparently leaked by, but not attributed specifically to, lawyers in the case, and in the Paula Jones sexual harassment lawsuit that had caught Lewinsky in its web.

On network television on Friday, taste went out the window. ABC News correspondent Jackie Judd reported that "a source with direct knowledge of" Lewinsky's allegations said she "would visit the White House for sex with Clinton in the early evening or early mornings on the weekends, when certain aides who would find her presence disturbing were not at the office." Judd went on: "According to the source, Lewinsky says she saved, apparently as a kind of souvenir, a navy blue dress with the president's semen stain on it. If true, this could provide physical evidence of what really happened."

That phrase "if true" became a gateopener for any rumor to make its way into the mainstream. Judd's report ignited a round of stories about a search for such a dress. Despite disavowals of its existence by Lewinsky's lawyer, William Ginsburg, stories soon appeared about a rumored test for tell-tale DNA by the FBI.

The *New York Post*, under the headline Monica Kept Sex Dress As a Souvenir, quoted "sources" as saying the dress really was "a black cocktail dress that Lewinsky never sent to the cleaners," adding that "a dress with semen on it could provide DNA evidence virtually proving the man's identity—evidence that could be admissible at trial." The newspaper also reported that "Ken Starr's investigators searched Lewinsky's Watergate apartment, reportedly with her consent, and carried off a number of items, including some clothing," which Ginsburg subsequently confirmed. He later said that the president had given Lewinsky a long T-shirt, not a dress.

The *Village Voice*, in a scathing retracing of the path taken by the ABC News report of a semen-stained dress, labeled Judd's account hearsay and noted it had nevertheless been picked up by other news organizations as if such a dress existed. Six days after the original ABC story, CBS News reported that "no DNA evidence or stains have been found on a dress that belongs to Lewinsky" that was "seized by the FBI from Lewinsky's apartment" and tested by "the FBI lab."

ABC, the next day, reported that "according to law enforcement sources, Starr so far has come up empty in a search for forensic evidence of a relationship between Mr. Clinton and Lewinsky. Sources say a dress and other pieces of clothing were tested, but they all had been dry cleaned before the FBI picked them up from Lewinsky's apartment." In this comment, ABC implied that there had been stains, and it quoted an ABC spokesperson as saying, "We stand by that initial report" of a semen-stained dress.

A close competitor for the sleaziest report award was the one regarding the president's alleged sexual preference. On Wednesday, January 21, the Scripps Howard News Service reported that one person who had listened to the Lewinsky-Tripp tapes said Lewinsky "described how Clinton allegedly first urged her to have oral sex, telling her that such acts were not technically adultery."

That night, on ABC News's *Nightline*, Ted Koppel advised viewers gravely that "the crisis in the White House" ultimately "may come down to the question of whether oral sex does or does not constitute adultery." The question, he insisted, was neither "inappropriate" nor "frivolous" because "it may bear directly on the precise language of the president's denials. What sounds, in other words, like a categorical denial may prove to be something altogether different."

Nightline correspondent Chris Bury noted Clinton's "careful use of words in the matter of sex" in the past. He recalled that in 1992, in one of Gennifer Flowers's taped conversations offered by Flowers in her allegations of a long affair with the then governor of Arkansas, she "is heard discussing oral sex with Clinton." Bury went on, "during this same time period, several Arkansas state troopers assigned to the governor's detail had said on the record that Clinton would tell them that oral sex is not adultery."

The distinction came amid much speculation about whether Clinton, in his flat denial of having had "sexual relations with that woman," might be engaging in the sort of semantic circumlocution for which he became notorious in his 1992 presidential campaign when asked about his alleged affair with Flowers, his draft status, smoking marijuana, and other matters.

The Washington Post on Sunday, January 25, reported on the basis of the Tripp tapes that "in more than 20 hours of conversations" with Tripp, "Lewinsky described an eighteen-month involvement that included late-night trysts at the White House featuring oral sex." The story noted in its second paragraph: "Few journalists have heard even a portion of these audio tapes, which include one made under the auspices of the FBI. Lewinsky herself has not commented on the tapes publicly. And yet they have been the subject of numerous news accounts and the fodder for widespread speculation." Nevertheless, it then added: "Following are descriptions of key discussions recorded on the tapes, information that *The Washington Post* has obtained from sources who have listened to portions of them."

The story went on to talk of "bouts" of " 'phone sex' over the lines between the White House and her apartment" and one comment to Tripp in which Lewinsky is alleged to have said she wanted to go back to the White House—as the newspaper rendered it—as "special assistant to the president for [oral sex]." The same story also reported that "Lewinsky tells Tripp that she has an article of clothing with Clinton's semen on it."

On television, these details led some anchors, such as Judy Woodruff of CNN, to preface some reports with the kind of unsuitable-for-children warning usually reserved for sex-and-violence shows like *NYPD Blue*. But comments on oral sex and semen may have been more jarring to older audiences, to whom such subjects have been taboo, than to viewers and readers from the baby boom and younger.

The tabloids were hard-pressed to outdo the mainstream, but they were up to the challenge. Borrowing from *The Sun of London*, the *New York Post* quoted Flowers in an interview saying "she reveals that Clinton once gave her his 'biblical' definition of oral sex: 'It isn't "real" sex.' " The headline on the story helped preserve the *Post*'s reputation: GOSPEL ACCORDING TO BUBBA SAYS ORAL SEX ISN'T CHEATING.

Meanwhile, the search for an eyewitness to any sexual activity between Clinton and Lewinsky went on. On Sunday, January 25, Judd on ABC reported "several sources" as saying Starr was investigating claims that in the spring of 1996, the president and Lewinsky "were caught in an intimate encounter" by either Secret Service agents or White House staffers. The next morning, the front-page tabloid headlines of both the *New York Post* and the New York *Daily News* shouted, CAUGHT IN THE ACT, with the accompanying stories attributed to "sources."

Other newspapers' versions of basically the same story had various attributions: the *Los Angeles Times*: "people familiar with the investigation"; *The Washington Post*: "sources familiar with the probe"; *The Wall Street Journal*: "a law enforcement official" and "unsubstantiated reports." The *Chicago Tribune* attributed ABC News, using the lame disclaimer "if true" and adding that "attempts to confirm the report independently were unsuccessful." *The New York Times*, after considering publication, prudently decided against it.

Then on Monday night, January 26, *The Dallas Morning News* reported in the first edition of its Tuesday paper and on its Web site: "Independent counsel Kenneth Starr's staff has spoken with a Secret Service agent who is prepared to testify that he saw President Clinton and Monica Lewinsky in a compromising situation in the White House, sources said Monday." The story, taken off the Internet by The Associated Press and put on its wire and used that night on *Nightline*, was retracted within hours on the ground that its source had told the paper that the source had been mistaken.

Then there was the case of the television talk show host, Larry King, referring to a *New York Times* story about a message from Clinton on Lewinsky's answering machine—when there was, in fact, no such story. Interviewing lawyer Ginsburg the night of January 28, King told his guest that the story would appear in the next day's paper, only to report later in the show: "We have a clarification, I am told, from our production staff. We may have jumped the gun on the fact that *The New York Times* will have a new report on the phone call from the president to Monica Lewinsky, the supposed phone call. We have no information on what *The New York Times* will be reporting tomorrow."

Beyond the breakdown in traditional sourcing of stories in this case, not to mention traditional good taste, was the manner in which a questionably sourced or totally unsourced account was assumed to be accurate when printed or aired, and was picked up as fact by other reporters without attempting to verify it.

For days, a report in *The Washington Post* of what was said to be in Clinton's secret deposition in the Paula Jones case was taken by the press as fact and used as the basis for concluding that Clinton had lied in 1992 in an interview on *60 Minutes*. Noting that Clinton had denied any sexual affair with Gennifer Flowers, the *Post* reported that in the deposition Clinton acknowledged the affair, "according to sources familiar with his testimony."

Loose attribution of sources abounded. One of the worst offenders was conservative columnist Arianna Huffington. She offered her view on the CNBC talk show *Equal Time* that Clinton had had an affair with Sheila Lawrence, the widow of the late ambassador whose body was exhumed from Arlington National Cemetery after it was revealed he had lied about his military record. Huffington, in reporting on the alleged affair, confessed that "we're not there yet in terms of proving it." So much for the application of journalistic ethics by journalistic amateurs.

While CNN and other twenty-four-hour cable outlets capable of breaking stories at any moment and Internet heist artists like Drudge poised to pounce on someone else's stories, it wasn't long before the Internet became the venue of first resort even for a daily newspaper. *The Wall Street Journal* on February 4, ready with a report that a White House steward had told a grand jury summoned by Starr that he had seen Clinton and Lewinsky alone in a study next to the Oval Office, posted the story on its World Wide Web site and its wire service rather than wait to break it the next morning in the *Journal*. In its haste, the newspaper did not wait for comment from the White House, leading deputy press secretary Joe Lockhart to complain that "the normal rules of checking or getting a response to a story seem to have given way to the technology of the Internet and the competitive pressure of getting it first."

The Web posting bore the attribution "two individuals familiar with" the steward's testimony. But his lawyer soon called the report "absolutely false and irresponsible." The *Journal* that night changed the posting to say the steward had made the assertion not to the grand jury but to "Secret Service personnel." The story ran in the paper the next day, also saying "one individual familiar with" the steward's story "said that he had told Secret Service personnel that he found and disposed of tissues with lipstick and other stains on them" after the Clinton-Lewinsky meeting. Once again, a juicy morsel was thrown out and pounced on by other news outlets without verification, and in spite of the firm denial of the *Journal* report from the steward's lawyer.

One of the authors of the story, Brian Duffy, later told *The Washington Post* the reason the paper didn't wait and print an exclusive the next morning was because "we heard footsteps from at least one other news organization and just didn't think it was going to hold in this crazy cycle we're in." In such manner did the race to be first take precedence over having a carefully checked story in the newspaper itself the next day.

White House press secretary Michael McCurry called the *Journal*'s performance "one of the sorriest episodes of journalism" he had ever witnessed, with "a daily newspaper reporting hour-by-hour" without giving the White House a chance to respond. *Journal* managing editor Paul Steiger replied in print that "we went with our original story when we felt it was ready" and "did not wait for a response from the White House," because "it had made it clear repeatedly" that it wasn't going to respond to any questions about any aspect of the case.

Steiger said at that point that "we stand by our account" of what the steward had told the Secret Service. Three days later, however, the *Journal*

262 ◆ In the News

reported that, contrary to its earlier story, the steward had not told the grand jury he had seen Clinton and Lewinsky alone. Steiger said that "we deeply regret our erroneous report of the steward's testimony."

On a less salacious track, the more prominent mainstream dailies continued to compete for new breaks, relying on veiled sources. *The New York Times* contributed a report on February 6 that Clinton had called his personal secretary, Betty Currie, into his office and asked her "a series of leading questions such as: 'We were never alone, right?' " The source given was "lawyers familiar with her account."

The *Post*, "scrambling to catch up," as its media critic Howard Kurtz put it, shortly afterward confirmed the meeting "according to a person familiar with" Currie's account. Saying his own paper used "milder language" than the *Times* in hinting at a motivation of self-protection by the president, Kurtz quoted the *Post* story that said "Clinton probed her memories of his contacts with Lewinsky to see whether they matched his own." In any event, Currie's lawyer later said it was "absolutely false" that she believed Clinton "tried to influence her recollection."

The technology of delivery is not all that has changed in the reporting of the private lives of presidents and other high-ranking officeholders. The news media have traveled light years from World War II days and earlier, when the yardstick for such reporting was whether misconduct, alleged or proved, affected the carrying out of official duties.

In 1984, when talk circulated about alleged marital infidelity by presidential candidate Gary Hart, nothing was written or broadcast because there was no proof and no one willing to talk. In 1987, however, a *Newsweek* profile reported that his marriage had been rocky and he had been haunted by rumors of womanizing. A tip to *The Miami Herald* triggered the stakeout of his Washington townhouse from which he was seen leaving with Donna Rice. Only after that were photographs of the two on the island of Bimini displayed in the tabloid *National Enquirer* and Hart was forced from the race. Clearly, the old rule—that questions about a public figure's private life were taboo—no longer applied.

But the next time a presidential candidate ran into trouble on allegations of sexual misconduct—Bill Clinton in 1992—the mainstream press was dragged into hot pursuit of the gossip tabloids that not too many years earlier had been treated like a pack of junkyard dogs by their supposedly ethical betters. The weekly supermarket tabloid, *Star*, printed a long, explicit first-person account of Flowers's alleged twelve-year affair with Clinton. Confronted with the story on the campaign trail in New Hampshire, Clinton denied it but went into extensive damage control, culminating in his celebrated *60 Minutes* interview. With the allegations quickly becoming the centerpiece of his campaign, the mainstream press had no recourse but to report how he was dealing with it. Thus did the tail of responsible journalism come to wag the dog.

From then on, throughout Clinton's 1992 campaign and ever since, the once-firm line between rumor and truth, between gossip and verification, has been crumbling. The assault has been led by the trashy tabloids but increasingly accompanied by major newspapers and television, with copy-cat tabloid radio and TV talk shows piling on. The proliferation of such shows, their sensationalism, bias, and lack of responsibility and taste have vastly increased the hit-and-run practice of what now goes under the name of journalism.

The practitioners with little pretense to truth-telling or ethics, and few if any credentials suggesting journalistic training in either area, now clutter the airwaves, on their own shows (Watergate felon G. Gordon Liddy, conspiracy-spinner Rush Limbaugh, Iran-Contra figure Oliver North) or as loudmouth hosts and guests on weekend talkfests (John McLaughlin, Matt Drudge).

In the print press and on the Internet as well, journalism pretenders and poseurs feed misinformation, speculation, and unverified accusations to the reading public. The measure of their success in polluting the journalism mainstream in the most recent Clinton scandal was the inclusion of Drudge as a guest analyst on NBC News's *Meet the Press*. The program also included Isikoff, the veteran *Newsweek* investigative reporter.

Playing straight man to Drudge, moderator Tim Russert asked him about "reports" that there were "discussions" on the Lewinsky tapes "of other women, including other White House staffers, involved with the president." The professional gossip replied, dead-pan: "There is talk all over this town [that] another White House staffer is going to come out from behind the curtains this week. If this is the case—and you couple this with the headline that the *New York Post* has, [that] there are hundreds, hundreds [of other women] according to Miss Lewinsky, quoting Clinton—we're in for a huge shock that goes beyond the specific episode. It's a whole psychosis taking place in the White House."

Drudge officiously took the opportunity to lecture the White House reporters for not doing their job. He expressed "shock and very much concern that there's been deception for years coming out of this White House. I mean, this intern relationship didn't happen last week. It happened over a course of a year and a half, and I'm concerned. Also, there's a press corps that wasn't monitoring the situation close enough." Thus spoke the celebrated trash-peddler while Isikoff sat silently by.

Such mixing of journalistic pretenders side-by-side with established, proven professional practitioners gives the audience a deplorably disturbing picture of a news business that already struggles under public skepticism, cynicism, and disaffection based on valid criticism of mistakes, lapses, poor judgment, and bad taste. The press and television, like the Republic itself, will survive its shortcomings in the Lewinsky affair, whether or not President Clinton survives the debacle himself. The question is, has the performance been a mere lapse of standards in the heat of a fast-breaking, incredibly competitive story of major significance? A tapering off of the mad frenzy of the first week or so of the scandal gives hope that this is the case.

Or does it signal abandonment of the old in favor of a looser regard for the responsibility to tell readers and listeners where stories come from, and for standing behind the veracity of them? It is a question that goes to the heart of the practice of a trade that, for all its failings, should be a bulwark of a democracy that depends on an accurately informed public. Journalism in the late 1990s still should be guided by adherence to the same elemental rules that have always existed—report what you know as soon as you know it, not before. And if you're not sure, wait and check it out yourself.

Those news organizations that abide by this simple edict, like a disappointed *Newsweek* in this instance, may find themselves run over by less scrupulous or less conscientious competitors from time to time. But in the long run they will maintain their own reputations, and uphold the reputation of a craft that is under mounting attack. To do otherwise is to surrender to the sensational, the trivial, and the vulgar that is increasingly infecting the serious business of informing the nation.[4]

Curtains for Conventions?

Other issues becloud the horizon of journalism as we enter a new millennium, and one concerns the ritual every four years of political conventions. Their days may be numbered since the advent of widespread primaries makes them redundant. More important, in the opinion of Sandy Grady, longtime political correspondent for the *Philadelphia Daily News*, the public relations specialists, or "spin-doctors," have done them in by overly scripting what once were largely spontaneous affairs. The greatest interest these conventions arouse today seems to be, "When are the balloons coming down?" Once again, as in the Simpson murder trial or the Clinton political trial, overkill engendered public apathy, if not resentment. As Mexico's Octavio Paz, winner of the Nobel Prize for Literature in 1990, observed in 1994, "politics borders on the one side with theater and on the other with religion."[5] With an astute eye, Sandy Grady sounds the death knell for political conventions—as they are now programmed, at least—from the standpoint of a journalist in the following selection based on his observations at the 1996 Republican National Convention in San Diego.

Walk behind the convention hall and you see them lined up like mastodons, the huge white vans with the logos of CBS, ABC and NBC. Their maze of cable connects to the skyboxes and the network demigods, Dan, Peter and Tom. Well, wave goodbye.

Those white vans, symbols of the power TV networks pour into political conventions, are dinosaurs soon to be extinct.

I suspect the televised convention is dead. This will be the last summer the major networks play patsy for political parties' image-makers.

And this 1996 Republic dronathon—scripted as tightly as a beer or auto commercial—helped kill the beast.

Oh, the Republican managers are proud of what they candidly call their four-day "infomercial." They brag about their MTV-styled convention with its 15-foot screens, video clips, cutaways and rapid-fire speeches.

But they've gagged any dissent—Democrats will be just as guilty—and murdered the friction, spontaneity and life that makes good TV.

Well, let's ask David Brinkley, the silver-haired ABC-TV eminence who's covered these rituals since the black-and-white era. Last TV convention, Dave?

"Probably the last one we'll see in such an extravagant way," says Brinkley, who's retiring after this presidential season. "Nobody watches, at least not many. The novelty's worn off, and not much really happens."

Like Brinkley, I remember—either from watching on the tube or being there—conventions full of juice and tension. The 1964 Goldwater convention when NBC's John Chancellor was carried off the floor by guards; the tear-gas-clouded 1968 Democratic bedlam over Vietnam, the '72 George McGovern fiasco in Miami, the 1976 Reagan-Ford feud in Kansas City. Goodbye to all that. Instead, we've got the 1996 Republicans staging an electronic pep rally—nice, antiseptic, all the dirty laundry kept off screen.

Typically, last night was dull as a toothpaste ad—wooden oratory from governors (Tom Ridge, too) and a nice keynote from Susan Molinari, considered wildly daring because she was a woman.

Come on, where were Pat Buchanan and his peasants with pitchforks? Where were Gov. Pete Wilson and William Weld with their pro-choice rebellions? All barred. In truth, the only memorable '96 moment was Colin Powell's passion.

My hunch is that most of the 1,990 delegates (only 54 black) roared cheers for Powell to break the boredom of their own infomercial.

But Michael Deaver, the ex-Reagan imagemeister who joined with Paul Manafort to contrive this artificial convention, swaggers about its success.

"Look, our enemy is the channel changer. We're competing with 70 channels," Deaver said. "We're targeting the 18 percent of voters who are undecided. They're young working people with families. We're fighting for their attention."

Boasts Ron Walker, who managed seven GOP conventions, "We've scripted them tighter than a gnat's ass."

Trouble is, even the click-click, balloons-and-bunting 1990s video rally isn't working. CBS's ratings for the San Diego convention are down from 5.6 four years ago to 3.9; NBC has dropped from 5.1 to 4.5. For comparison, a show like "Seinfeld" draws a 14.1.

No wonder the networks are restless—CBS, to the GOP managers' chagrin, rebelled by carrying only a snippet of Monday's Ronald Reagan video. And the Big Three nets are chopping the convention into mini-bites. Their coverage is down from 100 hours in 1980 to under 20 hours for San Diego.

"Yes, this will probably be the last time the top networks cover a convention on this scale," said NBC producer Jeff Zucker. "At least until something significant happens."

That means, unless there's a real slugfest between two candidates (hasn't happened in twenty years) or a thunderous national debate (not since Vietnam), conventions will be demoted to C-SPAN, CNN and Pat Robertson's Family Channel.

"No reason for the major networks to be doing conventions anymore," argues ex-NBC president Reuven Frank, a veteran since the Ike era. "There hasn't been any news in four cycles. They're fancy political ads."

The resentment is shared by the 12,000 reporters here, including 3,000 newspaper stiffs, 1,000 magazine types and 750 foreign journalists. We're all here, with our rental cars and laptops, hunting a story.

The dirty little secret: There ain't no story.

I don't blame the Dole-Kemp team for conniving this script so Republicans cover up all the sour hatreds of Houston '92 and look like a big, happy Walton family. Ironically, though, by vetting every speech and squelching their messiness, they've sucked out the convention's life—dissent, debate, drama—and left a boring husk.

You can bet Democrats will be just as overrehearsed. But by the year 2000, these pep rallies will be off the major screens—just tribal rituals like Elks or Rotarians in funny hats.

The media-slick pols have killed off the dinosaur. So pack up those network vans, haul 'em away. And take me with them.[6]

Who Is More Equal?

In 1962, British economist Barbara Ward predicted in her book, *Rich Nations and the Poor Nations*, that the poverty-stricken countries would not accept forever their misery. She pointed out that while the industrialized north remained an island of plenty in an ocean of poverty, the have-nots of the south eventually would come battering down the doors of the United States and western Europe. At the time, critics scoffed at the idea that the unwashed masses with pitchforks and sticks could challenge the military-industrial complex of the north, but that was before the proliferation of nuclear weapons in India and Pakistan and their likelihood elsewhere. Yet this story goes largely unreported while we expend our talent, time, and resources to cover the "blockbuster" Simpson and Clinton stories, crowding foreign news off the air or out of the print medium. Even more startling is the fact that the networks are cutting back on their foreign correspondents when they are needed most. Moreover, editors send reporters overseas who are not qualified to cover the stories to which they are assigned.

Americans traditionally have not been interested in international news, experiencing long stretches of isolationism or sheer indifference. Editors say that readers or viewers are not interested in foreign stories. There are notable exceptions, of course, in newspapers such as the *Christian Science Monitor*, *New York Times*, and *Washington Post*, but many readers are not given access to international material to whet their interest. It is a vicious circle, fueled also by ethnocentrism or national bias. To many Americans, most people in the global village live on the wrong side of the tracks where they are conveniently out of sight and out of mind.

One publication, the monthly *World Press Review*, corrects this myopia by culling world news from the global press, thus presenting solid reporting or comment on the most important issues of the day from many international sources. It lists the newspapers or magazines from which material is selected as liberal, centrist, or conservative, and there is a balance. Editor Larry Martz comments here on nationalistic reporting in his editorial, "Who Is More Equal?" from the June 1999 issue of *World Press Review*. This publication should be required reading in all university journalism classes because, as H. G. Wells once said, "Human history becomes more and more a race between education and catastrophe."

One night in early March, a story from Africa got more time on America's network evening news than any other news of the day—"even more attention," reported Rome's Inter Press Service, "than Monica Lewinsky's first televised interview since her affair with President Bill Clinton became headlines!" But no, Jim Lobe wrote sardonically, the big story wasn't Nigeria's peaceful election or one of Africa's myriad wars with their millions of victims. It was about eight white tourists who were killed by Hutu guerrillas while trekking to the famed "gorillas in the mist."

This sort of thing comes easily to Americans, as the war in Kosovo is proving again. Call it chauvinism, ignorance, racism, navel-gazing, or all four; the fact is that we look at the world and see only what interests us, which is mainly ourselves.

There are good reasons for taking a hand in the Balkans, but they don't play well to a public that simply doesn't want to get involved. Thus, NATO's intervention in Kosovo is proclaimed as a moral imperative, a unique situation that justifies interference in the internal affairs of a sovereign nation. Never mind the fact that at least a dozen other conflicts around the world— all with larger death tolls, many with more refugees—are going on all but ignored. There's nothing wrong with trying to help the refugees and trying to stop ethnic cleansing (NATO's tactics are another matter). But the thing could be done with less righteous bluster and more acknowledgment that, after all, the West is acting in its own self-interest. That might cut the whiff of hypocrisy and racism—the suspicion that, as with killings in Africa, some victims are more equal than others. And in the end, it might make for more sensible policy.[7]

Notes

1. *Philadelphia Daily News*, February 12, 1999.

2. Jeffrey Toobin, "Cash for Trash," *The New Yorker* (July 1994): 34–36.

3. Toni Morrison, "The Talk of the Town," *The New Yorker* (October 5, 1998): 31.

4. Jules Witcover, "What Went Wrong," *Columbia Journalism Review* (March/April 1998): 19–25.

5. Octavio Paz, "All the World's a Stage—and an Audience," *Los Angeles Times*, March 23, 1994.

6. Sandy Grady, "Image-makers Have Finally Killed It All," *Philadelphia Daily News*, August 14, 1996.

7. Larry Martz, "Who Is More Equal?" *World Press Review* (June 1999): 3.

Acknowledgment of Sources

Bagdikian, Ben H. "Rupert Murdoch." *The Nation* (June 12, 1989): 806. Reprinted by permission of *The Nation*.

Baker, Ray Stannard. *American Chronicle: The Autobiography of Ray Stannard Baker*, 94–95. New York: Charles Scribner's Sons, 1945. © 1945 by Ray Stannard Baker; renewed 1972 by Rachel Baker Napier. Reprinted by permission of Scribner, a Division of Simon and Schuster.

———. *Following the Colour Line: American Negro Citizenship in the Progressive Era*, 9–11. New York: Harper and Row, 1906.

Bennett, James Gordon. *Memoirs of James Gordon Bennett and His Times*, 180–81, 184. New York: Stringer and Townsend, 1855.

Bradlee, Ben. *A Good Life: Newspapering and Other Adventures*, 405–9. New York: Simon and Schuster, 1995. © 1995 by Benjamin C. Bradlee. Reprinted by permission of Benjamin C. Bradlee.

Brinkley, David. *David Brinkley, A Memoir*, 155–58. New York: Alfred A. Knopf, 1995. © 1995 by David Brinkley. Reprinted by permission of David Brinkley.

Browne, Junius Henri. *Four Years in Secessia: Adventures within and beyond the Union Lines*, 13–19. Hartford, CT: O. D. Case and Company, 1865.

Clarke, John Henrik, Esther Jackson, Ernest Kaiser, and J. H. O'Dell, eds. *Black Titan: W. E. B. Du Bois, An Anthology by the Editors of Freedomways*, 268–73. Boston: Beacon Press, 1970. © 1970 by David G. Du Bois. Reprinted by permission of David G. Du Bois.

Cobbett, William. *The Democratic Judge: Or the Equal Liberty of the Press*, 89–90. Philadelphia: Peter Porcupine, March 1798.

Commander, Lydia Kingsmill. "The Significance of Yellow Journalism." *Arena* 34 (August 1905): 150.

Cronkite, Walter. *A Reporter's Life*, 373–76. New York: Alfred A. Knopf, 1996. © 1996 by Walter Cronkite. Reprinted by permission of Walter Cronkite.

Davis, Richard Harding. "The War Correspondent." *Collier's* (October 7, 1911): 21–22, 30.

Du Bois, W. E. B. *John Brown*, with a new introduction by Herbert Aptheker, 101–2, 104–6. Millwood, NY: Kraus-Thomson Organization, 1973. © 1973 by Herbert Aptheker. Reprinted by permission of Herbert Aptheker.

Dunne, Finley Peter. *Observations by Mr. Dooley*, 239–44. New York: R. H. Russell, 1902.

Duster, Alfreda M., ed. *Crusade for Justice: The Autobiography of Ida B. Wells*, 63–67. Chicago: University of Chicago Press, 1970. © 1970 by the University of Chicago Press. Reprinted by permission of the University of Chicago Press.

Ford, Paul Leicester, ed. *The Journals of Hugh Gaine, Printer*. Vol. 1. *Biography and Bibliography*, 74, 83. New York: Dodd, Mead and Company, 1902.

Garrison, William Lloyd. *The Abolitionists, and Their Relations to the War*, 43–45. New York: E. D. Barker, 1862.

Gellhorn, Martha. *The Face of War*, 1–4. New York: Simon and Schuster, 1959. © 1959 by Martha Gellhorn. Reprinted by permission of Martha Gellhorn.

Glessing, Robert J. *The Underground Press in America*, 53, 108–10. Bloomington: Indiana University Press, 1970. © 1970 by Indiana University Press. Reprinted by permission of Indiana University Press.

Grady, Sandy. "Image-makers Have Finally Killed It All." *Philadelphia Daily News*, August 14, 1996. Reprinted by permission of the *Philadelphia Daily News*.

Greeley, Horace. *Recollections of a Busy Life . . .* , 136–40, 142–43. New York: J. B. Ford and Company, 1868.

Harris, Benjamin. *Publick Occurrences Both Forreign and Domestick*. In Willard Grosvenor Bleyer, *The History of*

American Journalism (New York: Houghton Mifflin Company, 1927), 46.

Heaton, John L. *Cobb of "The World," A Leader in Liberalism*, 239–42. New York: E. P. Dutton and Company, 1924.

Hemingway, Ernest. "Old Newsman Writes a Letter from Cuba." *Esquire* (December 1934): 25–26. © 1934 by the Hearst Corporation. Reprinted by permission of *Esquire*.

Hopkins, Ernest Jerome, ed. *The Complete Short Stories of Ambrose Bierce*, 471–74. Garden City, NY: Doubleday and Company, 1970.

Howe, E. W. *Ventures in Common Sense*, 134–35. New York: Alfred A. Knopf, 1919.

Hughes, Langston. "Langston Hughes Recalls Triumphs and Tragedies of a Race as Told by the Defender." *Chicago Defender*, August 6, 1955. Reprinted by permission of the *Chicago Defender*.

Isaacs, Arnold R. "Ernie Pyle, Poet of the Infantry: How Would He Cover Modern War?" *Philadelphia Inquirer*, April 16, 1995. © 1995 by Arnold R. Isaacs. Reprinted by permission of Arnold R. Isaacs.

Ivins, Molly. "With U.S. Media, Malice Is Absent—But So Is Attention," *Fort Worth Star-Telegram*, September 20, 1992. Reprinted in *Nothin' But Good Times Ahead*, 146–48. New York: Random House, 1993. © 1993 by Molly Ivins. Reprinted by permission of Molly Ivins and Creators Syndicate.

Kronenberger, Louis. "The Solar Perch" (editorial). *PM*, June 19, 1940.

Laird, Ruth. "Examination of Newspaper Accounts of Indian Activities in Selected South Dakota Weeklies, 1887–1920." Unpublished paper, Library of South Dakota State University, n.d.

Lippmann, Walter. *Liberty and the News*, 68–72. New Brunswick, NJ: Transaction Publishers, 1995. © 1995 by Transaction Publishers. Reprinted by permission of Transaction Publishers.

Lord, Arthur A. "Why Television News Is on the Decline," *Philadelphia Inquirer*, March 30, 1993. © 1993 by Arthur A. Lord. Reprinted by permission of Arthur A. Lord.

Lovejoy, Joseph C. and Owen. *Memoir of the Rev. Elijah P. Love-joy: Who Was Murdered in Defence of the Liberty of the Press, at Alton, Illinois, Nov. 7, 1837*, 181–83. New York: John S. Taylor, 1838.

Martz, Larry. "Who Is More Equal?" *World Press Review* (June 1999): 3. Reprinted by permission of *World Press Review* and Larry Martz.

Matthews, Herbert L. Speech at City College of New York, March 15, 1961, 1–5, 7, 9, 15–16. Matthews Papers, Butler Library, Columbia University, Cuban Revolution, Box 2. Reprinted by permission of Eric Matthews and Columbia University Library.

McWilliams, Carey. *The Education of Carey McWilliams*, 213–14, 220–21. New York: Simon and Schuster, 1978. © 1978 by Carey McWilliams. Reprinted by permission of Harold Ober Associates.

Penn, I. Garland. *The Afro-American Press, and Its Editors*, 448–50. Springfield, MA: Willey and Company, 1891.

Phillips, David Graham. "The Treason of the Senate." *Cosmopolitan Magazine* 40, no. 5 (March 1906): 487–88.

Pyle, Ernie. *Ernie's War: The Best of Ernie Pyle's World War II Dispatches*, ed. David Nichols, frontispiece, 153–54. New York: Random House, 1986. Reprinted by permission of Scripps Howard Foundation.

Reed, John. "Villa Accepts a Medal." In *Insurgent Mexico*, 113–15. New York: Simon and Schuster, 1969.

Rowan, Carl T. *Go South to Sorrow*, 10–13. New York: Random House, 1957. © 1957 by Carl T. Rowan. Reprinted by permission of Random House.

Rutherford, Livingston. *John Peter Zenger, His Press, His Trial and a Bibliography of Zenger Imprints*, 238–40. Gloucester, MA: Peter Smith Publisher, 1963. Reprinted by permission of Peter Smith Publisher.

Scripps, E. W. "Is Honest Journalism Possible?" In *I Protest: Selected Disquisitions of E. W. Scripps*, ed. Oliver Knight, 243–45. Madison: University of Wisconsin Press, 1966. © 1966. Reprinted by permission of the University of Wisconsin Press.

Sevareid, Eric. "What's Right with Sight-and-Sound Journalism." *Saturday Review* (October 2, 1976): 18–21. © 1976 by

Eric Sevareid. Reprinted by permission of Don Congdon Associates, Inc.

Sinclair, Upton. *The Brass Check: A Study of American Journalism*, 32–36. Pasadena, CA: Privately printed, 1920.

Snow, Edgar. "China Will Talk from a Position of Strength." *Life* (July 30, 1971): 22–26.

The Speeches at Full Length . . . of General Hamilton, In the Great Cause of the People, against Harry Croswell, on an Indictment for a Libel on Thomas Jefferson, President of the United States, 63–64. New York: G. and R. Waite, 1804.

Steffens, Lincoln. "Hearst, the Man of Mystery." *The American Magazine* 63, no. 1 (November 1906): 3–4, 12, 20.

Stickney, William, ed. *Autobiography of Amos Kendall*, 370–74. Gloucester, MA: Peter Smith Publisher, 1949. Reprinted by permission of Peter Smith Publisher.

Swisshelm, Jane Grey. *Half a Century*, 139–42. Chicago: Jansen, McClurg and Company, 1880.

Tarbell, Ida. *All in the Day's Work: An Autobiography*, 234–37, 239–42. New York: Macmillan, 1939.

Toobin, Jeffrey. "Cash for Trash." *The New Yorker* (July 11, 1994): 34–36. Reprinted by permission of Condé Nast.

Twain, Mark. "License of the Press." In *The Complete Essays of Mark Twain*, ed. Charles Neider, 10–14. Garden City, NY: Doubleday and Company, 1963. © 1963 by Charles Neider. Reprinted by permission of Charles Neider.

White, Theodore H. "When He Used the Power of TV, He Could Rouse Thunder." *TV Guide* (January 18, 1986): 13–14. © 1986 by the *Los Angeles Times* Syndicate. Distributed by the *Los Angeles Times*. Reprinted by permission of the *Los Angeles Times* Syndicate.

White, William Allen. "Editors Live and Learn." *The Atlantic Monthly* (August 1942): 56–60.

Witcover, Jules. "What Went Wrong." *Columbia Journalism Review* (March/April 1998): 19–25. © 1998 by *Columbia Journalism Review*. Reprinted by permission of *Columbia Journalism Review* and Jules Witcover.

Index

ISBN 0-8420-2760-2

9 780842 027601

90000 >